LEAVING PIPE SHOP

Memories of Kin

Deborah E.
McDowell

SCRIBNER

SCRIBNER
1230 Avenue of the Americas
New York, NY 10020

SCRIBNER and design are trademarks of Simon & Schuster Inc.

Designed by Deborah Kerner

Set in Garamond No. 3

Manufactured in the United States of America

10   9   8   7   6   5   4   3   2   1

Library of Congress Cataloging-in-Publication Data.
McDowell, Deborah E., date.
Leaving Pipe Shop : memories of kin / Deborah E. McDowell.
p.   cm.
1. McDowell, Deborah E., date. —Childhood and youth. 2. Afro-American women—Alabama—Besse-
mer—Biography.   3.   Afro-Americans—Alabama—Bessemer—Biography.   4.   Afro-Americans—
Alabama—Bessemer—Social life and customs. 5. McDowell family. 6. Bessemer (Ala.)—Biography. I.
Title.
F334.B5M38   1997
976.1'78—dc21
[B]   96-48173
CIP

ISBN 0-684-81449-8

The author and publisher gratefully acknowledge permission to reprint the following material:
    From *Duino Elegies* by Rainer Maria Rilke, translated by J. B. Leishman/Stephen Spender. Translation
copyright 1939 by W. W. Norton & Company, Inc., renewed © 1967 by Stephen Spender and J. B. Leish-
man. Reprinted by permission of W. W. Norton & Company, Inc.
    "Don't Explain." Words and music by Billie Holiday and Arthur Herzog © copyright 1946 by
Duchess Music Corporation. Copyright renewed. Duchess Music Corporation is an MCA company. International copyright secured. All rights reserved.
    "Somewhere Along the Line." By Dinah Washington and Walter Merrick © by Longitude Music Co.
All rights reserved. Reprinted by permission of Longitude Music Co.

IN REMEMBRANCE OF ALL OF MY KIN
LONG GONE, TOO SOON
"I am all of them, they are all of me."
    —Etheridge Knight,
        "The Idea of Ancestry"

My memory stammers but my soul is a witness.
—James Baldwin,
   The Evidence of Things Not Seen

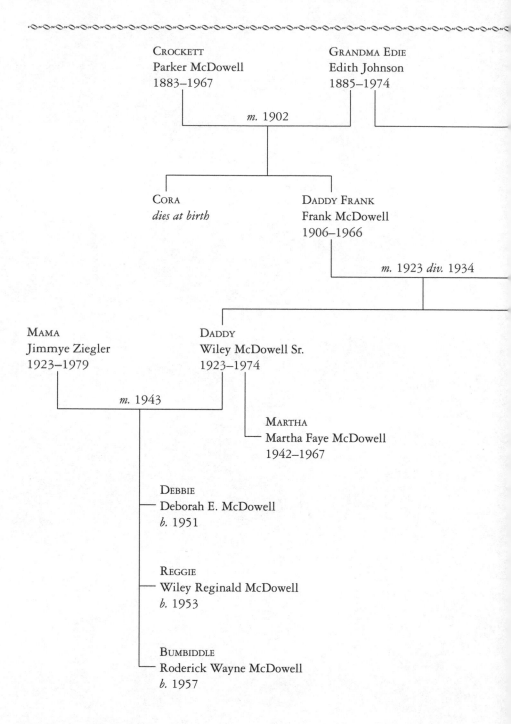

CROCKETT
Parker McDowell
1883–1967

GRANDMA EDIE
Edith Johnson
1885–1974

m. 1902

CORA
dies at birth

DADDY FRANK
Frank McDowell
1906–1966

m. 1923 *div.* 1934

MAMA
Jimmye Ziegler
1923–1979

DADDY
Wiley McDowell Sr.
1923–1974

m. 1943

MARTHA
Martha Faye McDowell
1942–1967

DEBBIE
Deborah E. McDowell
b. 1951

REGGIE
Wiley Reginald McDowell
b. 1953

BUMBIDDLE
Roderick Wayne McDowell
b. 1957

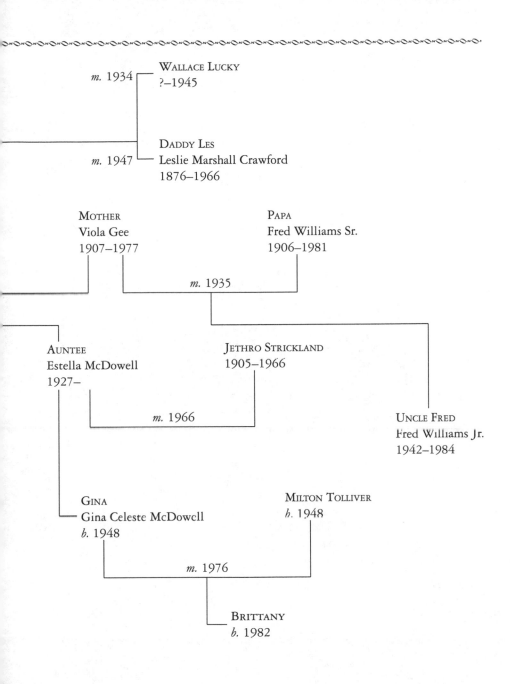

WALLACE LUCKY
?–1945

m. 1934

DADDY LES
Leslie Marshall Crawford
1876–1966

m. 1947

MOTHER
Viola Gee
1907–1977

PAPA
Fred Williams Sr.
1906–1981

m. 1935

AUNTEE
Estella McDowell
1927–

JETHRO STRICKLAND
1905–1966

m. 1966

UNCLE FRED
Fred Williams Jr.
1942–1984

GINA
Gina Celeste McDowell
b. 1948

MILTON TOLLIVER
b. 1948

m. 1976

BRITTANY
b. 1982

Contents

Respite

Daddy and I are in the dusky kitchen, seated in the green-and-gray crushed ice chairs from the 1950s, the vinyl ones with thick-padded seats and chrome-metal tubing to brace the legs and back. We face each other across the divide of the oven door, open to reveal its dark-blue-and-white-flecked inside, spattered with hardened food spills that have stained the white flecks brown. A cast-iron skillet rests atop the stove, along with Daddy's black hump-backed lunch box with the metal latches. We both wear coats buttoned tight against our necks: I in the green wide-wale corduroy car coat with the quilted lining that Mama made when I was in fourth grade; Daddy in his khaki-colored double-breasted army coat with brass buttons. His stub-toed leather boots are unlaced, the tongues flapping lankly down.

Light blue smoke plumes from the oven and clouds the room, which feels ice cold and damp. We are shivering but arguing heatedly over the correct pronunciation of r-e-s-p-i-t-e. I insist that it's pronounced ree-spite. "Re" as in "return" and "spite" with a long "i" — as in "Don't cut off your nose to spite your face." He hears me out and laughs the way he always does, from way down in his throat, and after drawing on his cigarette and stomping his foot, he shouts, "That's just plain wrong, Miss Know-It-All." And reaching for the dictionary, he says, "Let me break it down for you. It's like you were going to say 'rest' without the 't,' then 'pit.' The 'e' of the last syllable is silent. Respite."

I awake from this dream drenched in sweat.

PART
ONE

Summons

Memorial Day Weekend 1994

You got to come home."

Whenever Auntee calls, I always cringe, then lock my knees and brace myself for the bad news, and the news is almost always bad, even if she is calling just to check on me or to keep in touch. She rushes through questions about my job, the weather, what I ate for lunch or dinner, then settles comfortably into talk of gloom and horror. I bite my tongue as she plies her way through one account after the other of brutal stabbings, fatal gunshot wounds, near-death escapes, ravaging diseases. Someone is either wasting away from terminal cancer, covered with rotting, pus-filled sores, or has suddenly yielded up the ghost, without prior warning. Like Miss Lovie Stoudimire, who had a massive heart attack while watering her azaleas ("Nobody even knew she had heart trouble") or Mr. Cleveland Fleming, crushed to death beneath a dump truck on a muddy back road in Muscoda. Years later, when rumors surfaced that his own son was driving the truck and had meant to run him over ("accidentally on purpose," Auntee said), she even called to tell me that.

Auntee is preoccupied with death and dying. Maybe it's because she's seen so much of both up close and acted as their willing messenger, always late at night. She was the one who had called to tell me Great-grandma Edie was gone, and then she had called about Daddy, then Mother, then Mama, then Papa. Most in May, around Memorial Day, except for Daddy, who died in winter, on December 5, leaving us bereft and in no spirit to celebrate Christmas. The stroke had killed him almost instantly, barely an hour after he collapsed in a heap on the sidewalk in front of the Moore and Handley hardware store. The others—Crockett, Daddy Les, Daddy Frank, and Martha Faye had all died before I went away to college in 1968. But before I left, in that fifteen-year period from 1974 to 1981, someone close had died, one after the other. Uncle Jr. broke the stretch three years later in 1984. We had expected him to die—he had diabetes, an enlarged heart, and a drug habit he couldn't shake—but his passing at forty-two years old still left all of us in shock and wondering who would be the next to go. Almost ten years had elapsed since Uncle Jr.'s passing and one of Auntee's late-night death-angel calls. So when I heard those dreaded and familiar words in May 1994, "You got to come home," and the heavy pause that followed, I was sure the long reprieve had ended. Swallowing hard, I tried to steady myself for the worst.

"I ran into Buttercup up at Bruno's Food Store and he told me that the Pipe Shop is giving out settlement money."

"What?" I heaved a sigh of relief. At least no one had died. To keep from yelling at her, I drew another deep breath before asking, "Who in the world is Buttercup?"

"You know Buttercup. Theotis Sanders is his name, but he goes by Buttercup. Your daddy used to work with him up in the Pipe Shop. Married one of the Miller girls, Maxine."

"I don't remember anybody named Buttercup or Maxine."

"Well, I don't know how you could forget Buttercup, many times as he came to y'all's house. Don't you remember? He and your daddy knocked around together, belonged to the same club, the Esquires. Card partners. Anyway, he was one of the ones who just got money from the government for asbestos poisoning. You and Reggie and Bumbiddle can probably get some too, seeing as how you your daddy's next of kin. Seems to me that since Wiley worked out there for all that time with Buttercup, he was bound to get the asbestos too. Pokie just got some of the money because her daddy died of lung cancer."

"Auntee, Auntee, slow down. I don't know any of these people. Anyway, Daddy had a stroke."

"Don't matter. The asbestos could have caused it."

"I doubt it."

"You don't know until you look into it. Buttercup said that if a man had died, the money would go to his widow, and if she had died, it would go to his children. So now that's you and Reggie and Bumbiddle, and you the right one to see about it. You the oldest and you know how to stand up to these plant folks. You got to have enough gumption to deal with these peckerwoods."

"Auntee, this is bound to end up just like the pay discrimination suit did. I'll go through a lot of toil and trouble—making phone calls, gathering documents, writing letters—for a measly twelve hundred dollars."

When the Justice Department settled its 1970s class-action suit against twelve Birmingham locals of the United Steel Workers of America, that's all we got for all the years Daddy had suffered wage and job discrimination. Like all the other plaintiffs, he had been systematically and routinely assigned to dead-end jobs that paid half the average white man's wage. They were all trapped in a racially segregated system designed to exclude blacks from jobs requiring higher skills. If they tried to advance to better units, they lost all seniority at the plant.

"Auntee, I repeat, I don't have the time for this. Not for chump change."

"You don't know how much you'll get until and unless you try. Plus twelve hundred dollars was more than you had."

I wanted to get off the telephone and finish reading the chapter of a dissertation I had promised to return the next day, but Auntee refused to let me off the hook. "Look into this" and "Check on that," she commanded, as I shifted impatiently from foot to foot to keep my bladder from exploding. Hoping to placate her for the moment, I asked a few more questions.

"Did this Buttercup tell you who to contact?"

"No, he didn't. But you can call him. Hold on, let me look up his number. Wait a minute. I can't see these little numbers anymore. Let me call Brittany."

"Don't wake her up."

"She's not sleep."

"Well, she oughta be. What is she doing up this late on a school night?"

"They don't have school tomorrow. The teachers have some kind of in-service. Brittany, come here and look up a telephone number for Grandma."

I jotted down the number as Brittany read it to me.

"Buttercup can tell you who to call. Just tell him you Wiley's daughter. He'll remember you. I still can't believe you don't remember Buttercup. He used to call you 'Thin Thighs.'"

"Oh, yeah. Now I do. He lived up near Cox and Autry Food Saver. Had a lazy eye."

"Yeah, that's him. Nice man. Do anything for you. Give you the shirt off his back."

"Auntee, I didn't even know the Bessemer plant was still open."

"Oh, yeah, it's open. Ain't too many folks working out there, but they still open."

"Well, I'll call the plant tomorrow."

"You know, this might not be the kind of thing you can take care of on the telephone. You might need to be here, you understand. If I was you, I would come home and do my business that way, face to face. When you do your business face to face, folks ain't as quick to try to mess over you."

"Auntee, I just can't drop everything and come running home every time you hear rumblings about money at the Pipe Shop. And, anyway, the school year just ended and I still have a lot of loose ends to tie up."

"When will you be through?"

"In about three weeks."

"Well, come then."

"I can't. I have to go to Berlin and then I have to teach summer school."

"Berlin? In Germany? For what?"

"For a conference."

"What kind of conference? I sure do hate to see you doing all this ripping and running back and forth overseas. What with all these people shooting airplanes out the sky and bombing up everything, I just can't believe that you want to be traipsing all around the world all by yourself. Just like Mother."

"I won't be by myself. Other people are going."

"Don't matter," she said, then proceeded with more bizarre imaginings. "You need to settle down and move back home. Have a family. Your mama gone. Your daddy gone, and it ain't gon' be too long before my head gets cold. You need to come back home amongst your own folks."

Auntee would not let this subject loose. She needled talk of my moving home into every conversation, pleading with me to come back to Alabama—for good. Since I'd gotten as far as Virginia—at least I was back in the South, she said—she still clung to the hope that I would eventually wend my way home. After eight years in the flatlands of Indiana, I had moved to Waterville, Maine, a few months after Mama died.

"Maine? That's up near Canada, ain't it?"

"Yeah, Auntee."

"Then you might as well be in another country."

During the eight years I stayed in Maine, bundled up and blanketed against the cold for most of the year, Auntee never missed an opportunity to remind me of just how far I was from home. "Why you want to live in a place with snow coming all the way up to your window that's got you looking like some kind of Eskimo?" she wanted to know when I sent her a picture of me in a hooded parka, standing knee-deep in snow outside the house I lived in. It was the day after one of the worst blizzards in the state's history.

"It's not always that high."

"Hmmph, if it only got that high one time, that would be one time too many for me."

I had trekked to Colby College to teach African-American literature to the sons and daughters of the upper class. Many hailed from places like

Darien and Greenwich, Park Avenue and Central Park West. The faculty shared the opinion that the students had selected Colby only because of its proximity to Sugar Loaf Mountain, where they skied when they were not jetting off to the slopes of Cortina. Though skiing had seemed to be their primary preoccupation, the students learned to love the works we read, especially Toni Morrison's *Sula* and James Baldwin's "Sonny's Blues."

When I left Maine eight years later and headed for Virginia—this time a blizzard did run me out—Auntee wanted to know why I couldn't just come on home. There were perfectly good universities in Alabama. What about the University of Alabama at Birmingham, where all the Acoff girls had gone? They were now all engineers, all four of them. And what about Tuscaloosa?

"You know, it's changed a whole lot since George Wallace was down there raising Cain." I laughed as we remembered that day in June 1963, when she, Gina, and I huddled tensely in front of the black-and-white television to watch the showdown in Tuscaloosa: Governor George Wallace versus a federal court order. The all-white Alabama National Guard rolled onto the Tuscaloosa campus armed with M-1 rifles, in readiness for a riot. And as the phalanx of uniformed soldiers thickened, we wondered aloud whether Wallace would take his stand in the schoolhouse door and thus keep his inaugural promise of "segregation now, segregation tomorrow, segregation forever." Now, of course, all the world knows he didn't. Knows all about his face-saving gesture. While he grandstanded in one door, Vivian Malone and James Hood marched right through another, without incident. Defiant to the end, Wallace sped back to Montgomery, vowing that he would "never surrender" the fight to keep segregation the law and the custom of Alabama.

"Oh, it almost slipped my mind. Buttercup say you will need your daddy's death certificate before you can file a claim." She had segued back to the subject of asbestos, and this time it set my teeth on edge.

"Auntee, look, Daddy's been dead and gone, soon will be twenty years. I just don't want to stir all that stuff up again." I could tell from the tone of her voice that her face had taken on that familiar pinched and sullen cast. Silence always follows.

"Well, then, good night."

Auntee Estella—most of the family calls her Stella—is my oldest living relative, my father's only sister. She and her only daughter, Gina, and Gina's only daughter, Brittany, are my closest relatives left in Bessemer, Alabama, where I was born March 14, 1951, in a rural industrial community called the Pipe Shop, twelve miles from Birmingham. Short for the U.S. Pipe and Foundry, Pipe Shop gave our neighborhood its name and the men of Bessemer menial employment while the steel industry hung on, paying a barely livable wage. Health care has now replaced ferrous metals as the city's main employer, but in the boom times, the men of Pipe Shop donned sooted overalls and poured molten iron into spinning molds for casting pipes sold all around the world.

From a distance, U.S. Pipe looks like a school grounds. Even the grassy slope at the west end of the complex resembles a giant green chalkboard. Bright white letters, stretching high above street level, are cemented into the grass:

U.S. PIPE AND FOUNDRY. EST. 1890.
MORE THAN A PLACE TO WORK

Once, skipping alongside Daddy on a run to Gober's package store, we passed the group of hulking, fenced-off, red-brick buildings that spanned two long blocks. Yanking on his arm, I remember asking, "What does that mean, Daddy?"

"What?"

"The sign. More than a place to work."

Now I can't remember what he answered, but those white letters remained a puzzle throughout my early years.

U.S. Pipe dominated our neighborhood, which was bounded (and crowned) by the plant at Nineteenth Street on the north, Twelfth Street on the south, Seventeenth Avenue on the east, and Twenty-second Avenue on the west.

When I left Pipe Shop to go to college in September 1968, I vowed never to come back, except for brief visits to see my loved ones. By escaping Pipe Shop, I would permanently put the images, slights, and restrictions of racial segregation far behind me (or so I naively thought).

Why would I want to return to Alabama? I had always silently asked myself whenever Auntee laid the pressure on. While summer's palette, its sounds and smells, had framed my childhood memories in Pipe Shop, at least from adolescence onward, the place looks sere and desolate in my mind's eye and conjures up the sadness I often feel when roses shed their petals and magnolia blossoms turn from cream to rust.

As the years have galloped by, my trips back home have been few and far between. I must admit that, at times, it's only duty that compels me to visit when I do—the duty owed an elder who helped to raise me from a gangly, knobby-kneed girl and taught me to love Dinah Washington's blues.

*   *   *

Sleep deserted me that night. Between midnight and morning, memories, roiling, roiling, roiling from the deep, pried my eyes wide open. First, I watched the play of dogwood branches silhouetted on the pleated shade, then tried to read but could not concentrate. In this agitated state, I picked my way in the darkness down the stairs to search for Daddy's death certificate. I was certain that I still had a copy somewhere in my house. I first searched underneath the cabinet in my study, opening the big battered manila envelope with meaningless dollar figures scribbled on the outside, red ink soaked into the fibers of the paper.

I am a serious pack rat. Large envelopes, brown paper bags, and pasteboard boxes are my intermediate filing systems. Not for nothing am I Mother's granddaughter. I learned from her the habit of stuffing clippings and mementos into cavernous bags. The only difference is that in Mother's case, they often made their way from paper bag to photo albums and scrapbooks. Mother was famous for her scrapbooks. When the Bessemer Voters League honored Mr. Asbury Howard for all his hard work as its president and for his courage as a leader, I vaguely remember that Mother's clippings from the *Birmingham World* helped to compose "This Is Your Life," the large scrapbook chronicling his career as a Civil Rights activist. I plan many scrapbooks in my head, but the last time I actually pieced one together was at high school graduation. Since then, my clippings have remained in this disorderly zone, stuffed into wrinkled envelopes shoved into corners of cabinets and closets of my study and behind the sofa bed.

Inside the envelope were old playbills, the stubs of concert tickets, my dried corsage from the junior prom, still pinned to lime green tulle. My medal for proficiency in Spanish, various newspaper clippings from the *Birmingham World*. Funeral programs and sympathy cards, Mama's spiral club book, a copy of the recipe for Papa's famous lemon pound cake, pages of a 1956 speech by Martin Luther King Jr., mimeographed in fading purplish elite type.

There was the photograph of Daddy we used on the front of his obituary. A young man in military uniform, his hair close shaven, his pants stuffed down in knee-high, stub-toed boots, hands clasped behind his back. He had signed the photograph "To Mother, With Love, Wiley."

Everything but the death certificate. Maybe it was in the large grocery bag in the cabinet's corner. I unfolded its zigzag lip, but the death certificate wasn't in there either. Just a sandwich Baggie of random snapshots and my faded pink baby book.

This was actually the second time the baby book had surfaced as I searched for something else. The first time I found it, it lay inside the cedar chest, buried underneath piles of fabric, stray pattern pieces, Daddy's honorable discharge papers, and pictures of his German girlfriends. That day I was looking for a pattern piece for Miss Ezell Wilkerson's shawl-collared jacket, smoothing out wad after wad of caramel-colored tissue paper. Although a great seamstress, Mama was forever losing pattern pieces or stuffing them, distractedly, into the wrong envelopes. My guess is that after finishing one of her intricate garments with bound buttonholes, or mutton sleeves, or tiny tucks setting off the bodice of a dress, or accordion pleats with precision spacing, she couldn't be bothered with folding pattern pieces and tucking them neatly away.

"You still didn't find it?" Mama asked impatiently, then broke into a tirade: "This is absolutely the wrong style for Ezell. Her chest is entirely too big for this jacket. It's just gonna gape wide open and expose her sagging titties for everybody to see. Folks always trying to wear what God didn't give 'em the shape to wear. Coming in here with pictures from these magazines wanting to look like these models. But ain't no way for them to look like these models who ain't no bigger than a zipper." Next to open-necked garments on the buxom, Mama hated sleeveless ones on women whose upper arms had melted into jiggling flesh. Even if the soft pockets of fat had only collected just above the elbow, Mama still insisted that the woman's arms be covered up—for good.

The day she told Miss Ezell that she shouldn't wear a sleeveless dress to Pokie's wedding, even though it was planned for the middle of July in Alabama, I thought she had taken her dressmaking dos and don'ts a bit too far. I know she embarrassed Miss Ezell in front of Baby Jean, our neighbor from across the street. One of the few "kept" women in Pipe Shop, Baby Jean was bored, and when Mr. Willie, her common-law husband, went to work, she often drifted over to our house in the late morning. With a pack of Camels, crimped aluminum foil for an ashtray, and a bottle of Royal Crown Cola, she perched on the edge of the bed while Mama sewed. That day she was wearing a sleeveless duster, which prompted Miss Ezell to protest: "Look at Baby Jean; her arms ain't covered." Mama lost no time in quipping, "That's right, but look at your arms, then look at Baby Jean's. She ain't got chick nor child. You got eight, and nothing will ruin a woman's arms for sleeveless dresses like having eight children. Now look here, Ezell, this is your oldest child and your only daughter, so when the usher walks you down the aisle, you better not have your arms wiggling and jiggling all over the place like Jell-O." Miss Ezell put up some resistance, but the dress of ice blue silk brocade ended up with cuffed three-

quarter-length sleeves. Mama had won again, just as she would the following Christmas when Miss Ezell wanted a leopard-skin pillbox like
Jackie Kennedy wore. Mama simply said, "Your head's too big and your
neck's too short."

I can't remember whether or not I found the missing pattern piece
curved like a scythe's blade, but I did find the baby book with the pink-
satin-padded cover and a garland of hand-painted red roses.

Aunt Queen Esther Harris, who wrote life and burial insurance for
North Carolina Mutual, had given the baby book to Mama when I was
born. Although she had never had children of her own, she was fond of
them, so Mama chose her as my godmother. Throughout my childhood,
whenever she came to collect the insurance money, she brought me all my
favorite things—bags of Big Moon cookies, tins of sardines, boxes of Crayola crayons, coloring books and jigsaw puzzles, loose-leaf pastel paper, and
pencils inscribed with my name in gilded letters. She even gave me my
first savings bank, a mottled ceramic pig with a plastic stopper underneath. But my favorite present of them all was Cindy, the "Walking Bridal
Doll" in white lace gown and veil, with rooted hair like stiffened bristles
and a dark brown face that dented to the touch.

When I first found the baby book, each page was blank. There were no
first pictures, no print of feet and hands, no record of contagious diseases
or vaccinations, no names of pets, no record of athletic events, not even
how much I had weighed at birth, the date I was christened, what my first
words were or my first prayer or who had taught it to me.

"Mama, why didn't you ever write in the baby book?" I wanted to know
the day I first found it.

"Oh, child, I never had time for all that. That's for folks ain't got nothing else to do but sit around all day. I been too busy working."

That day I commenced to writing in the book myself. I must have been
about fourteen when I started filling in the blanks, for the "Height and
Weight Chart" is clear up to that line, where I recorded being 5 feet, 8 and
a half inches tall, an inch short of my current height, and weighing 122
pounds. I would have been in ninth grade then at Brighton High.

I put the baby book into the paper bag and carried the stack of snapshots back up to my room. By the muted yellow light of the bedside lamp,
I shuffled through them, lingering, as always, over that one of us at
Mother's house. My brothers, Reggie and Bumbiddle, were not yet born.
My guess is that the picture was taken after one of Mother's famous Sunday dinners, held after church when she was home from Mountain Brook,
where she worked as a live-in private-duty nurse for a wealthy family

named the Bergers. Daddy, Mama, and my half sister, Martha Faye, are seated on the camelbacked sofa. Daddy wears an ivory-colored jacket and a printed bow tie and holds me round my waist between his knees. I look to be about three, although still gripping a pacifier in my mouth. Mama smiles admiringly at Daddy, who stares straight into the camera.

Martha Faye does not seem happy. She hugs the sofa's bulky arm, almost escaping from the picture. Martha Faye was the daughter Daddy had fathered before he married my mother. Her mother, Ernestine, was only sixteen when she was born. As Auntee tells the story, Daddy would have married her, but Mother begged him not to. According to Mother, *everybody* knew the girl was fast and wild and opened her legs for anything warm and breathing. To make amends for not marrying Ernestine, Daddy adopted Martha Faye soon after he returned from his army stint in Germany, but she remained with her mother and visited every now and then. When Ernestine eventually married a brawler and a boozer, who was mean to Martha Faye, she came to live with us in Pipe Shop when I was six years old.

"She looked so thrown-away," Mama would say when she remembered the day Martha Faye moved in. "Great big moon eyes and would jump if you called her name for going on I don't know how many months. But I raised her just like she was my own flesh and blood. I didn't make a bit of difference between you. Not a bit. If I made you a dress, I made one for her. If you got shoes, she got shoes."

I remember the day Martha Faye left Pipe Shop for good as one of the saddest of my life. She had been in our lives for many years—in the same house for almost three—and I'd grown quite attached to her. She went to live in Buffalo with Ernestine, who had moved there with her husband, now born again and preaching. It was too soon, so sudden, just like her death from bone cancer when she was only twenty-five years old.

We buried her in Buffalo. It was my very first trip North. Ever since Martha Faye had left Pipe Shop, I had dreamed of going to Buffalo, pickling my fantasies of the grand time I would have once arriving. After being cramped in the backseat of the car, bickering through the night with Gina, we arrived in Buffalo near dawn the next day and I discovered just how much it resembled Birmingham, except the houses were stuck together like rows and rows of Siamese twins.

Gina's in the picture taken at Mother's house, standing opposite Martha Faye. She must have been around six and about to go somewhere, since she is buttoned up in a plaid coat, a velvet tam slanted on her head. She clutches the pole of the torchère lamp and grins to expose two missing teeth.

There was the snapshot of Reggie and Bumbiddle. Pictured together as they usually were when we were children. Reggie must be four here, seated behind the infant Bumbiddle on the kitchen floor. For some reason, they are poised between the refrigerator and the kitchen cabinet, where jelly-glass tumblers of cartoon scenes are upended on the counter. A head taller, Reggie faces right, on the side where the scar would later be from when the dog almost ripped his eye out. He grips his baby brother tightly round the belly. Here they are again in much the same position, this time on the front porch, where long shadows dance across the knotted floorboards and around the window frame.

One by one, I studied each of these cherished pictures—my first-grade picture, the only one in Daddy's wallet the day he died. Gina and me in matching dotted swiss dresses, standing with Uncle Jr. the day before he went away to college. The ninth-grade class picture of me in the dark brown shift that buttoned down the side and hung loosely on my slender frame, my wiry hair tamed by a bright gold headband. Mama in her high school robe and mortarboard, posed stiffly against a wintry wooded back-drop. She sits sideways, curls touching the white collar. A ten-year-old Auntee looking forlorn, a huge bow pinned in back of her head, drooping down like rabbit ears. Auntee as a young woman in white cafeteria uni-form, a lace handkerchief stuck in the pocket. Her hair is freshly pressed and curled and she smiles, as always, with lips pursed tightly together. Reggie in his eighth-grade class picture. Bumbiddle, in his seventh-grade equivalent, the corners of his mouth turned up in that familiar devilish grin. Several pictures of Mother. More of Mother than of anybody else. In one she's standing in one of her trademark suits on the steps of an Eastern Airlines jet, looking over her shoulder and waving at someone below. Mother in California in a floral bathing suit, seated on the steps of a huge swimming pool, her legs dangling in the shimmering blue-green water. Mother holding the Bergers' grandbaby, Laney, in a receiving blanket, the baby's bald alabaster head resting on Mother's shoulder.

Mother, who was my paternal grandmother, insisted that her children and their children call her Mother, a departure from the Southern black custom of "Mama" or "Muddeah" (for Mother dear). This oddity created some confusion throughout my childhood, not so much because of the naming but because of what it signified. Who was responsible for mother-ing me? It wasn't always clear. So many "mothers" were answerable for my care, and all too often, least of them my own. Mama's authority was con-stantly usurped by Mother, who was strong-willed and brooked no op-position, and certainly not from her generally quiet and unassuming daughter-in-law. This situation created divided loyalties in me, but in the end I let Mother's claims prevail. Almost everybody did.

What happened to the rest of the pictures, I don't know. The family's photographic archive just stops at a certain point, leaving everyone frozen at a much earlier moment in time. It's such a mystery. I know Mother snapped pictures at Auntee's wedding and at Gina's debutante's ball. And I know there were several of Uncle Jr.—different shots of him the day he left for the citizenship tour, the day he graduated from Dunbar High, and many of the day in August 1959 when he left home for Howard University. Pictures of him in ROTC uniform, cords of braided gold dangling from the epaulets.

These were all in a scrapbook I helped Mother put together soon after Auntee's wedding. She spread the pictures over the dining-room table, arranging them in special order, then I pasted the chevrons on pages of black construction paper and secured the photographs in the four pointed corners. Just below each one, I wrote in silver ink the cursive captions Mother dictated: "Wiley in Uniform," "Mother with Baby Laney," "Mother Takes Her First Flight," "Mother and Papa at the General Conference, Buffalo, New York," "Mother in Florida," "Mother in San Francisco," "Mother in New York with Mark Goodson," "Estella's Wedding, May 1967," "Fred Jr. in Officer's Uniform," and many others. Where was the picture of Great-grandma Edie and her two sisters standing on the banks of a reflecting pool? All swathed in long, glistering white dresses, they looked like apparitions rising from the water's mists.

"Here is the number you need to call to get the death certificate." I played Auntee's annoying message on my answering machine the next afternoon. As much as I wanted to ignore it, I was compelled, despite myself, and for reasons that I still cannot explain, to dial the number I had scribbled on an index card. "This is the Bureau of Vital Statistics, Jefferson County, Alabama," announced the official-sounding voice. He instructed me to request a search in writing, including the name of the deceased, race, sex, place of death, date of death, and funeral home, if known. Send a $12.00 money order for each search to:

Death Records
Jefferson County Health Department
P.O. Box 2648
Birmingham, Alabama

The Magic Mineral

Shuffling through the rubber-banded stack of mail awaiting my return from the conference in Berlin, I found a large brown envelope with a white label, a bold red letter "A" bleeding through:

ASBESTOS VICTIMS SPECIAL FUND TRUST

This must be the package Auntee had mentioned in her last call. I stared absently at the letters before opening the envelope. Inside was a white pamphlet with more large red lettering:

THE INSIDE STORY: ASBESTOS EXPOSED

and several pages about asbestos, "the magic mineral," and the symptoms of asbestosis—breathlessness, dry coughing, and chest constriction.

According to the pamphlet, only the spouse of a deceased victim or a child who was a dependent at the time of the victim's death would be eligible to file claims. Bumbiddle was a dependent when Daddy died, but now he was ensconced in Guam where he had remained after a stint in the navy. He is the only one of us with children—three boys who look just like Daddy, except for their mother's Asian eyes. My other brother, Reggie, wouldn't be eligible to file claims, because he was already grown and gone and in the army by the time Daddy died, then roaming from Germany to San Francisco to Chicago to Jamaica, where he grew dreadlocks that hung to his hips. Now settled in Detroit, Reggie is a determined (read "starving") artist, who makes sculptures of steel trees and carves spoons of pregnant women with featureless faces and arms cut off at the elbows.

Could I file on Bumbiddle's behalf? The pamphlet didn't say. The plaintiff would need a death certificate, medical records, letters from physicians, and a host of other documents to accompany the application. Yes, this was surely a long shot. Daddy seldom went to doctors, except for the company doctor who certified each year that he was well enough to work. The time he had pneumonia, he did go to Dr. Calloway, who gave us our shots and attended Mama when both Reggie and Bumbiddle were born, and when she lost the other baby, but Dr. Calloway had died long before Daddy. No. It made no sense to waste my time with this, and Auntee couldn't make me. I would stand my ground. Anyway, I was almost certain the death certificate had said "cerebral hemorrhage."

Could asbestos poisoning trigger a stroke? A remote possibility, but then it struck me that, knowing as little as I did about asbestos, how could I be so sure? All I knew was that it was heavily used in the industry that brought Birmingham its fabled distinction as "The Magic City," the mineral that had made U.S. Pipe and Foundry one of the largest pipe manufacturing plants in the state of Alabama and, according to *Fortune* magazine, one of the top industrial firms in the nation.

I looked up "Asbestos" in the *Brittanica* Mother had given me for high school graduation in 1968. I saw headings for VARIETIES, USES, PRODUCTION AND CONSUMPTION, but there was no category for DANGERS or HEALTH CONCERNS.

Long before I was born, my ancestors had yoked their prospects for survival to the might of steel, just as they had once been yoked to cotton in the sweeping fields of rural Alabama.

1885. This was the year Henry de Bardeleben, dubbed "King of the Southern Iron World," established the rural industrial town of Bessemer, naming it after Henry Bessemer, the British industrialist who had discovered how to make steel from pig iron. This very year my great-grandmother on my father's side, Edith Johnson, was born in the farming town of Greensboro in Hale County, Alabama. Grandma Edie, as we called her, married her first husband, Parker, whom she and everybody else called Crockett, although I never understood just why. They had a son, Frank, who became Mother's first husband and "Daddy Frank" to me and all of his other grandchildren. As fate would have it, they ended up in Bessemer around 1905, following in the tracks left by hordes of others who had also wrenched themselves away—some were forced off the land—from the rich, waxy soil of cotton country and into the satellite towns of Birmingham: Bessemer, Dolomite, Jonesboro, Muscoda, Ishkooda, Acipco, Black Diamond—where the men labored in blast furnaces and foundries and rolling mills or crawled on their bellies with lights on their heads, digging in the veins of mine shafts.

For mysterious reasons, Crockett didn't last long at U.S. Pipe and Foundry, although I have never been able to learn the straight of why he left there to haul furniture for Walker/Handley and Sons. Throughout my childhood, two stories made the rounds about Crockett's time at U.S. Pipe. The first one came from Daddy Frank, who boasted that his father had slapped a white foreman for calling him an ape. "Daddy slapped the somabitch," he would brag. "When the somabitch called him a gorilla, Daddy told him he could have his gorilla job and stick it where the sun don't shine." In another version of the story that my father heard years later from a man long retired from Pipe Shop, Crockett was fired for labor organizing. Of course, it is conceivable that they could both be true.

When Daddy Frank started at Pipe Shop in 1921, he was sixteen years old. He worked there for forty-four years, his tenure ending abruptly with the stroke that paralyzed him the evening after the morning he put in his last shift there. The year Daddy Frank began to work at Pipe Shop was a momentous one in the plant's history, the year U.S. Pipe purchased the rights to a centrifugal casting method, which revolutionized the production of cast-iron pipe. Dimitri Sensaud de Lavaud, a French engineer, was the inventor and he must have been to cast-iron production what Eli Whitney was to cotton. Two years later, in 1923, my father would be born and eventually tied to "the de Lavaud," the section of the plant where he spent almost the entirety of the nearly thirty years he worked there. The last line of his service record reads

> Union on Strike Since 10-31-74 through date of death
> 12-5-74. Removed from payroll. DECEASED.

In the ensuing weeks, the demands of summer school crowded out all but fleeting thoughts of Daddy and the plant and asbestos. Although Auntee's calls had slackened, her mission raged unchecked, and I felt her ghostly hand behind a rash of unsolicited mailings. One came from a law office in Birmingham.

Asbestos Diseases Steal Your Dreams
This country owes its very existence to the strength and courage of its working men and women. With your energy and craftsmanship, you created America's industrial base. You built homes. Made the American dream a reality. Unfortunately, many worked in areas contaminated by asbestos. Asbestos caused mesothelioma, asbestosis, lung, throat, colon and intestinal cancer and occupationally related illnesses.

Call the Law Offices of Mitchell, Mitchell, and Graham if you or a loved one has been diagnosed with any asbestos-related disease. Call, we want to help.

In the inset of the flier was a photograph of a thick-shouldered black man, with pockmarked face and grizzled beard. Wearing a white hard hat and what looked like a denim jacket, he squints at the viewer through black thick-rimmed glasses—a searing and accusing stare. I half expected a call from Auntee to see if I had gotten this latest mailing, but when two weeks passed without a word from her, I knew what that meant: She was waiting for me to call. To my surprise, she did not mention asbestos, not even once, just the state of her own health. She wasn't feeling well, she said, and her talk was riddled with references to death. I'd heard them all before.

Auntee always exaggerates any ordinary ache or pain or even a bona fide medical complication. She always worries that they all foretell impending death, but in all my years of listening to her litany of complaints, I must say that seldom has even one been serious. But that night in late June, I heard a subtle and unfamiliar timbre in her voice, and when she pleaded with me to come home, because she was "feeling poorly," I promised, without a moment's hesitation, to make it there in time for the Fourth of July.

Arrival

I scanned the crowd and spotted them from a distance down the jet way. Out in front of the crowd, three abreast. Brittany, Gina's twelve-year-old daughter, was much taller than when I had last seen her just two years before. She moved slightly forward as I came through the gate, but Auntee pulled her back. As I approached, both Auntee and Gina stood protectively behind her, each resting a hand on her shoulders. We hugged and chitchatted. The trip had been fine. No, the flight wasn't too bumpy. Did they serve a snack? Just peanuts and Coke these days. "That ain't enough food for a sparrow. You must be starving."

"No, I'm all right. I ate breakfast."

"Well, I know what kind of breakfast you eat. Just a handful of berries and some oatmeal ain't got no butter or milk or nothing in it." Auntee was remembering the last time I cooked breakfast at home. "You call this cooking?" she had asked. "Get out the way." Then she flattened rounds and rounds of Ziegler's sausage patties in a frying pan.

"I hope you ain't stopped eating barbecue."

"Oh, no, I haven't. Did you barbecue?"

"Not yet. But for the Fourth. I started making my sauce last night, so by Monday all the flavors will be good and settled in. Where's your baggage ticket?" Auntee asked.

"I only have this bag."

"That little bag all you brought? You must not be planning to stay long."

"Until Wednesday."

"Shucks, that ain't hardly no time."

We found the car, piled inside, and zigzagged through the airport maze. Gina had said very little, so I nudged her. "Cat got your tongue?"

She laughed and said, "No, I'm concentrating on getting out of this airport; it's so confusing up in here since they remodeled, plus with Estella in the car, can't nobody squeeze a word in edgewise." She was partly right. Auntee crammed the minutes with chatter and news about the neighbors, church members, coworkers, even strangers whose misfortunes had been featured on the evening news. She quieted for a few minutes while Brittany told me about her piano lessons, but at the next lull, she revved up again with talk of gloom and doom.

Auntee hates riding on the interstate, so Gina took the long way home, over the Bessemer Super Highway, past where Miss Pigrom's music studio used to be, past the Twenty-fourth Street Grill and Bessemer's two oldest black funeral homes—standing side by side: Coleman and Sons and Stansell Brothers. As we proceeded across the bridge, I stared down on the mean shotgun houses that squatted on either side underneath the bridge's metal and concrete.

Turning right off the highway, we passed Macedonia A.M.E. Zion Church, which my family had attended since migrating to Bessemer, and in minutes, we were on the outskirts of Pipe Shop. There the interstate picks up again. When the 59/20 freeway cut through Pipe Shop, it displaced our neighbors at the easternmost edge, which is now smattered with fast-food joints on either side of the interstate.

You have to drive through Pipe Shop to get to Auntee's house, just three miles west of U.S. Pipe and Foundry. We flashed past boarded-up houses where junked cars without tires stood out front on cement blocks. Each time I return, more houses are torn down. Mama Lucy's house is gone, along with Miss Georgia's shot house. Those remaining are in need of paint, repairs, reseeded grass, and flowers. During my childhood, in almost every yard, there were planters hewn from asphalt tires and bursting with red and yellow zinnias, and elephant ears, growing three feet tall, reaching the porch's edge.

As we pulled into Auntee's driveway, I could see the effects of the Alabama drought. The grass was brown, dry, patchy, and Auntee's blue hydrangeas were barely hanging on to life. There was no sign of rain. Inside the dejected-looking house, all the curtains were drawn, enveloping each room in darkness. The air conditioner groaned and blasted stale refrigerated air.

We changed into shorts and lounged in the backyard underneath the shade tree until our sweaty thighs began to stick to the plastic straps of the folding chairs, and we tracked back indoors. There in the daytime darkness, the din of the air conditioner competed with the television audience, roaring as the sumo wrestlers fought to pin each other to the mat, and with the constantly ringing phone. At Auntee's house, the phone rings from morning to night, lengthy one-way conversations running back to back. No one was watching the television, so when Gina and Brittany left the room, I turned it off. I needed some peace and quiet. But from her perch on the telephone, Auntee called out, "Don't turn it off."

"But nobody's watching it."

"That's all right. Leave it on. Willie Fred left Cookie? When? Wait, Ruby, let me call you back; they saying something about O.J. on Channel Seven."

Auntee cannot tolerate silence; it has to be annulled. After the television has ceased to blare and phones have shut off for the night, the radio's static lulls the house to sleep, and first thing in the morning, rouses it again with news of drive-by shootings and ads for cemetery plots.

The O.J. blip now past, Auntee cast her eyes my way and asked, "Did you call out to the Pipe Shop?"

"No, but I was planning to call today." I had been planning no such thing, but, as usual, I felt the need to placate Auntee. I took the portable telephone from its cradle and dialed information for the plant's number. In less than a minute, I returned the phone to its cradle. What a blessing. I was freed of this nettlesome asbestos burden.

"What happened? You got a busy signal?"

"No."

"What, then?"

"They are in a vacation shutdown."

"What? Until when?"

"July fifteenth."

"Well, you got to stay until then."

"Auntee, I can't. I told you that I have to move to Washington at the end of August. I have a million things to do before then."

My feeble explanations just urged her on.

"What's more important? Moving to Washington or your own daddy?"

"That's not the point, Auntee. Anyway, Daddy's dead. I don't understand why you can't just leave this alone and let us enjoy our visit. Why are you so caught up in this asbestos mess?"

"I want you to know that I'm not trying to get nothing for myself. I don't want not one thin dime of whatever you might get . . ."

"We might not get a dime."

"I'm just thinking about my brother, your daddy. Wiley worked himself into the ground out there at that plant. Worked himself for that union, and what good did it do him? Well, since you don't want to handle it, let me leave it alone, but if it was my daddy, I would at least look into it.

Right is right any way you look at it. If they didn't give me some kind of settlement, they would have to give me some kind of reason why. I would march right out to that Pipe Shop and make them give me what was mine."

"Time out, Auntee. I'm going outside."

"In this hot, browsing sun?"

"It's hot in here." I sat, seething, on the porch. It was easy for her to say what she would do, "If it was her daddy," who had been moldering in the grave for almost thirty years. Besides, Auntee was only four years old when Daddy Frank and Mother separated, and he had never been much of a presence in her life.

Everybody always said that Auntee looked just like Daddy Frank, right down to the bulging bags under her rheumy eyes. She even had his bandy legs. His hair-trigger temper too. At the slightest provocation (or none at all) she would flare, like now, into conniption fits, tiny droplets of perspiration collecting on the bridge of her nose.

Daddy Frank was quite a cussed character, with a fierce appetite for rotgut liquor. He came to visit his mother, Grandma Edie, every Saturday, no matter what, generally staggering from Georgia's, the local shot house. Sometimes he was too drunk to make it up the steps, and just plopped down on the walkway. Grandma Edie would often drag him up the steps, scolding him all the while about what a lousy son he'd turned out to be, despite his proper Christian upbringing. And didn't it look mighty bad for him to be staggering and foaming at the mouth and smelling like a whiskey still right in front of his grandchildren? What kind of example was that to set? Her appeals were all lost on Daddy Frank, whose head lolled as he slobbered and slurred the famous words that often punctuated his arrival: "I'm Ethiopian, and the meanest motherfucker ever walked the earth."

With each passing year of my childhood, I warmed to Daddy Frank and, while I never came to regard him as my grandfather—Mother's second husband, Papa, fulfilled that role—in time he became an endearing and harmless old man. But in the early days, he could scare the living daylights out of me. Reggie always laughed when Daddy Frank drew him tight against his body, spewing Prince Albert tobacco juice in his face. And giggled when Daddy Frank thundered, "Don't you never forget these two things: I'm your granddaddy and you Ethiopian. You Ethiopian." But when he hugged me to his body, I trembled and cried to be released. There he'd be, sitting on the steps and holding forth about hard work and hard-headed women, when he would pitch his voice to that falsetto range that so aggravated Grandma Edie and say, "Mama, Mama, Miss Edie, please give your child some corn bread and buttermilk." When she'd bring the soupy mixture to him in his favorite sky blue bowl, he'd slurp it up, then lean his back against the brick pillar and drop off to sleep.

This was the very brick pillar that eventually took his life. After the stroke, Miss Cleo, Daddy Frank's common-law wife, would bring him to our house during the day while she worked, or on weekends, when she went fishing with her buddies on the Tombigbee River. For a while, it was a taxing scene. We already had our hands full with Daddy Les, Grandma Edie's third and final husband, now lingering in the last stages of senility; now we were hit with Daddy Frank, paralyzed on his whole right side.

If Daddy wasn't working the graveyard shift—from midnight to morning—he would meet Miss Cleo at the green Rambler and lower his father's shriveling body gently into the wheelchair. But when Daddy wasn't there, some other man in the neighborhood would carry Frank's body, as pall-bearers do a fallen potentate. Miss Cleo was grateful for the help, but, as she insisted, she could handle Frank herself. She was a short, but hefty, broad-hipped woman who had transformed Daddy Frank. Grandma Edie said it was all because she was his pea-liquor cooler, neither fearing his feistiness nor submitting to his controlling will. Each year they stayed together, his hot temper seemed to cool. That is, until he had the stroke that brought the rage right back and made it worse, because it could not be numbed with alcohol. Sometimes, despite her preachments about the evils of liquor, Grandma felt sorry for her only child and sneaked him shots of gin. I had seen her do it many times, holding the shot glass to his lips while Daddy Frank sipped the liquid, some dribbling down his chin. Although Grandma denied it to the bitter end, it had been widely bruited about that Daddy Frank was actually drunk the day he tumbled off the porch. Our next-door neighbor, Eddie James Floyd, remembered that he reeked of liquor that last day.

That day, Miss Cleo had brought him to our house before sunrise. From my bed I heard the wheelchair trundling over the wooden floor, the creak of the mattress as he was eased into the daybed; then the house was still again. After breakfast Daddy left for a union meeting and Mama for her job at Dixie Cleaners, and Reggie and Bumbiddle joined the boys in the neighborhood who rolled car tires up and down the street. I sat for a while with Daddy Frank on the porch, lighting his cigarettes, then placing them carefully in his good hand. He had been restless all that day, first wanting to sit under the chinaberry tree, then on the porch, then back out in the yard. Eddie James patiently lifted him up and down, up and down the steps.

I finally escaped to my friend Linda's yard just a few houses away, and was absorbed in a game of jacks when the siren's wail jerked my head around. "It's stopping in front of y'all's house," Linda gasped, and I leaped from the porch and bolted home. There he was, lying very still on the ground, Grandma Edie and Eddie James standing over him. Over the years, whenever she told the story, Grandma would always blame herself, but she never owned up to giving him gin.

"I gave him his dinner 'round two o'clock and then I rolled him out on the porch so he could get some sun. I know I put the catch on the wheelchair. I swear 'fore God I did. Lord knows, I wouldn've left my child out there on the edge of that porch to roll off and hit his head. I wasn't gone no more than five or ten minutes. No more. No more. I just went in the house to put clean sheets on the bed, so he could lay down. And then I heard the chair fall. *Bam-a-lam-a-lamma.* And I come a-running to see my child laying down on that muddy ground on his bad side. I cried, 'Oh Lord, have mercy,' screaming till Eddie James heard me and came running again and called the ambulance.

"Frank snagged his pajama leg. Must have got it caught in the chair. You know the last thing he said to me? He said, 'Mama, I'm tired. I want to lay down.' He knew then, before he even tumbled off that porch. He knew his time had come. When the ambulance man turned him over, I could see he was bleeding from his head. His eyes was open, but when I said, 'Frank, Frank, this Mama. Here Mama,' he didn't say nothing. It was like he couldn't see me or didn't know who I was. He never came to. I will believe to my dying day that Frank was already gone when they took him out of this here yard. Never came to."

Grandma Edie never forgave herself for Daddy Frank's fall. She should have been watching him, she insisted. When she wasn't blaming herself, she was blaming Mother, although, by that time, she couldn't have been serious about his accident being Mother's fault, because Mother and Daddy Frank had been divorced for years.

Grandma Edie had long reserved a special place in her heart for Viola Gee, her first daughter-in-law, who was born February 12, 1907, in Epps, Alabama, Sumter County. She had met the beak-nosed, waiflike girl at church. Mother had just run off from Meridian, Mississippi, where she was being cruelly mistreated by an aunt who had taken her in when her own mother died. Grandma Edie took to her immediately and thought she would make a nice wife for her son Frank, grown more wayward by the day. He was spending a good part of his Pipe Shop earnings on women and the other part on gin, but Grandma Edie was convinced that a good woman could straighten him out. Soon after she introduced them, on a day she dragged Daddy Frank to church, they started keeping company. By the time they were married in 1923, Mother was sixteen years old and four months pregnant with my father. Auntee was born four years later. When the six-year marriage frayed beyond repair, Mother set out, with great determination, to remake her life.

Grandma Edie tried her best to keep Daddy Frank and Mother joined together, if only for the sake of the "poor little children," but Mother's mind was made up. She was leaving Frank. First, she tried to earn a living at something other than polishing staircases or, as she often put it, "washing other people's dirty drawers." She had a hankering for something more dignified. Not finding it in the environs of Birmingham, she left Pipe Shop just days after her twenty-fifth birthday, February 12, 1932.

As Mother used to tell the story, it was something she had to do. Long, long after she left Daddy Frank, she was still defending her decision. "When he almost split my head wide open and Wiley saw him do it, I knew I had to go. Miss Edie said, 'Daughter, how can you leave your little bitty children?' but I said, 'Miss Edie, I rather leave 'em for a little while than leave 'em for good. And as sure as I stay with Frank, I'll be dead.'" And so she boarded a train for the School for Colored Nurses in Stymon, West Virginia, leaving Daddy and Auntee with Grandma Edie. The story goes that she came back two years later wearing a crisp white shirtwaist uniform and a navy blue cape lined in red. In short order, she divorced Daddy Frank and vowed to erase him and all his drunken, womanizing ways from her life, even if it killed her. And it did kill her, eventually, or so thought practically everybody in the family.

Fourth of July

The next day was the Fourth of July. Back home in Pipe Shop, Fourth of July was—after Christmas and Easter—the most important holiday of the year, a time for new shorts and sandals and cool-offs in bathing suits.

"Spray us, Daddy, spray us," we are squealing. "Whee-e-e-e." He turns the hose on us. It tickles my belly button. The water from the outside hydrant is very cold. I remember that we would hop from foot to foot, pretending to dodge the water as Daddy chased us around the yard and we took cover behind the fig tree leaves. At nightfall, we ran up and down Eighteenth Street with bunches of long, thin sparklers irradiating the purpled darkness and crackling in our hands.

Fourth of July also marked the beginning of the watermelon season. According to Grandma Edie, watermelon couldn't be eaten a day before then, because it wasn't really ripe, and if you ate it, it would give you cramps or maybe even kill you. Among the many strict rules of food consumption, this one was right up there with warnings against drinking gin with watermelon. Cousin Red made the warning famous, when I offered her a piece of watermelon one Fourth of July. "No, Sugar, I don't eat watermelon when whiskey season's in." Whereupon her husband, Bubba, laughed and said, "Well, I guess that means you won't never eat a slice of watermelon, 'cause whiskey season is every day the good Lord sends, for you."

The scent of barbecue sauce simmering on the stove led me to the kitchen, where Auntee stood scraping potato skins still hot from boiling water. I dipped my finger in the pot and tasted the barbecue sauce.

"I see you're still using Daddy's recipe."

"It's not your daddy's recipe," she snapped. "And anyway, how you know he didn't get his from me?"

"No, Auntee, you never used to put Worcestershire in your sauce."

"Yes, I did. Why you think your daddy had to come up with everything?"

"Auntee, I didn't say he did, and I didn't mean anything by it. I was just teasing." I left Auntee rattling pots and stomped down the hill to Buddy's Place to get a copy of the *Birmingham World*. Of course I knew her tantrum was not at all about a barbecue recipe. She was still on a slow boil from yesterday. As I passed the rock quarry, stirring up clouds of red dust and gravel, I muttered to myself, "I don't care what she says. It *is* Daddy's recipe."

Daddy always mixed his famous sauce in a dented aluminum boiler, simmering over the blue gas flame. The sauce would scent the house with lemon juice and the smokiness of Worcestershire.

"It's pronounced Wooster-sheer."

"No, Daddy, it has four syllables."

"I know."

"Well, what happened to 'cest'?"

"It's silent."

Daddy barbecued for almost all the neighbors on our block. They would lumber into the yard with new-cut slabs of pork ribs wrapped in white butcher paper or mutton or Cornish hens. Most turned out with packages of Bruno's chicken thighs, nestled in yellow Styrofoam and priced for buying in bulk, or just-thawed stacks of pork chops. Daddy always set up the grate the night before, yanking it from the back fence, choked with vines of kudzu and morning glories.

When Daddy first brought the grate home, roped to the back of Mr. Mitchell's truck, we watched him transform it into a barbecue grill by propping it on four corners of cinder blocks stacked six deep. He squirted a steady stream of lighter fluid on charcoal briquettes, scraps of kindling, and crumpled newspapers piled underneath. When Reggie and Bumbiddle and I fought with each other over who would drop the lighted match down through the grate and hear the whoosh as it ignited, Daddy solved the problem by giving each of us a match.

"Cup your hand to keep the flame from blowing out."

As I reached the crest of the hill, on my way back to Auntee's, I could hear the funky growling of the blues. "Been searching. Been searching. Been searching every wh-i-i-ich a way-ay-ay-ay."

I tromped around the house to the backyard, where friends and neighbors had already sprawled around the barbecue pit, six-packs and fifths of gin around their feet. We fanned ourselves with the bottoms of cardboard boxes, hoping to stir a cooling breeze. I danced two times with a gold-toothed man in a baseball cap, already soused at noon.

"You want to ride in my brand-new car?"

"No, sir, another time."

Auntee's next-door neighbor, Pee Wee, and Pee Wee's back-door man trickled in with other cousins all afternoon, who bantered over whether I had grown to resemble Daddy more than Mother. "It's the same," Red insisted. "'Cause your daddy looked just like Aunt Curly, and you look just like both of 'em, except you done got stout." Red had brought some back ribs from last year's hog killing down home in Boligee. Most of the hog killings took place "down home," as the people referred reverently to the hamlets they had lived in before migrating to Bessemer.

I had witnessed one hog killing and never hoped to see another. Actually, the hog had already been slaughtered back behind Daddy Frank's and Miss Cleo's house. Mama had told me to go directly there after school. I was shocked to see the animal scraped to pinkness and hoisted upside down by its feet, the blood still on the ground where it had drained. Because I could not bear to watch the pig, I leaned over the black cast-iron wash pot to let the water's steam moisten my face.

Auntee wiped the sweat collecting on her brow and mopped the slab of ribs with sauce, then cut off a tip for me to taste. I read it as a peace offering. Just then, the portable phone rang and Gina passed it to me.

"Long distance," she said, and snickered. "A man." It was difficult to hear over the music, the popping beer cans, and wolf tickets that everybody was hawking at the card table. "Boston time. Boston time. Give 'em here. Every last single book." I put my hand over my ear and sidled toward the back steps.

"I'll be back on Wednesday on U.S. Air flight 210. At six-thirty in the evening. Yeah, I'm having a good time. We're outdoors barbecuing right now. I'll call you later."

"Who was that on the phone?" Auntee wanted to know.

"Just a friend who's going to pick me up from the airport."

"A special friend?"

"Not really."

"What kind of answer is that? Are you going together?"

"Not exactly."

"Oh, I see. I don't understand all this newfangled courting. In my day, you either went together or you didn't." She kept basting the ribs with the miniature mop that the sauce had dyed rust red.

"How long you known him?"

"Not long. Just about two years."

"Well, give it some time. Is he nice?"

"Nice enough."

"Well, I can see you ain't gon' say too much about this man. Maybe he ain't the one." She looked up at me from her basting and asked, quiet-like, "He ain't white, is he?"

"No, Auntee. Stop it. You're embarrassing me in front of all these people."

She laughed. "Well, then he must be married."

"No, Auntee, he's not married either."

"Well, that's good. Don't go getting yourself tangled up with no married man. You can do bad all by yourself. You don't need no help with that."

Lurking just behind this quip was the ghost of Mr. Lige, the man Auntee had loved for many years. His name was Elijah Honeycutt, but everybody called him Lige. Against Mother's fervid objections—he was already married—Auntee would not let him go, nor would she give up her hope that he would marry her one day. But when some mysterious muscular ailment finally claimed his wife, he ditched Auntee and married Wilhelmina Polk, who had graduated with Gina from Carver High, no less. Auntee took years to recover from this blow. And you might say she never did. While she had lots of other men over the years, she trusted not a one. They became, for her, mere means to other ends, like rings and watches, new shoes and washing machines.

When the rib fest ended just at dusk, the good timers ambled to their cars and headed with the children for the fireworks. Auntee didn't want to go and persuaded Gina and me to stay at home with her. She has always been afraid to be alone.

"Why didn't you want to see the fireworks, Auntee?"

"I don't like sitting in the dark with a bunch of people I don't know."

"But you know all the people who went from here."

"I might know them, but I don't know all these other folks and what they might do. Round holidays folks get crazy, carrying knives and guns and all. That's why I wasn't so hot on the idea of Brittany being up in that crowd," and turning to Gina, she said disapprovingly, "but if her mama wants her to go, why . . ."

Not wanting to be provided with a reel of the measureless disasters unwinding in Auntee's head, I dropped the conversation and, with Gina, patrolled the yard for crumpled paper napkins, beer cans, Dixie cups, stray rib bones, and sparklers strewn like pick-up sticks all along the roadside. After all the signs of celebration were finally choked inside one big black plastic bag, we hugged around the shade tree, where the flickering glow of citronella candles channeled us back in time.

"Auntee, do you ever see Mr. Lige?"

"No, not since Mr. Fred died. I was surprised to see him at the funeral, but I guess he came because Mr. Fred was always decent to him, even when he thought he was in the wrong. And he knew that Mr. Fred was just like a daddy to me. I might not have been his flesh and blood, but he never throwed that up in my face. Once he married Mother, he treated me like a daughter. Didn't you see him at the funeral?"

"I'm sure I did, Auntee, but I just don't remember."

"You probably didn't recognize him, 'cause he was looking so old—older than dirt or leastways like he might have been one of the folks walking behind Jesus on the road to Calvary. I could tell just by looking at him that he wasn't 'bout nothing by then. You see, all these young women had done used him up, squeezed him dry, got everything they could out of him. He had some kinda nerve showing up at the funeral. Anyway, I didn't want him. What business I got with a broke-down man?"

Gina ribbed her, "You didn't always think he was a broke-down man." Gina was right, and I was determined to ask Auntee something I had wanted to know all my life: What made her cling to Mr. Lige for all those years? I asked her point-blank.

"Mother always wanted to put me with these goody-goody types," Auntee began, "like Arthur Rutledge and Enoch Ravizee, who always acted so sanctified, like they had just been dipped in holy water. She always wanted to pick my friends for me. Something was always wrong with anybody I picked out for myself. With Mother, nothing I ever did was right. Not my clothes, not my hair, not my friends. Didn't matter. If I liked it, it wasn't right. No way, no how.

"Well, I was never interested in the boys she thought I should have. I wanted somebody tougher than that, not always letting their mamas pull 'em first one way and then another. You know, women need men who look like they got some backbone, look like they could chop some wood. Lige was like that, or so I thought at the time.

"I met him at Georgia's house. He came walking in there looking like Big Daddy Lipscomb. I never will forget it. He was wearing a straw hat with a stingy brim—I think it was tan-colored. He had on a starched white shirt open at the neck—he always wore white shirts—and some black pants that he kept hiking up. He had come down to Pipe Shop to see his sister Ovetta, and she brought him round to Georgia's for a shot of gin. He had just come back from up the country. He was working for General Motors up there in Detroit. Making good money, but when his wife got down sick, he couldn't take care of her by himself, so they moved back down here where her people could help see after her. He got on out there at the rolling mill.

"I liked him 'cause he had some pride, some get-up about him. Always had on clean, pressed clothes, shined shoes. Shaved. Smelled good. Always had a nice car. And he could take me more places than the ball diamond and the Lincoln Theater and fried-chicken dinners at Macedonia Church.

"Now I know I should have known better than to believe in a man who would scratch me in my hand the first time he saw me. You know, that's what men would do back then to let you know they liked you. They would do it in a secret kind of way, like when they shook hands with you, they would scratch. Well, anyway, I went riding with him that very day and that's how it all got started. If I had it to do all over again, I'd've left him alone, left him right back there in Georgia's kitchen. But that day, Lord, I thought he was the best thing since a pocket full of crisp new dollar bills.

"Don't get me wrong now. I had some good times with Lige, you understand. He was my sho-nuff spodeeodee, but I got tired of sneaking 'round. Annie Laura would come get me. She had a piece of a car, and she would drive me to meet Lige. We went around to all the nicest places—the Madison Night Spot, before it went downhill, the city auditorium to hear the bands. He gave me money, sometimes a fifty-dollar bill. He was making good money in those days at the rolling mill. Sometimes he would take me uptown and let me get things on his bill. Dresses. Shoes. Hats. Slips. Whatever I wanted. I wasn't working then, no more than a little day work, so Mother suspected he was buying me clothes, and she liked to had a conniption fit. She said I had no business letting no man I wasn't married to buy me clothes. The first time Mama Edie saw him, she called me in the kitchen and said, 'Stella. You keeping company with this man?' And I said, 'Yes ma'am, Mama.' And she said, 'Stella, that's a gap-toothed man. You can't trust no gap-toothed man. He'll lie just as soon as look at you.'

"Everybody told me to leave him alone. Mama Edie, Mother, even your own mama told me. They all tried to sense me into leaving him alone. Mother said, 'Don't fool yourself. Men have good-time women and then they have wives. They run the streets with the good-time women and then go home to their wives.' She was right too. You could stick a pin in that. But did I listen? No, sirr-ee.

"But to tell you the truth, I didn't want him to leave his wife, her being disabled and all. That wouldn't have been right. He didn't mistreat her, never left her by herself. Back then, folks didn't expect no more than that. There always was men around that had sick wives, but as long as they made sure they were looked after and clean, folks didn't look down on them for needing the company of another woman. Now if a man ran around with lots of women, that wasn't good, but if he had a steady woman he kept company with, folks looked the other way.

"When Sadie died, I still didn't put no pressure on him to marry. That wouldn't have looked right either, her just dead and all. But then, he upped and married that young hussy young enough to be his daughter, and Sadie's head wasn't no more than five months cold. Liked to knock the wind outta me when Wiley told me. Lige didn't even have the common decency to let me know. He just stopped coming round. Changed his phone number. I didn't know what had happened to him. Weeks went by; I was so worried that I sent Wiley round looking for him, to see what he could find out. Well, sir, Wiley went out to that rolling mill to find out when his shift ended, and that's how he heard. Lige told him. Wiley said, 'Stella, forget about Lige. You have wasted too much time with him already. Any man who ain't got enough respect for you to give you a call and tell you what's happening ain't worth a drop of spit. He's a coward. What you want with a coward?'

"After that, I lost interest in everything, but I remember as plain as I'm looking at you, the day I started coming back around to myself. It was after me and Mr. Fred had a long talk, sitting in the kitchen at Mother's house. Just us, by ourselves, without Mother screaming and fussing and stomping through the house. He just let me talk to him. I told him it looked like I had lost everything and didn't have no future. And he said, 'Stella.' I never will forget it. He had just come in from prayer meeting. I was laying on Mother's couch in the living room when he came in. I didn't answer him at first, 'cause I knew he was gon' start in on me 'bout drinking. So I pretended like I didn't hear him, but he called me again. This time, he called my whole name, and the only time Mr. Fred ever called my whole name was for something serious. He said, 'Estella Louise, come in here in the kitchen.' And I went on back there. He said, 'Estella, you can't just roll up and die over no man, 'specially when you got a child to see after. You know, sometimes you can't look back at what you done lost, but pray to keep your mind on what you got left. You got a child, and you need to start paying more attention to her. I want you to get up from this table and make your mind up to forget about Lige Honeycutt. Don't take no more thought of him.' He said, 'If you keep wasting your time with Lige you'll look up one day and wonder where your life done gone, but then, it'll be too late to get it back.'

"I never forgot that talk we had. It still took me a long time to really get over Lige, but from that very day I started coming back to myself, and it was Mr. Fred that helped me do it."

*   *   *

I left Auntee's house five days later. In all, I had been there just over a week. I extended my stay beyond the weekend I'd allotted, because Auntee was complaining again about knife-like stomach pains. At first, I humored her along, thinking it was plain old manipulation, at which Auntee is quite adept. She gets this tendency from Mother, who had also habitually feigned sickness, alternately to get sympathy and in order to be left alone. But when I caught a glimpse of Auntee's stomach as she dressed for the doctor, a bitter chill came over me. I could not help but be reminded of Mama and the physician's description of her stomach the night he sent her home with an envelope of Demerol. She was dead by daybreak.

Black female, age 55. Temperature. Stomach noticeably distended.

That's how Auntee's stomach looked to me.

Leaving Brittany with the next-door neighbor, Gina and I drove Auntee to the emergency room, where she received a vague diagnosis and pills to line up alongside the other amber plastic bottles that filled a two-tiered lazy Susan atop the kitchen counter.

Auntee was somber throughout that afternoon and bound and determined to talk to Gina and me about "her business." She answered our attempts to deflect this fixation with, "I just don't want you-all to have to be scrambling around here looking for burial policies and suchlike." She handed me the insurance cards—Booker T. Washington and North Carolina Mutual. "I want you to know where everything is, so when my head gets cold, you won't have to worry." Now that I think of it, she might have said, "When I'm laid out on the cooling board." It was one or the other.

Years had passed since I'd heard either of these expressions, both of which I associated with Grandma Edie. Now they had found their way to Auntee's tongue, right down to the words of the song that Grandma often lined at prayer meeting: "This may be the last time. Maybe the last time, I don't know."

"Oh, Estella," Gina pshawed, "you'll still be around here kicking and snapping and nagging long after the rest of us are gone." I laughed in agreement, although I had a vague presentiment that this was an unlikely pass and, for the first time, the sensation frightened me.

I hung around for three more days until her symptoms had subsided and her feisty mood returned. I knew it was safe to leave when she resumed the daily round of telephone calls.

She came into the bedroom as I was cramming my things into the duffel bag. "Here. Let me fold these clothes. You pack just like Mother, just jamming everything together." I stepped aside and watched Auntee as she carefully folded my clothes, and joked with her to chase away the sadness that was palpable in the room. Over the years I've come to understand this quality in Auntee, which runs through me as well. She is saddened by any kind of separation—even from the person at the other end of the telephone line. Many a time I've moved to end a conversation with her and heard her say, "Wait, before you go, let me tell you this. I'd almost forgot about it." And I listen to the remembered item and we resume the round once more: "Wait, before you go . . ."

That day, as she squeezed the last newly laundered T-shirt in the corner of the bag, she turned to me and said, "I don't guess you ever intend on coming back home, do you?"

I could not bring myself to say, "No, Auntee, I don't," and so I said, "Who knows, I might. Maybe even soon," and that seemed to satisfy her for the moment.

Our good-byes were brief, but as I hugged Auntee I let myself feel the pangs of future loss. Until this visit in July 1994 I had taken for granted that Auntee would go on forever—needling, haranguing, erupting like Mount Vesuvius at the most unexpected moments. But this time I noticed signs of her fragility that I had not seen before.

I returned home and began preparations to move to Washington. I had received a fellowship from the Woodrow Wilson International Center to begin a book called "Viewing the Remains: On Violence, Mourning, and the Symbolics of Loss." But in the ensuing months, I slowly came to understand just how deeply this intellectual project was rooted in an emotional need to view the remains of my own past, a viewing long postponed. Auntee had been the catalyst, first with her frantic, late-night call in the wee hours of Memorial Day, the call that sent me combing through the contents of crumpled paper bags in search of a death certificate. And over the course of one long year, she spurred the process on as she gave voice to fears of her own mortality, transferring those fears to me. As my oldest living relative, she was my last link to memories of my family in the days before my birth. For years, throughout my life, death or its imminence had interrupted study, and so I surrendered to the pattern once again. I researched one book by day, but by night, I scoured the columns of my memory and pressed all my fragile band of remaining kin to do the same, so that I, long the family's reader and its scribe, could piece together the history of our family, there in Pipe Shop, one story at a time.

PART
TWO

Pipe Shop

If you ever hope to amount to anything, you have to break out of Pipe Shop." That's what Mother always said. She had hammered this into my head for as far back as I can remember. But no matter how much Mother disdained it, Pipe Shop was the center of my world for all my formative years. In fact, I have no memory of my life before Pipe Shop, when we moved there as a family of four—Daddy, Mama, Reggie, and me—so that Daddy could be close to his new job at U.S. Pipe. It was January 1955. My memory begins there, at 1805 Long Eighteenth Street, where we lived with Great-grandma Edie and her third and last husband, Daddy Les. By September of that same year, Martha Faye had come permanently to stay. Then in April 1957 Bumbiddle was born and we all crowded into this white wood-framed double-tenant house.

As I recollect the world of Pipe Shop now almost thirty years later, I seek not to cast it in a nostalgically sentimental light, complete with clichéd references to a "closely knit" community in which everybody got along, pulling together and in harmony against the might of an oppressive white world outside. And yet, Pipe Shop did possess these qualities in some measure, though they were often tested along the way.

Nearly everybody in the community worked at "The Pipe Shop" but also had some sideline job to hustle extra money, because the Pipe Shop didn't quite pay a living wage. And so Mr. Renfrew cut almost everybody's grass. Mr. Mitchell used the back of his dump truck to haul manure, stacks of Sheetrock, rolls of linoleum, a used refrigerator or living-room suite. Mr. Odell Richards was about the only person in the neighborhood who wasn't forever in a tight. He lent money, stashed throughout his house, to people laid off or needing an extra little bit to stretch to payday. Grandma Edie claimed that he squirreled money away in socks, in empty cans of Prince Albert tobacco, and between the pages of the Bible. It was even rumored that he buried money underneath the house in case of a fire.

During tax season, neighbors filed through our front door with 1040 and W-2 forms and sipped beer while Daddy calculated on scratch paper. Would there be a refund? Would it be enough to pay off a nagging debt? To put down on a car or a child's piano or clarinet or maybe to take a vacation up the country? When Daddy said that the IRS owed them and not the other way around, he was elevated to a wizard in their eyes and mine.

When Miss Minnie Lee Sturdivant, the Avon Lady, came to call, we ordered bubble bath, talcum powder, lipstick, and perfumes that Mother insisted we should never wear. "Avon is absolutely too loud," she said before instructing me to wash it off one Sunday before we went to church. "A body can smell you coming a mile away. I'll get you a little bottle of perfume that's not so loud." It was a lost cause, though. When I told Mama about what Mother thought of Avon, she sneered, "When Miss Viola starts buying my perfume, then she can tell me what kind to wear." And that's just what Mother did one Christmas, but Mama left the bottle of L'Air du Temps standing unopened on the dresser, just for spite.

Miss Ruby Seal had a newspaper route, pulling rubber-banded bundles of the the *Birmingham News* and the *Birmingham World* from a rusty basket bolted to her son's red bicycle. Published every Tuesday and Friday, the *World,* subtitled a "standard race journal," was Alabama's oldest black semiweekly newspaper, and we turned to it for reports and announcements of community happenings and for an angle on local and national events missing from the majority paper, the *Birmingham News.*

It seemed that everyone looked to the *World* for something different: Grandma, for the weekly Bible lessons; Mama, for laughs at Eugenia Boone's "Society" column. When Mother went to the general conference held at Mother Zion Church in New York City, the paper covered her bon voyage at the airport, making it sound as if she were off on a diplomatic mission to a flashpoint of the world. The *World* was the main source for Mother's scrapbook clippings and for the poems Mrs. German and Mrs. Harvey, the leaders of the church's youth club, clipped for Sunday afternoon recitations. Women in Pipe Shop combed L. S. Craig's column for advice about their troubled marriages, and, based on what they found, speculated as to whether L. S. was a woman or a man.

While the *Birmingham World* kept us all abreast of "outside goings-on," for the local Pipe Shop scuttlebutt, the women and girls of the neighborhood flocked to Ophelia's to get their hair straightened and styled. While a few women went to Willie Bell's, the other black beautician in Pipe Shop, who lived up near Daddy Frank, most went to Ophelia's. Because she had so many customers (as well as another job), Ophelia was often rushed and thus sometimes grazed someone's scalp or ear with the straightening comb, then blew to cool it off.

"Did 'Phelia burn you? Oh, honey, I'm sorry. I didn't mean to. You so tender-headed, I can't hardly get down to the roots. Whoo-whoo. That better?"

You'd better eat before you went to Ophelia's, though (or pack a snack), because you were sure to sit all day long, as other girls and women trickled into the house to wait impatiently for Shirley Temples or bangs and kissy curls held down by shiny black crisscrossed hairpins. Sometimes, people lost patience with the wait and the crowd thinned out. At those times, gossip flowed more freely and Miss Ophelia stopped for lunch.

"Is anybody hungry?"

Heads would nod and the curling irons stop clicking just long enough for her to drop a dozen hot dogs in a pot of boiling water before sending me and her daughter, Peaches, to Blankenship's for buns and Coca-Colas.

"Don't get the sixteen-ounce," she would say. "They try to fool you like you gettin' a whole lot more drink, but you ain't. Plus, they taste flat, 'cause they half drink and half water. So be sure to get the eight-ounce."

"Yes, ma'am."

In the evenings, Miss Ophelia worked as a waitress at Pearl Harbor, Mr. Robert E. Lee's bar and grill. The only bona fide black business in the neighborhood, it lived up to its red hand-lettered sign: BEST BAR-B-QUE IN TOWN.

Sometimes I tagged along with Daddy when he went to Pearl Harbor for take-out sandwiches on bread soaked through with tangy sauce. At night, the pendant lights above each booth tinted everybody red and the boom of the jukebox set the whole floor a-shaking and a-shimmying like the waitress's jellied hips. When Jack's Hamburgers and the colonel's chicken crept into Pipe Shop, Pearl Harbor was one of the first small businesses to fold. Mr. E. Lee sold the jukebox to Miss Addie Pearl Ferguson, and her son, Fellow, rigged up wires from the house to the backyard. On Friday and Saturday nights in summer, grown folks gathered there, and way into the wee hours of the morning you could hear their laughter ringing through the air. Grandma Edie condemned Miss Addie Pearl's place as a den of iniquity, Sodom and Gomorrah there in Pipe Shop, right down to the blues that belted from the vibrating box.

But then the police started issuing summonses to Miss Addie Pearl for disturbing the peace. People swore it was Miss Eula Martin who had called the law—she had complained enough—and so they decided to boycott the little business she ran from the porch of her pink A-frame house, selling lace-edged handkerchiefs and stockings to the women who didn't want to take the bus all the way downtown. The stockings were cheap anyway and never held their shape; they sagged behind the calves like outsized blisters and creased along the instep. And the shades Miss Martin stocked for black women were never quite right; when they weren't "flesh," meaning a cross between pink and beige, they were Red Fox, the color of the Alabama dust that clashed with the pale bananas, pearl pinks, and other soft pastels that color the clothes of this period of my memory. Mama often sent me to buy her stockings, and as she hooked them to her girdle or dotted nail polish just above her heel to halt a run, she would grumble that Miss Eula Martin must truly be color-blind.

Mr. Hezekiah Burns barbered all the boys and men's hair in our neighborhood. "Be sure you pee before you go to get your hair cut," people would joke, signifying on his wife, who was suspicious and afraid of everybody and everything entering her house, especially anybody who might need to pee. It was too chancy to have just anybody sitting on her toilet stool. Somehow, one day, my classmate Cleophus Diggins stole in there, before Mr. Hezekiah could stop him. Cleophus kept us laughing for days in the lunch line about the pink tile, pink tub, pink commode, pink curtains, pink toilet paper, pink soap. "Who wants to piss in a pink toilet, anyway?" said Cleophus when he was ordered out.

Mr. Pat's, one of two white-owned Mom-and-Pop businesses (the other was Blankenship's), sold cold cuts and pullets picked clean, then stacked breast side up on mounds of glinting ice garnished with sprigs of parsley. Mr. Pat chalked his prices on a board swinging from a rope over the counter. Several times a day somebody, generally me, dropped into Blankenship's to buy whatever we needed between Saturday trips to the A & P or Bruno's Food Store—potatoes, Baby Ruths, cigarettes, and Goody headache powders. You scurried across Eighteenth Avenue, a narrow two-lane blacktop road perpendicular to Eighteenth Street, and in four or five giant steps you were at Blankenship's.

I see the rusted thermometer, advertising Coca-Cola, just outside the door. See the giant plastic red-lidded jars that crowded the vinyl-topped counter of the one-room store. See my comfort on those hot and humid Alabama afternoons—Tom's potato chips, Big Moon cookies, and stage planks, the large gingerbread squares with pink frosting scalloped on the edges. If I had gotten a nickel or dime or quarter for running errands in the course of the day, I tore to Blankenship's, the bell overhead clanging as I burst through the door. And without even drawing breath, I asked for a nickel's worth of jawbreakers or two-for-a-penny cookies.

On a good day, I had a quarter that some adult had given me for an end-of-year report card sprinkled with A's or for a "recitation" at church, or for running an especially long and challenging errand. Then I would ask for two oatmeal cookies and a cup of strawberry ice cream sold in waxed cups printed with blimpy snowmen wearing stovepipe hats. The days of quarters were quite rare, for more often than not, I had run an errand for Miss Lillian Butler, known by every child on our block as the "stingiest woman in all of Pipe Shop." Even if you had walked all the way to Walgreen's in downtown Bessemer to pick up her high blood pressure medicine, she still only wanted to pay you a dime. After a time, I was about the only child in all of Pipe Shop who would run errands for her, she was so cheap. The trips to Walgreen's were generally only once a month, so I could bear the hop across the street to Blankenship's for her daily order: a Goody headache powder and an eight-ounce bottle of Coke. Always impatient to see the sum of my reward, I shifted from one foot to the other, waiting for her to retrieve from her bosom the sweat-stained handkerchief in which she wrapped her "small change," as she put it. In those seconds from bosom to lap to opened handkerchief, I planned my goodies in my head. Sometimes Mr. Blankenship would say, "Too many cookies will rot your teeth," but I never paid him any mind. Clutching the tiny grease-stained brown paper bag tightly in my hand, I looked left and right for rushing cars, then prepared my bare feet for the sprint back home on the blistering pavement.

My fondest memories of my earliest years in Pipe Shop are all laced with the sounds and smells of summer. After a year of walking to school and standing in lunch lines behind moldy-headed boys with runny noses and girls whose socks always scooted down, like mine, to expose an ashy heel, the summer's images were light and breezy, filled with roisterous sun-splashed days and scented with honeysuckle so strong it burned your nostrils. We romped and somersaulted up and down Eighteenth Street, which stretched from Miss Evaline's, our next-door neighbor's house, to Valley Creek, where we fished for crawdads. We lay spread-eagled on the grass or did headstands in someone's yard, our legs gaped open wide to receive the warm rays of the sun—that is, until some woman passed and said, "Get up from there. That ain't nothing for a nice girl to be doing."

For almost the whole of one long summer, we scavenged the roadside for soft-drink bottle caps, hoping that the branded corks of the crinkle-edged caps had not been peeled away. Squealing in delight if we found one intact, we scraped away the grime to reach the cork and dreamed about the ever elusive prizes we would win. I had entered the "Write Your Own Ticket" sweepstakes several times, placing an "X" in the box beside the prize I was sure to win. Once I checked "Spectacular Spending," which would bring 1,001 shopping certificates. Another time I checked "Luxurious Driving." Of course, I would give the car to Daddy, because I couldn't drive and Daddy needed a car. For years we had borrowed Mother's car, until my sophomore year in high school when Daddy bought a used dark green Oldsmobile 98 that turned out to be a lemon.

The category I most wanted to win, though, was "Adventure"—a trip to the French Riviera via Air France. When Mr. Blankenship said the sweepstakes was over, and Daddy declared it a commercial swindle, I flew into a rage and threw most of the caps into the garbage can. When I calmed down, I fished a few out to replace the plastic checkers pieces constantly disappearing from the set.

Plunged back into quotidian routines, we listened for the tinkling bell of the ice cream man or someone peddling vine-ripened tomatoes, watermelons, pole beans, speckled butter beans, or just-picked ears of silver queen corn from the backs of rattling trucks. Grandma knew how to thump the watermelons in just the right way, to test for ripeness. Sometimes the man on the truck would cut a triangular plug and give it to one of us to taste. Then juice dribbled between our fingers and down our arms to mingle with the dust caked on from hours of playing outside. I always hoped for a sugar baby. Round like a soccer ball, sugar babies were rarely on the truck, but when they were, Grandma picked one and gave me my favorite piece right from the end. After spooning out the red flesh and spitting out the seeds, I slurped the nectar collected in the bottom of the green-striped rind.

We passed long sultry July evenings in the age-old Southern way: rocking rhythmically back and forth on porches. Brandishing rolled-up sections of the *Birmingham News,* we swatted at mosquitoes buzzing round our ears. Grandma Edie called this interlude of evening "first night," the time before day's sunflower light turns slowly from tender gray to gunmetal to purple. While Reggie and the other boys shot marbles in the vanishing light and Daddy rested up for the night shift, the girls and women on our street crowded on someone's porch. Miss Hattie's was everybody's favorite.

Miss Hattie lived directly across the street from us in a big rambling house with dark brown shingles. Her two granddaughters and two great-granddaughters lived with her. People in the neighborhood often muttered, "That house needs a man." But just as often, someone would chime in with, "What man could last in a house with so many bossy women?" Of some indeterminate age, Miss Hattie had frizzy gray hair with that dingy cast of yellow that the blue rinse was supposed to "highlight." Always hidden behind the curtain in the kitchen window, the blue rinse, just like the Sears and Roebuck catalogues, passed from Miss Hattie's house to ours, and then on to Miss Mae Walker's, Grandma Edie's best friend. I never understood why the women used it, because it dyed their hair from yellow-gray to a hideous lavender that made them look like dead women, lying in coffins, powder blue satin pillows underneath their heads. When I allowed as much to Grandma, she answered simply, "If the good Lord blesses you to get as old as me and Miss Hattie and Mae Walker, you'll understand."

Flashing a habitual gold-toothed grin, Miss Hattie often smiled and teased me about being nothing but a "little switch of a thang." Her granddaughter Wig was a scrawny, bow-legged, meriny woman of about twenty-five with a thick black mane of hair. That's why they called her Wig. We called her meriny because her skin was light and tinged with yellow. She often sat on the floor between Miss Hattie's legs to get her dandruff scratched and the pungent-smelling pine tar rubbed into her scalp. As Miss Hattie pulled strands of feathery hair from the plastic comb, she passed them down to Wig, who rolled them into balls between her fingers and stuck them in the pocket of her duster, lest they be wafted on the wind and fall into devilish hands hell-bent on hexing. People used to say that the right hex or "fix" could steal a wife or husband or cause a lingering illness that no doctor could explain or cure. It was even rumored that somebody had fixed Crockett, but Grandma swore it wasn't her. They had been divorced long before he took sick, she said, so why would she want to hex him? If anything, she felt sorry for him. He had paid with his guts for leaving her, and her Christian discipline forbade her to seek vengeance or take any solace or lip-smacking delight in the knowledge that colon cancer had condemned him to a form of social isolation, and forced him to tote his bowels in a sack on his side.

Like everybody else on Eighteenth Street, I loved Miss Hattie's stories about spells and hexes. As her slat-backed rocker creaked on the splintery floorboards of the porch, and she gazed on the deepening purple sky, we all surrendered to the spell of these numberless stories—of people cussing out their boss ladies (or perhaps only pretending that they had). Of the Johnson twins killed in a mine explosion. Of a schoolteacher from Wetumpka whose nature went to her head as she tarried on the mourner's bench.

When Wig went to join her serviceman husband, she left her two little girls with Miss Hattie, who delivered them to their mother a few months later. Miss Hattie returned from Frankfurt, regaling everyone with stories of the trip—her first time on an airplane—and the frozen collard greens she had smuggled overseas. Two years later, Wig was back in Pipe Shop with her daughters, and people who lived several blocks from Miss Hattie's house found some excuse to stop at the edge of her porch in order to hear these little colored girls "talk German."

I feigned sophistication and indifference, since I had already learned one German phrase from Daddy when I found pictures of his Frankfurt girl-friends from the time he was stationed there. One had dark hair piled in a bun high atop her head, and the blond waves of the other fell all around her shoulders like a shawl. Each held a look of longing and bittersweetness in her eyes. Daddy seemed embarrassed when I pointed to the scrawl in the lower right corner of one of the pictures and asked him what it meant: *"Ich liebe dich, Ariane."* He answered, "It means, 'I love you.'"

When he said, "I love you," I launched into the game I often played with Mother.

"Do you love me, Daddy?"

"Of course, I do."

"How much do you love me?"

"What kind of question is that?" he asked and kept working the crossword puzzle.

"Mother always wants to know how much I love her, and I say rivers and rivers, oceans and oceans, and miles and miles."

Daddy said, "That's a silly game."

"What happened to the ladies in the pictures, Daddy?"

"Quit asking so many questions."

"Tell me a word to guess," I said.

"This is a grown folks' puzzle," he answered. "We'll do one tomorrow," and the promise was enough to hold me until then.

1805 Long Eighteenth
Street

Our move to 1805 was to be a temporary stopover while Daddy searched for a bigger place to live, but for one reason or another—Daddy was laid off, an emergency had consumed the moving fund—we never left that house. Built to accommodate four, maybe five people comfortably, 1805 Eighteenth Street stretched to fit eight, spanning three generations. In addition, a revolving band of aunts and uncles, cousins, and other distant kin came for visits, short and long, throughout the year. Grandma Edie's brother, Uncle George, and his wife, Corine, bused up from Cosimo every summer, and Aunt Lucy, Grandma's sister, came several times a year from Greensboro. Wearing trademark gold-hooped earrings and walking with a cane, Aunt Lucy always stepped off the Greyhound bus complaining of the rheumatism in her knees. At times impatient with her younger and least favorite sister, Grandma said that she was just plain lazy and wanted to escape the demands of farm life with her husband, Perry. For sure, she drowsed away each day in Pipe Shop, reclining on the sofa and watching soap operas with the volume turned up to a deafening pitch, which ruined quiet time for reading or a nap in the afternoon.

The walls of the house were thin partitions through which, it seemed, even the sound of crumpling paper could penetrate. As siblings will, Reggie, Bumbiddle, and I fought raucously, which always brought Mama bursting into the back room that we shared. Clucking us to attention, she tried to affect a blustering tone and an edge of parental seriousness that she could never quite pull off: "If you-all don't hush up all this fuss, I'm gonna get on you like cockleburs on cotton." Or sometimes, "All right, in five minutes I want it to be so quiet in here that you could hear a rat piss on cotton." I would think to myself, that's definitely possible in this house.

Sometimes even Aunt Fang, Grandma Edie's former sister-in-law, came. It never ceased to amaze me and almost everybody else in our family that Grandma still maintained close ties with Aunt Fang, many years after her divorce from Crockett. She used to say that since she had married Crockett, and not his sister, Fang, whom she had always dearly loved, it made no sense for them to give each other up, just because Crockett had had the evil mind to leave.

According to Grandma Edie, Crockett had left her because she was black and had big hands. That amazed me too. Plus, it made no sense. When I first heard the story, I had asked, wasn't she black before he married her? Didn't they hold hands when they were courting? The grown folks never answered me, brushing my questions away with the axiom that silenced me so frequently in those early years: "This is grown folks' business. You don't need to know."

After he divorced her, Grandma Edie married a Mr. Wallace Lucky, a man I never knew, but I heard many stories told about this hypochondriac, who sounded like he might also have been agoraphobic, for not long after he and Grandma married, Mr. Lucky became petrified of leaving home. Just plain wouldn't go out of the house. He was eventually diagnosed with some other mysterious ailment that no one ever named, which left him malingering for several years before he died.

Once divorced, then widowed, Grandma Edie was cool on the idea of marrying for a third time, but after much persuasion, she eventually married Daddy Les, the man I called my Great-grandfather. Grandma Edie had met him when she got a steady job making lunches in the Pipe Shop cafeteria on the three-to-nine shift. Himself a widower with a grown daughter who taught school in Tuscaloosa, Daddy Les came in one day to order his lunch and noticed her. Actually, as she described it, he first noticed the mole on her upper right lip and started teasing her about it. Each day that he came in for his sandwich, they exchanged a few more words, until she whipped up the nerve to invite him to Women's Day at Macedonia Church. He accepted, and was soon parking his brown felt hat at her house some part of every day. He proposed three months later and often teased her about the three more months she wasted before deciding to make him her third husband. As she explained it, how could she be sure that he wouldn't leave her just as Crockett had? After all, Daddy Les was what she called a high yellow man. What would possess him to want a dark-skinned woman for a wife? These days, when I picture Daddy Les, he still has skin so thin and fair it seems almost translucent, and eyes that are bluish-gray and kind.

Time proved Grandma's decision wise, for Leslie Marshall Crawford showed himself to be as faithful a husband as Crockett had been wild. Daddy, who had grown up with Grandma in the leanest times, always claimed that Daddy Les had loved her back to life. Before he came along, no man had ever tickled her so lightly at the small of her back and called her E. so sweetly. He loved all her relatives too, including Cake Pie, Grandma Edie's prickly cousin, who irritated everybody else.

Her real name was Eldora, and, according to Mama, she was good for nothing but crunching on white nuggets of Argo starch and regaling us with stories of hog killings and two-week-long revivals. Mama also thought Cake Pie always stretched the truth a bit and was not shy about voicing her skepticism. "You-all sure do have long revivals in Demopolis. I guess everybody in the whole county could get saved in two weeks' time."

Such a comment was a clear signal that Cake Pie's story had broken Mama's concentration at the sewing machine. From a corner of hers and Daddy's bedroom, just to the side of a four-paned window, Mama ran a cottage sewing industry. I now think sewing transported her to the brink of meditation, for whenever she was sewing, I always had to ask her any question a second time. She seemed especially deaf to my appeals for a nickel or a dime to run to Blankenship's. If I found her in a good mood, she'd joke around with me, answering my request for money with, "Baby, your Mama's poorer than Job's turkey." Or, "I can't even win a nickel bet." Or, "Your Mama's so broke she can't buy a flea a wrestling jacket, low cut and no sleeves."

In her heaviest seasons—Christmas and Easter—Daddy helped her. He generally handled alterations and restyling for men in the neighborhood, narrowing the lapels of jackets and pegging the legs of trousers that still had more years of wear. Sometimes he designed whole garments, like the matching sky blue linen jackets for Reggie and Bumbiddle when they were still in short pants and white high-top shoes.

Kitty-cornered to the cedar chest and flush against the footboard of the bed, the wrought-iron treadle sewing machine commanded the room. When company was expected or it was Daddy's turn to host his Friday night card game, the black machine, embossed in gilt, folded down into the cavity of the cabinet. And the three drawers on either side, always pulled open in easy reach of tangled thread, extra bobbins, hooks and eyes, and other sewing notions, were closed shut for the night.

As a child, I thought sewing was paper dolls and jigsaw puzzles for grown folks. I could sit for hours watching Mama sew, bewitched by thread unspooling and the treadle whirring up and down. By the end of the day, the putty-colored linoleum floor was littered with scraps of every shape and hue and texture, which had cascaded from the scissors' edge. When Daddy had the machine electrified, it wasn't nearly as much fun to watch her sew. Once both her feet and calf muscles had pumped the treadle and propelled the fabric through the teeth of the machine; now it only took the lightest pressure of her toe.

Once a month on Saturdays, we shopped for notions at Goldstein's Fabric Store—thread, cards of seam binding, bias tape, and twill tape and interfacing and beading needles and tailor's chalk. Every inch of Goldstein's was crammed with fabrics, chockablock from floor to ceiling. Some bolts lay crosswise, stacked one atop the other, on shelves recessed in dark, wood-paneled walls. Others stood vertically on tables in the middle of the floor and formed a carousel of colors as brilliant as a peacock's plumes. There, in the store's shadowy light, I fingered coarsely woven linens, organzas, brocades, bouclés, velvets, and batistes, mohair and alpaca, merino and serge, watered-silk moiré, and Alençon lace, delighting in a hodgepodge of sensations that shifted with the seasons.

When people came to be measured, clutching rumpled pictures torn from *Vogue* and *Mademoiselle,* I was often installed at a table in the corner of the living room, cranking out my homework or coloring or writing in my diary, and unless I looked up from my occupation and into a pair of grown-up eyes, I could sit for hours drinking in what Mama called "grown folks' talk" and processing the snippets of their "private business." When she began to take in mending from Dixie Cleaners, much of what I'd heard spill from the women's mouths found its way into the stories Reggie, Bumbiddle, and I invented about the garments in the bundle and the people they belonged to.

If Mama didn't bring the mending home, her boss delivered it, and Mama would punctuate his arrival with a familiar line: "Here come the pole cats," a reference to the men's trousers that dominated the heap and always smelled like pee. No sooner had Mr. Shannon unloaded the mending and proceeded through the door than Mama would launch into her weekly tirades. Normally an even-tempered woman of few and measured words, she often vented her frustrations while inspecting moth-eaten garments, some too tattered to hold a patch: "I'm tired of sewing patches on top of patches"; "Now whoever this coat belongs to oughta' just give it up. It won't even make a good dust rag." Or one of my favorites: "Can't these men tell the difference between a crotch and a toilet stool?"

"You right, Mama. Oo-wee, these pants is hooning," Reggie would say. "Hooning" was one of the many words he invented and used to describe the piss-stained pants.

Once there was a long, red-sequined evening gown in the mending pile, its zipper off the track. Just as we'd begun to spin some fantastic story about the zipper, Mama interrupted: "Ain't nothing to this—just another middle-aged woman eating too many slices of sweet-potato pie trying to squeeze her fat butt into a dress she outgrew a long time ago."

How did the gray pin-striped trousers get ripped from seat to crotch? "That's easy," I said. "He was somebody's back-door man who split them climbing out the window when her front-door man came home."

The day I offered this speculation, Mama looked up from her needle and said, "What you know 'bout somebody's back-door man?"

"Nothing," which was partly true, but from eavesdropping on the gossip that Mama's customers swapped, I had heard of men (and sometimes even women) caught in outlawed beds, who took off like jackrabbits, sometimes snagging their clothing as they made their getaways.

Wresting
the Alphabet

Both devout, God-fearing Christians, Grandma Edie and Daddy Les infused the spirit of religion throughout the house. To their eternal mortification, Daddy and Mama had forsaken the church. On Sunday mornings, they lingered at the breakfast table, reading the morning papers, granting themselves sacrilegious relief from Reverend Miree's droning sermons and the choir's soporific strains. We children, on the other hand, were carted off to church services at Macedonia A.M.E. Zion that stretched from 9:30 in the morning until 1:00 in the afternoon.

Grandma Edie took special interest in my religious conduct because I was her namesake. She wanted me to be named Edith, and Mama compromised by making it my middle name. I never thought "Deborah Edith" had a euphonious ring, but at least it kept peace in the family. Grandma Edie felt justified in insisting that I bear her name, since she had marked me, she said, with a mole just above my upper right lip, in the same spot as hers.

While Mama and Daddy were "backsliders," in Grandma Edie's words, they did not block Grandma and Daddy Les from exposing their children to the word of God. In truth, they couldn't have prevented it, even if they'd wanted to, for in Pipe Shop, as throughout many parts of the South during the 1950s, everyone obeyed the unspoken laws of gerontocracy, which ceded authority to the elders in almost every aspect of life. It was understood and seldom questioned that, because Daddy had been left in Grandma Edie's care since he was a young boy still in short pants, he remained her charge, even though he now had children of his own.

I thought it supremely unfair that Mama and Daddy were exempt, while we children endured the rigors of religious discipline from two old people, who began each day with prayer and insisted that grace be said at every meal, followed by a round of Bible verses from everybody at the table. Bumbiddle's is still the most memorable, because it never changed in all the years: "Jesus wept." It was the first verse Grandma Edie taught him, as soon as he could talk, but as he grew, unlike Reggie and me, he didn't feel the need to impress Grandma Edie and Daddy Les with longer and longer verses. These two words sufficed. If we happened to be out of Grandma's watchful sight, either Reggie or I would snicker after Bumbiddle said his verse and then add every child's blasphemous addendum to "Jesus wept": "Moses crept and Peter fell out the back-door step."

Some part of every afternoon Daddy Les retreated to his and Grandma's bedroom to read the black Bible in a zippered case that he always took to church. But while Daddy Les was content to read the Bible to himself, Grandma Edie demanded that she be read to—mainly by me. Far more often than either Reggie or Bumbiddle, I was yanked from play to read her the Bible. I felt persecuted by this arrangement and often wondered (silently, of course) just who performed this office for her before I learned to read.

With the equivalent of a fourth-grade education, Grandma Edie could read, but preferred to hear the rhythms and the cadences of the scriptures that she coaxed out of me, and long before my tender years afforded me an understanding of their meaning.

"Go get the Bible." It didn't matter what I was doing when Grandma Edie summoned me. When my feet could barely touch the braided rug, she sat me down in the slat-backed rocker in the living room, stretched the heavy, cracked-leather Bible open on my lap, and commanded me to read. Her favorites were Job, then Psalms, then First Corinthians. I remember that the words were often strange—Bildad the Shuhite and Eliphaz the Temanite. One day, now comfortable with the sound of these foreign names on my tongue, I broke into "A-hab, the A-rab, sheik of the burning sands"—when Grandma interrupted the reading session to take a telephone call. When she came back into the room, I was still singing the song whose rhymes reminded me of what I had been reading.

"What you doing? Stop that mess," she thundered.

"I was just playing, Grandma Edie."

"Well, you ain't got no business playing when you reading the Lord's word. Stop your wrassling."

And so I resumed my reading, my index finger inching its way—word by word—across the pages. At times, even now, whole passages and snatches of the verses come back to me unbidden. "Blessed is the man that walketh not in the counsel of the ungodly, nor sitteth in the seat of the scornful. . . ." "The waters wear the stones." "Because I was flesh, and a breath that passeth away and cometh not again." "From everlasting to everlasting, thou art God." "The work of our hands, establish thou it."

Mama offered little sympathy when I complained to her about these command performances of reading and reciting. She'd just laugh and say, "You asked for it. You wouldn't rest until you learned to read. You know, you always wanted to be grown before your time." The story of my determination to read was one Mama recited, with little prompting, over the years. "You were about four years old," Mama would begin. "I kept you home from Sunday School because you were running a little fever. You were the one of my children always whining about first one thing and then another, and this day you were whining because you didn't want to stay in the back room. I guess you thought you would miss something. We were reading the newspapers—your daddy and me—and we handed you the want-ads section so we could have some peace and quiet for a change. 'Cause you know, if you were awake, Lord have mercy, you were a regular motormouth. 'Why is this, Mama?' and 'Why is that?'

"'That's a big girl. You can read too,' your daddy said. That had always pacified you, but this particular day it didn't work. You were stretched on your back on the floor, with your knees bent, the newspaper spread between your arms. Somebody had given you some old wire-framed eye-glasses with the lenses punched out—I think it was Miss Queen Esther—which you liked to wear when you were play-reading. But this day, noth-ing could hold you still. Your daddy had gone to get a pack of cigarettes, and I left you in the living room while I went to start my dinner. No sooner do I get in the kitchen and turn on the stove than I hear you howling loud enough to wake the nations of the dead.

"I come a-running from the kitchen, thinking that you might have choked on something, 'cause I would have heard if anything had fallen on you. There you were, still stretched out on the floor, your face screwed up in a knot. 'What's the matter? What's the matter?' I asked. You stopped screaming just long enough to catch your breath and say, pounding your little fists on the floor, 'I can't read, I can't read.'"

According to Mama, the convulsion occurred in May, and although she had planned to enroll me in kindergarten at Canaan Church the following fall, she decided neither of us could wait that long. "I knew that if I didn't take you somewhere, I was gon' have to run away. Miss Garrett told me to bring you to Vacation Bible School, since your daddy had already taught you your ABC's and how to spell your name. And so, that very June, that's where I took you, and right there in the basement of Macedonia, you started to learn to read."

It was there in Macedonia A.M.E. Zion Church that religion became yoked in my mind to the rudiments of social doctrine. The beatitudes and the Ten Commandments that children printed on white construction paper and taped all around the concrete walls were not mere exercises in penmanship, but abiding instructions for living. There in Macedonia's basement, before I could add my hand to those represented around the wall, I learned that God made me, Jesus wept, and I would too if I didn't behave like a good little girl. In 1950s Alabama that meant speaking only when spoken to, and in all, as little as possible. Eventually, of course, the elders granted exceptions to the rule: the lines in Easter and Christmas pageants, in which all children had to perform. These we had to memorize, along with the late Sunday afternoon recitations or "Inspirational/Educational Readings," as Mrs. Harvey called them.

This was a culture that placed great store on rote memorization, which must surely explain just how much I remember from those early days. It was not enough to read. You must remember what you'd read and be ever at the ready to recite it, line by line, with all the right intonations and stresses, with diction perfectly clear.

When I entered Pipe Shop Elementary in the fall of 1956, I was reading simple sentences from the Dick and Jane primer. The school faced Sixteenth Street and stood diagonally across from Antioch Church, where the renowned Reverend Mordecai Richey preached his annual "Shadrach, Meshach, Abednego" sermon that people came from miles and miles around to hear, whether they were Baptist or not.

Pipe Shop Elementary was still fully segregated when I first walked through its double doors in 1956, two full years after the *Brown* decision declared segregation unconstitutional. That was the year Alabama had joined Mississippi, Florida, and Georgia in taking legal action to declare Brown null and void. Nineteen fifty-six was also the year in which all but twenty-seven Southern members of Congress signed the infamous "Southern Manifesto" urging all states in the Union to resist integration.

Pipe Shop Elementary was still segregated when I left in 1963 to start junior high at Brighton. When what passed for desegregation made its sluggish way to Bessemer, long after Brown was the law of the land, the school did not survive the change, but in 1956 it was alive with learning about Alabama, the "Cotton State" deep in the "Heart of Dixie." And about the Pilgrim fathers. We drew harvest scenes on sheets of white butcher paper, peeled Pilgrims in black buckled hats from perforated cards, and tacked them onto bulletin boards trimmed with orange scalloped paper or burnished autumn leaves. I can hear the gathered dresses starched to stiffness, rattling through the halls. And see my cramped first-grade classroom, the green cardboard placards high above the chalkboard, large white alphabets printed perfectly on each card.

"I remember the first day I walked you to Pipe Shop School," Mama told me. "Now, that was another morning you pitched a hissy fit. You know that dress you have on in your first-grade picture? Well, I had made it. It was your Easter dress—bright blue like milk-of-magnesia bottles. Remember when I took you to Goldstein's? I asked you to pick out the color you liked, and that's where your little finger pointed, to that sparkling blue cotton bolt. You can't ever tell whether the weather will be warm or cool at Easter time, so I made you a red coat pleated in the back from the yoke.

"Well, I declare, you wanted to wear the whole outfit on that first day you went to Pipe Shop School. It was eighty-five degrees, but you pitched such a fit that I finally gave in, down to the patent-leather shoes. 'These your Sunday shoes,' I told you, but nothing would do you but wear them right up there to that school."

According to Mama, once I started to learn to read I nearly drove everybody stone crazy. "I'll have you know, once you started to school, many the day I had a great mind to hide every can and jar and bottle in this house and chop down every sign on the highway. I would get so tickled, you were so funny and particular, like a little old lady. We'd be riding along on the bus or just passing through a store and, clear out of the blue, you would pipe right up, reading the signs. Sometimes it would get on my nerves so bad, I would offer you a nickel just to be quiet for a few minutes. But that didn't do no good; you would just start lip-reading—Black and White Ointment, Argo Starch, Marlboro Man, Jack Daniel's, Gold Mine Pawn, Tires and Tires. Trojans. Didn't matter. And wouldn't know half of what you were reading. Just reading. Just reading."

Mama was right. I couldn't wait to learn to read, but there were times throughout my childhood when it seems that that was all I did—and not mainly for myself. Reading gave me my place in the family as well as in the neighborhood. When I wasn't reading the Bible to Grandma Edie or the morning scripture at Sunday School, I was reading the guide sheets of Simplicity patterns to Mama, when her eyes were strained from sewing. "Join front bodice to back at shoulder seam. Trim. Press seam toward back." And then I read off the prescriptions of her medicine bottles to Miss Lillian Butler, and although most times he seemed to know the recipe by heart, sometimes, after I'd helped to grate the lemon rinds, I'd read Papa the *Joy of Cooking* recipe for his famous lemon pound cake. Papa never made the cake exactly according to the recipe, though, which called for nine eggs. He used twelve, and instead of "2 greased 9-by-5-inch loaf pans lined with heavy waxed paper," he baked his in a fluted Bundt pan, unmolding it on Mother's favorite cake plate made from pink Depression glass.

Plaiting the Maypole

There is a gold star in the upper right-hand corner of my first-grade progress report—a half sheet of stiff, dingy paper. Pipe Shop Elementary. Jefferson County Public Schools. Birmingham, Alabama, the silhouette of Thomas Jefferson in ponytail in the center of the page. It is signed by Mrs. Vanetta Brown Foster and written in her hand: "She is progressing in her schoolwork, and reading above grade level. Her muscular coordination can be improved with more practice."

That I lacked "muscular coordination" was a fact made all too painfully plain the day Miss Skipwith herded the second-grade class to the playground to teach us to plait the Maypole. Unable to grasp the concept and bend my body to its will, I kept going over when I should have gone under. In frustration, Miss Skipwith took the ruler to my legs.

"Don't you know the difference between over and under?" she yelled as I dropped my head and focused on the red dust settling on my black patent-leather shoes.

I was humiliated by the snickers of the other children who held the streamers of crinkled colored paper in their hands. To this day, I remain self-conscious about any coordinated movement, and get my hackles up when anyone suggests I loosen up. "Relax." That's what Miss Skipwith said the day she left my legs in welts and exiled me to the edge of the playground while the others swayed gracefully through the May Day dance.

I was relieved when we all stood up beside our desks and sang the song that always marked the closing of the day:

Now the day is over
Night is drawing nigh
Shadows of the evening
Steal across the sky.

I rushed home and found Mama peering over the guide sheet of a pattern. When I began to tell her what had happened, she cut me off and said, "That teacher didn't mean anything by what she said. Quit wearing your feelings on your sleeves."

That night when Mother called to speak to Daddy, I told her about Miss Skipwith and the Maypole and the welts she scored into my legs. At 7:30 sharp the next morning, Mother barged into the house, all dressed up in her famous navy blue suit and white blouse with faggoting down the front. In her commanding way, she announced that she was taking me to school, and when Mama asked why, she snapped, as Mama remembered the morning, "Somebody's got to let these teachers know they can't be going around picking on defenseless little children." Mama thought she was making too much of a small thing, but never one to tangle with her mother-in-law, Mama let her have her way. Mother almost always got her way.

Clutching my hand, she walked me out to the green two-toned Chevrolet sedan and we drove the six blocks to Pipe Shop Elementary. As we climbed the wooden steps to my room, we could hear the class shouting in unison the last lines of the "pledge allegiance" that signaled the start of each day. When we walked into the room, Miss Skipwith was calling the roll, and she looked up and paused, no doubt surprised to see this unfamiliar citified woman whose high-heeled pumps clicked in four-four time down the center of the room. When Mother stopped at the edge of the desk, Miss Skipwith did not pause but proceeded down the list without acknowledging us. I answered, "Present," when she called my name. The roll call finished, Miss Skipwith removed her glasses and turned to Mother, who pulled herself up, straightened her back, and asked if they could step into the hallway. Still holding my hand in hers, she began, "I understand you beat my granddaughter all over her legs in front of the other children, just because she couldn't plait the Maypole. Now if she is acting up or gets out of line, it's all right to rap her on her knuckles, but you went a bit too far this time." Miss Skipwith started to sputter "But-but-buts," and Mother cut her off. "Furthermore, just in case you didn't know it, we send her to school to learn to read and write and speak correctly, not to plait some doggone Maypole."

Not finding the youthful Miss Skipwith sufficiently contrite or sufficiently respectful to a woman twice her age, Mother began an unsuccessful campaign to enroll me in St. Francis, the black Catholic school. It was then widely believed that children were better educated in parochial school, but Mama wouldn't hear of it. The nuns were much too strict, she said, and alleged to be especially so with little colored girls. As near as I recall, this struggle over where I should be schooled was one of the few times that Mama and Daddy stood up to Mother, without backing down. But as Mama always used to say, if Mother didn't get what she wanted one way, she'd get it another.

Mother came from a long line of black American women from the South who thought they could create the world in their own image. And if they met with obstacles along the way, why, they simply ignored them or took a detour. There was no such thing as "knuckling under," as Mother used to put it, or conceding defeat. And so, although I remained at Pipe Shop Elementary, I started to spend more weekends and holidays at Mother's house, a mere five miles east of Pipe Shop.

I grew up shuttling between these two worlds—of material want on the one hand and semiprivilege on the other, gilded with the absurd rituals of bourgeois social climbing—each competing for control of my identity. If Mother had her way, I would bear her imprint. I trotted around behind when she went antiquing, foraging in musty barns for dark, heavy claw-footed tables and cane-bottomed ladder-backed chairs, marble-top tables, bankers' lamps, and dusty chandeliers.

Mama swore up and down that while Mother might be concerned about what went on at Pipe Shop Elementary, she was even more concerned about what went on in the environs of the Pipe Shop community. She never thought Pipe Shop was quite good enough, or that the people there amounted to very much. But who in Pipe Shop could measure up in Mother's estimation when her standards were set in Mountain Brook?

When she had had a few beers, Mama was wont to say of her mother-in-law, "She spends so much time up on that mountain that she forgets about how folks are living down below." Sometimes I thought this was too harsh a judgment and I defended Mother against the charge. But it was true that my grandmother had long since hitched her dreams and values to Mountain Brook, that exclusive suburb of Birmingham tucked away in the Appalachian foothills, high above the clouds of foundry smoke. There in their gated estates that fringed Red Mountain, the well-to-do lived in segregated splendor and seclusion, broken only by the quiet presence of their black maids and cooks. The Bergers, the family Mother worked for, owned a Buick dealership in downtown Birmingham, but she was proud to announce to any inquiring soul that she was neither cook nor maid but a "private-duty" nurse who set the terms of her employment and whose services eventually came to be in high demand throughout Alabama and beyond.

She had started working for the Bergers in May of 1944, when she went to attend their daughter-in-law, Caroline, bedridden for most of a delicate pregnancy. She stayed on to care for the new mother and the Bergers' first grandchild for the first three colicky months of his life. Over the years Mother attended the other women who were busily producing heirs for the Berger fortune. I mainly knew them as faces in Mother's photo albums, except for Boots and Laney, with whom I occasionally played when Mrs. Berger came to ferry Mother back up the mountain after a weekend visit home. Sometimes Mother flitted in and out so fast that it could make you wonder whether you had actually seen her or she was just a figment of your mind.

The Bergers, who owned property all over Birmingham, lived on Saugahatchee Road. They also had a house in Mobile and another one in Florida. When Daddy once asked Mother how the Bergers got their money, she allowed as they both came from wealthy families who had left them set for life. According to Mother, Mrs. Berger had the greater inheritance.

Though Mother didn't know for sure, she had once whispered that Mrs. Berger was descended from one of the original founders of Red Mountain Iron and Coal. The company had opened a blast furnace at Oxmoor in 1863, manufacturing iron used in the production of confederate munitions. Whether Mrs. Berger's origins were tied to this company or not, her family had most certainly been industrialists in the early rise of Birmingham, not just in minerals that fed iron and steel, but in the foundations of the railway system, without which the industry would have been lost.

1404 Ninth Avenue

When Buster went mad and nearly bit Reggie's eye out, Mother seized the opportunity to vault me out of Pipe Shop. She reasoned that with both Mama and Daddy now working and Martha Faye gone back to Buffalo, something had to give. Grandma and Daddy Les were getting entirely too old to keep up with all three of us, and Grandma Edie had to go to Greensboro that very week to see about her sick sister, Lucy. What was it going to take for them to see that these two frail people had too much on their hands? For one of us to lose life and limb? After days of wrangling, it was decided that, at least for the rest of the summer, I would go to live at Mother's house. That was June 1959. I was eight and Reggie, five. Bumbiddle was a toddler. Although I didn't know it at the time, another baby was on the way, which Mama miscarried eight weeks later.

Nineteen fifty-nine stands out in my memory as a season of leave-taking. First Martha Faye just up and left right after Uncle Jr.'s birthday party. She didn't even stay long enough to go to the prom, and Mama had already finished making her evening gown, all except the facings and the hem. The day she left, the yellow satin strapless gown was still hanging on the door of the chifforobe, its layered flounces drooping down like the branches of a weeping willow tree.

Martha Faye was sniffling all that morning, but she wouldn't tell me why, and neither would Mama or Daddy or Grandma Edie. I knew they had to know, but no one would say a word to me, not until the morning before she was to leave. And they didn't say much even then. Just that Martha Faye was going to Buffalo to live with Ernestine and Leroy, her mother and stepfather. Just that. No more.

I still have vivid memories of that April Saturday when Martha Faye left Pipe Shop. The whiskey-colored suitcases with brass latches seemed to appear out of nowhere, and Daddy's long hairy arms loaded them into the back of Mother's station wagon. I condemned Martha Faye in my mind for leaving us, standing outside waving as the Greyhound bus pulled out of the Fourth Avenue station. That was the only time a double dip of black walnut ice cream on a wafer cone held no consolation for me whatsoever. My favorite taste was made bitter by her going, and whenever I tried to get it back—get back the taste that made me run to Blankenship's or Mae's Sundries, risking a beating for stealing away between Sunday School and the eleven o'clock service—it was gone forever. Now, just as spring had barely lengthened into summer, it was my time to go.

Although I had spent many weekends at Mother's house, I had never stayed longer than that. When they told me I was going there for the whole rest of the summer, I howled and said I did not want to go. I knew right then and there my tears would do no good, when the grown folks had made up their minds. My only role was to drop my head and hold my tongue. But never any good at holding my tongue, I spoke up for myself that day. I didn't want to leave Reggie and Bumbiddle behind and the girls who played jacks with me, and hopscotch and Little Sally Walker and Old Maids. I protested that you couldn't play hopscotch in the road at Mother's house, because it was on the highway where cars sped up and down, headed north and south, all day long. And what about the crossword games I played with Daddy? Of course, I kept my real reasons to myself. I didn't want to go for all that time because Auntee was too fussy, and sometimes Gina was mean to me when Mother wasn't around.

As I grew more and more inconsolable, Mother reached into her big straw bag with the palm trees on the front and handed Reggie a crisp green dollar to buy us popsicles at Blankenship's. My dismal prospects brightened for a moment when Mother announced that I didn't have to go for the whole summer, just until Grandma Edie came back from Greensboro. And Reggie and Bumbiddle would come to visit. And, yes, I could come back home for the Fourth of July. Plus, she promised, if Miss Florida Pigrom could fit me in, I could begin the piano lessons I had been eager to take ever since Gina started.

Still, when it was time to leave, Reggie and I lingered around Mother's blue station wagon, looking longingly at each other but saying nothing. I lacked then the words to express the feelings that leaving—even to chase the promise of piano lessons and days at Camp Nawaka, thick with pines— was not an unmixed good. As I began to cry again, this time a soundless cry, Mother tried to soothe me: "It's not like you're going away forever." And Daddy echoed her.

And so I left Pipe Shop that day, just before the Fourth of July, with a Bruno's grocery bag stuffed with a new pair of shortie pajamas, bloomer style, a new pair of shorts, a couple of T-shirts, and a new pair of sandals. I also had my crayons and coloring books, and the pink diary with gilt-edged pages that Larry Bates had given me the year before, when he pulled my name at the Christmas draw.

True to Mother's word, Bumbiddle and Reggie came to visit, and I went back to Pipe Shop for the Fourth, and we all played together just like I had never left, but we had already begun to view each other across a chasm of suspicion and childish misunderstanding—Reggie and Bumbiddle on one side and me on the other, or so I told myself. Actually, Bumbiddle was far too young to understand my being away, but Reggie spent that whole summer wondering why Mother did not take him (even though he was sometimes frightened in her presence), while I wondered why Mama and Daddy didn't let me stay. Reggie had thought my leaving meant that Mother favored me, while I had thought my leaving meant that Mama and Daddy favored him. So there it was. For different reasons, we had settled in our childhood minds what leaving really meant. He felt that the one who leaves is lucky and the one who stays is not, whereas, for a time, I felt just the opposite, but fought to keep the feeling down and make the best of that first summer at 1404 Ninth Avenue.

1404 Ninth Avenue was right on U.S. 11, or what we called the Bessemer Super Highway. The white A-frame wooden house with green shutters and green-and-white-striped awnings sat slightly back from the road and down in a hollow. Densely packed shrubs of abelia fronted the house, their blossoms like tiny white wedding bells. At the left front corner of the house, near the side porch, there was a bed of flowers that grew in shade—broad-leafed calladiums, begonias, forget-me-nots, and impatiens, always white impatiens planted every spring. Far down the driveway, on the other side, were Mother's famous tea roses. And far down the backyard, stretching almost to the railroad tracks that ran behind the house, wildflowers grew in profusion, along with daylilies, snapdragons, phlox, and blue hydrangeas. I wanted to know why some flowers came back every year, right in the very same spot as before. They were perennials, Mother told me, and I thought the word as pretty as the petals of the flowers.

Towering high above the roofline, on the other side of the backyard, stood a mulberry tree, its drooping branches overhanging the porch's edge. The purple berries stained the floorboards the color of Welch's grape communion juice that we drank from thimble-sized glass vials on every first Sunday morning as the preacher chanted, his crucifix sometimes clinking against the silver tray, "This do in remembrance of me."

Mother and Papa had bought the three-bedroom house soon after they married. Papa was the grandfather who was the most consistent presence in my life. Over the years I would hear repeatedly that Mother had married him because he was the very opposite of her first husband, Daddy Frank; just as Daddy Les had proved the opposite of Crockett. Many was the time Grandma Edie would say, "Fred Williams is a hard-working, God-fearing man." He was. He attended church regularly, served as superintendent of the Sunday School; never even drank a cup of coffee, much less a shot of gin. He had recently migrated from his birthplace in Montgomery, Alabama, when they met. He was working as an orderly at Bessemer General Hospital and renting Miss Pearl Garrett's screened-in back porch. The only one of Mother's friends from church who was not then married (although she later did when she was sixty-two), Auntee Garrett was a third-grade teacher at Paul Laurence Dunbar Elementary. She inspired the pity of those who had long ago abandoned the hope that she would ever find companionship. And thus the presence of Fred Williams, her single male boarder, provoked not a word of gossip that might insinuate a breach of the community's strict moral codes. It simply reassured them (people cared about these things back then) that, at last, she had some company and didn't have to rattle around in that house with no one to talk to but herself.

Papa always said, as soon as he spotted Mother at choir rehearsal, that he knew she would be his wife. Auntee Garrett introduced him to this natty-dressing, slim-hipped woman who spoke her mind, no matter what it cost her, and after a brief courtship, they were married on August 3, 1935, in the parsonage of the church. In time he came to call her "Miss Vi." It had started as a joke, the same way "Miss Priss," his name for me, had started, but after a while it stuck. Papa was the only person who referred to Mother as "Miss Vi," and it was a nice-nasty designation, shading to one side or the other, depending on his mood.

Papa soon left the hospital to work at Pyne Mine, an ore mine on the outskirts of Bessemer, going toward Muscoda. Yes, the conditions were more dangerous there (there had been some explosions), but the pay was more than he had ever earned. Mother found work as a practical nurse in a doctor's office and, within five years, they had saved enough to buy the three-bedroom house. Papa always joked with Mother about the time he took her to see the two-room tenements in the shadow of the mine. "'I know you can't be expecting me to stay here,' she said, her hands on her hips and her mouth poked out far enough to ride to town on. There was no way, no how, she was gon' live in a tenement, so we paid down on 1404 Ninth Avenue."

We always referred to 1404 as Mother's house, although she was seldom there. At least not for very long. This I now see in hindsight as the consummate irony. Mother kept up her crusade until she succeeded in moving me to her house so she could keep an eye on me, when meanwhile she was away in Mountain Brook for much of the time. Two weeks straight was the longest she usually stayed and then she was gone again. True, she came home practically every other weekend, or for longer, when the Bergers were away, but for the remainder of the time, Mother was not at home. That first long summer I spent at Mother's was an exception to the rule. She stayed home for one whole month while the Bergers were in Europe. Auntee said it was the longest she had ever stayed since starting at the Bergers in April 1944, when Uncle Fred Jr. was a knee baby.

Uncle Jr. was the only child Mother had with Papa, and just after his first birthday, not long after he was weaned, she took her first job away from home. She refused to settle for lower pay for equal work, which is what the local hospitals demanded of black nurses. "I had to be my own boss," she always said. Mother would insist that she hated to leave Uncle Jr., but she had to, just as she had had to leave Daddy and Auntee when she went away to nursing school. It was to make a better life for him, for all of them. And so while Mother worked in Mountain Brook, Auntee cared for Uncle Jr. with help from Mama.

Although she started out with the Bergers, and remained with them, off and on, until she had the stroke, in due course they spread the word about the mainstay they had in Viola. Soon others were soliciting her services, mailing her tickets to Alabama cities and eventually those flung far beyond. Mother was then in her mid-thirties and had fulfilled her dream to put those cold and brutal Pipe Shop years far, far in the distance.

Mother's ambition to escape a life of certain poverty and bruises too numerous to explain away had been admirable, but now some of her protracted absences were rumored to have nothing to do with work at all. Papa never said a mumbling word, at least not that anyone could hear. He was a worshipful husband, and "Miss Vi" always knew what was best. Besides, the "good money" that she made was shared with everybody in the family and brought distinction to her home.

When Mother was away, Auntee became the "woman of the house." People used to say that Mother was taking mighty chances, leaving her daughter in the ripening stages of young womanhood in the house with a stepfather, but Papa gave no one cause for worry. When he wasn't working, he was hunched over the kitchen table reading either the Bible or the newspapers, his penknife poised to cut clippings in clean, straight lines and store them in a basket atop the refrigerator until he delivered them to Mother or until she came home again.

Auntee cooked and cleaned, complaining bitterly about being her mother's slave, but with a tenth-grade education and no skills that would pay her more than menial wages, what else was she to do? Mother insisted that it was her own fault. She had brought it all on herself. She didn't need to drop out of high school. She could have gone to college, but she preferred rotgut liquor, outlaw men, and pregnancy out of wedlock. First Auntee had flatly denied that she was pregnant, but as her stomach puffed and puffed there was no hiding it. The story goes that when Mother learned of Auntee's pregnancy, she stayed away three months or more, and the job of tending five-year-old Uncle Jr. fell to Mama. The war was over and Mama and Daddy were now living in the apartments behind Town's Grocery Store, across the street and down from Mother's house. Daddy was working for North Carolina Mutual, selling burial insurance, while Mama worked half-days at a dentist's office in downtown Bessemer. When her shift ended around 2:00 in the afternoon, Mama would walk the short distance to Mother's house to tend Uncle Jr. and to help Auntee through the final weeks of pregnancy. She was right there when Auntee went into labor and Gina was born several hours later in the front bedroom of Mother's house.

Mother had refused to attend the birth, but as fate would have it, she got violently ill a few days later and Papa brought her home from Mountain Brook. Then all three generations—newborn baby, exhausted mother, and ailing grandmother—fell under Mama's care. For the first two weeks of baby Gina's life, Mother had flatly refused to lay eyes on her, and then, without warning, as Mama told the story, Mother woke up one morning, sponged herself off, put on her face powder, and asked to hold the baby, and from then on began to lavish on her new granddaughter the frilliest of dresses with hand-embroidered pinafores and satin ribbons for her hair. And from the time that Gina could walk and talk, Mother started molding her, enrolling her in dance classes and music lessons and sleep-away camp, but the molding never took. Gina resisted Mother at every turn, perhaps out of loyalty to Auntee.

For eleven whole years, Gina had been the only grandchild in Mother's house, and thus that first summer took some getting used to. She could accommodate my weekend stays, but the whole summer? Why, that was another matter. We fought constantly. From her perch at the kitchen window lined up with tiny terra-cotta pots of Mother's African violets, Auntee would yell, "Cut out that scrapping." And when the shouting didn't work, she ran out the back door, her slippers flapping on her heels, and headed for the mulberry tree to break a switch. Or sometimes she would storm out of the house with one of Papa's leather belts already wound around her hand. And then would start the whipping and more shouting in between the licks: "Y'all ain't supposed to be fighting one another. You're sisters' and brothers' children. You supposed to be looking out for one another." When we made up, we sat on Mother's pebbled cement porch imagining our weddings and our children, or watching the cars go by.

That summer we invented a game of reading tags and guessing state capitals. Gina could see things better from a distance, so she would generally read the tags: North Carolina, "First in Flight." And what's the capital? Illinois, "Land of Lincoln." And what's the capital? And so on, sometimes for hours, until Auntee called us in for hot dogs and lemonade. I could always spot the Alabama tags, although Gina swore I couldn't, not the writing anyway, just the bright red hearts on either side of the tin square, the "Heart of Dixie" embossed in between. We made up stories about where the people in the cars were going, how long it would take them to arrive, and whether they were going there for good.

Were the cars from Alabama going only as far as Tuscaloosa? Maybe they were going all the way to Florida. Mother went to Florida with Miss Berger lots of times; once or twice she even took Gina there with her. They brought us back View-Masters, with slides of beach scenes, and a matching pair of shells. Gina and I would hold the abalone shells against our ears, excited, yet not quite believing that we were actually hearing the plash and eerie howl of ocean waves.

When Mother was off in Mountain Brook, we played house inside, careful not to budge the furnishings from their appointed places. The whitewashed living room was spare and respectable. Just inside the door was a marble-topped table adorned in summer with fresh-cut flowers from the yard clumped in a clear glass pot-bellied vase with marbles in the bottom. A collection of silver candlesticks of graduated heights stood atop the mantel, along with Uncle Jr.'s first pair of shoes, the bronze and silver reflecting in the oval mirror with the filigreed frame.

To the left of the fireplace was a tall torchère lamp with a glass shade etched with frosted calla lilies. It was like magic to me as a child when I made the lilies go from dark to bright to brighter with each turn of the switch. A paisley shawl lay neatly folded on the arm of the camelbacked sofa, complementing the Persian rug that Mother had inherited from Mrs. Berger. A floor-model record player stood in one corner and a wing-backed chair with needlepoint doilies in the other. Smaller vases, bowls, more candlesticks, and ashtrays were arranged in built-in bookshelves above the King James Bible, copies of *National Geographic,* a set of *Funk and Wagnall's Encyclopedia,* and a first edition of Martin Luther King Jr.'s *Stride Toward Freedom* that Reverend Lockhart had given Mother.

Somewhere in the room was always a bunch of eucalyptus. Whenever I remember those remote days at Mother's house, I breathe the ambient air of eucalyptus and grow all warm inside.

My favorite room of all was Mother's room. When she was home in summer, she kept fresh-cut flowers right on her night table beside the copper lamp with the painted parchment shade. And in winter, dried hydrangeas filled the vase, their once blue petals now stained like snuff juice and as delicate as the wings of flies. And the fantasies I began to spin right there in that room were a balm against the fleeting bouts of homesickness I felt for Pipe Shop. My daydreams were inspired by oval bars of French-milled soap, crystal doorknobs, a silver handheld mirror with matching comb and brush, and a vibrant blue bottle of rosewater that sat serenely in the window.

In Mother's room I could wallow on the canopied bed when Auntee wasn't looking or play dress up, opening crystal bottles with skinny stems that looked like church spires, golden tassels hanging from their necks. I squeezed the atomizers and squirted perfume behind my ears, in the dent of my throat, and the bend of my knees and elbows—just as Mother did. And from the pile of clothes that I could use for fantasies, I almost always chose a long silver satiny nightgown with loose spaghetti straps that slipped down over my shoulders, exposing the hated bareness of my chest and the two dark mocking spots that took forever to grow to breasts.

As I used to do on weekends, I slept in the front bedroom with Gina, who always fell asleep before I did. Between the din of passing cars and transfer trucks, I was comforted and secured by the soft and lulling whistle of her breathing. Long after she had fallen asleep, I lay awake listening to the late-night noises just outside the window: the whistle of passing cargo trains or the squeaking brakes of cars. The crimson color of the stoplight glowed diffusely through Mother's white gauzy draperies trailing to the floor. On those summer evenings, as the humid breezes pushed the curtains softly outward from the shade, I would sometimes scoot out of bed, kneeling quietly on my knees at the window to see the headlights of passing cars and the lightning bugs glitter like so many diamonds studding the atmosphere.

The Hokey Pokey

That first long summer I spent at Mother's house, we went on many outings in between her shopping trips for Uncle Jr., who would be going to college that fall. My favorite was the trip to Mrs. Moss's Candy Cane Cottage at Springville Lake, which got its name from the pole of the tall gaslight out front, painted in red-and-white stripes.

That summer Mother enrolled Gina and me in the last session of day camp at Camp Nawaka. Gina was already a fearless swimmer, diving off into the deep end, but I was too scared to put my head under the water. I didn't even learn to float, a fact I still blame on the counselor, who told me I could float on my back and never have to put my head beneath the water. She coaxed me into deeper and deeper water by promising to keep her hand securely placed in the small of my back. "Can you feel my hand? I'm holding you." My body tensed as tightly as the corners of my eyes, which nearly squinted shut against the blinding sun. Just when I thought I might uncoil my muscles, she took her hand away and I sank down and inhaled water before she helped me stand up straight again. That was it. No more swimming until I was thirty-five, when I hired myself a teacher from the "Y," who succeeded in convincing me that my body could obey my will. At camp, when swim time came around, I either pasted leaves in a home-made scrapbook or jealously stood outside the chain-link fence and watched the other girls, their pink-and-yellow rubber caps bobbing in the aquamarine water.

When the Bergers returned from Europe, Mother left again for Mountain Brook. Miss Berger came to pick her up. I remember the day so well because, although I'd seen her lots of times in snapshots, that was the first time I saw her in the flesh. We were playing "The Hokey Pokey" when the shiny car slowed down, crawled into the graveled driveway, and Miss Berger toot-toot-tooted the horn. Miss Berger had a black Buick that looked almost like Mr. Lige's except that his had whitewall tires and long back fins just like torpedoes. I ran inside and shouted, "Mother, Mother, Miss Berger's here."

"What did I tell you about yelling? She's entirely too early; I told her two o'clock and here it is . . . Go see what time it is."

"The big hand on eleven and the little hand on one."

"I knew it; it's not even one o'clock and here she comes."

Mother was often running late, seldom ready when she said she'd be, but you'd never hear her own up to it; it was always somebody else who was early or who had gotten the time plain wrong. The house had been a welter of confusion and disarray all morning. The bowfront drawers of the dresser were pulled out, slips and gowns and camisoles draping over the edges. The doors of the old armoire, painted with faded pink and yellow roses, gaped open and stacks of clothing lay unfolded on the shelves. Mother moved in a frenzy from the dresser to the armoire, throwing things into the big gray suitcase that was open on the bed—nurse's stockings, regular stockings, girdles, jewelry, belts, uniforms all in a jumbled heap.

Mother shouted orders at everyone but Papa, who was home from work in Uncle Jr.'s bed, sick with a very bad summer cold that had kept him up three nights in a row with wracking coughs. When we tired of her "Run get this's" and "Run get that's" we—Auntee, Gina, and I—scattered in different directions. Auntee retreated to the side porch to read the new issue of *Bronze Thrills,* Gina went across the street to Cookie's house, and I went next door to find Pat and Cathy. We strolled back to Mother's house to play The Hokey Pokey. And that's what we were doing when Miss Berger pulled up, with Boots and Laney in the back.

"Run tell Mrs. Berger to come inside out of the sun."

"Miss Berger, Mother say for you to come inside out the sun." She would wait in the car, she said. As I walked away, I looked again at her broad-brimmed straw hat, the color of country eggs. Auntee inherited the cool hydrangea-blue dress that Miss Berger was wearing that day. When Mother brought home the annual box of clothes, Auntee plucked the pleated, scoop-necked dress from the box, and it seemed it never left her body. She washed and wore that dress, and when she could no longer zip it up, she gave it to our cousin Erie when she came up from Boligee.

"Mother, Miss Berger say she'll wait in the car."

"*Mrs.* Berger *says,*" she corrected me. "Well, if she wants to sit out there in that hot, browsing sun, let her do it. And if she gets sunstroke it sure won't be my fault. And I do hope she ain't got that little ugly yapping dog with her to be stinking up the car in this heat."

"Is it a little gray dog?"

"Yeah."

"Well, she got it."

"Well, I'll be doggone."

The dog was a little Yorkshire terrier named Chipper.

"Mother, why you always going to Miss Berger's house?"

"I have to work, Baby."

"All the time?"

"I don't work all the time. What's wrong?"

"I just wish you wouldn't go."

"I'll be back two weeks from now. That's not long. Run outside and play."

Back outside, I found Boots and Laney standing on the side of the car, amused by their own reflections, which widened and shortened in the glossy blackness of the car. I had heard all about these children—Laney, six, Boots, eight—and how spoiled they were. Mother thought it was nothing a good spanking wouldn't cure, but Miss Virginia, their Mother, said only barbarians hit children and so she wouldn't let anybody raise a hand to hers. "Spare the rod, ruin the child," would always put an end to Mother's latest account of the privilege and misbehavior of Boots and Laney.

That day they seemed standoffish and stuck up. But my curiosity got the better of me. I wanted to see up close these children that I had mainly seen in snapshots or peeking through the windows of a black-waxed car. Plus, Mother often said, you must always do your best to make strangers feel at home when they are visiting you.

"Do you know how to play The Hokey Pokey?" I asked.

The question startled Laney, who moved closer to her older brother as he turned around to stare at me.

"I said, do you want to play The Hokey Pokey?"

"We don't have that game."

"You don't have to have it. It's like a dance. Come on, we'll show you." Pat and Cathy seemed apprehensive initially, but soon we all joined in to play:

Put your right foot in
Take your right foot out
Put your right foot in
And you shake it all about
You do the hokey pokey and you turn yourself around
That's what it's all about.

They liked the game, especially Laney, who shook it so hard on the "put your whole self in" part that the sash of her pink sundress came undone and hung down almost to her lace-edged anklets. We were beginning another round when the car door slammed, and Miss Berger stomped over, her red-lacquered toenails peeking from the delicate white T-strapped sandals. While tying Laney's sash again, she said to me, "Run and ask Viola how long she intends to be; I have some people coming for dinner tonight."

"Mother, Miss Berger say how long you gon' be? How come she sound so saddity?"

"*Says. Sounds.* How many times do I have to tell you? Mrs. Berger says. Tell her not long. Run and get my uniform from the line. It should be dry by now and tell your Auntee to run a warm iron over it for me." I found Auntee still sitting on the side porch buried in *Bronze Thrills.* She snatched the uniform from my hand and muttered something underneath her breath. Mother called for me again and I ran into the bedroom, where she was standing in front of the mirror in a white lace-edged slip, putting her hair up in a French roll held in place by little tortoiseshell combs. When she finished, she turned around, holding the silver oval mirror in her hand so she could see her hair behind. Turning around again, she opened the tiny bottle of hair polish and brushed a thin silver streak just to the right of the front side. Then she clipped her cultured pearl earrings on and sprayed herself with perfume. Watching Mother dress was a form of hypnotism, and many of her dressing rituals have now become my own, although I no longer dust sweet white talcum powder on the inside of my thighs.

Auntee came just to the threshold of the bedroom door and hooked the shirtwaist uniform, hanging from a satin-padded hanger, over the top of the door. She left without uttering a word.

"Is my slip hanging?"

"No, Mother."

"Come here, I need you and Gina to sit on the suitcase," Mother said.

"Gina's over at Cookie's house."

"Well, run and get her. Never mind."

Throughout my childhood, when Mother finished packing for one of her long trips, the suitcase was always bulging. She would then summon Gina and me to climb atop the bed and press our weight against its lid. When she had snapped it shut, just above the silver initials of her name—"V G W"—she called for Papa or Uncle Jr. to lift the big gray leather suitcase to the car. But that day, with Papa sick in bed and Uncle Junior way up in New York, Mother had to lug the suitcase herself to Miss Berger's car.

I followed her in the hope that she would remember that I had asked her earlier for a quarter to buy a Baby Ruth. The Baby Ruth only cost a nickel, but I would pocket the rest. As she came down the steps, Boots and Laney ran toward her shouting, "Viola, Viola." Laney wrapped her tiny arms around Mother's knees, and her ponytail, more like a piglet's tail, bounced up and down. I did not like the way Laney was holding Mother and so I asked the question that forced her to turn to me.

"Mother, did you forget my quarter?"

"No, Baby, I didn't forget it." She took a change purse from her pocket-book and pulled out two quarters. "Give one to Gina now," she said, then leaned down to hug me tight against her chest. "Mother will see you soon—in two weeks—and I'll bring you back something real nice."

"Bring me back some colors and a coloring book, Mother," and she said she would. As Mother hefted the suitcase toward Mrs. Berger's trunk, I noticed that something was hanging from the back edge. Resting the suit-case on the grass, she opened the lid again. It was the cream-colored batiste blouse that Mother often wore with her navy blue suit. Cream like the color of newly opened magnolia blossoms. Mother had dragged the suit-case across the bedroom floor, then through the hallway, then onto the front porch, then down the sidewalk with clumps of weeds and volunteer impatiens growing through the stones, then finally over the grass. Dust had smudged the blouse, and the grass had left a dark green stain right down the front. Shaking her head, Mother handed the blouse to me and said, with exasperation in her voice, "Run ask your Auntee if she can bleach this out." Then she climbed into the backseat of the car with Boots on one side and Laney on the other.

Uncle Fred Junior

Near the end of that first summer, Uncle Jr. went away. He had held on to his job as a camp counselor until a scant two weeks before departing for college. During those two weeks, he kept mainly to himself. He wouldn't even play tonk with me, or gin rummy, or anything—just stayed closed up in his room with the brown-striped bedspread and black plastic treble clef signs hanging on the wall. He didn't even blow his trumpet. He could play any song by heart and often played along with Miles Davis on the record player. I can't remember what he played, but whenever I hear "Blue and Green," and the melancholy tremor that Miles strikes on the very first note, I think especially of Uncle Jr. blowing his trumpet. His eyes closed, the pimples on his face looking like they will burst wide open, he is blowing so hard. Then his jaw relaxes, but he holds the last trembling note.

Mother and Auntee were furiously getting him ready to go, but he took no part in the preparations. Whenever he came out to pour himself a glass of milk—he loved milk—Auntee, who was generally always somewhere near the kitchen, would ask with pleading in her voice, "What's wrong, Junior?" But he would only shake his head and answer, "Nothing." I would later learn what might have been bothering him, but at the time nobody knew and so we couldn't do anything to fix it, though we tried and tried.

His suitcases were open on the floor in Auntee's room, because she was mainly the one who was doing the packing. Mother had bought and then had monogrammed what seemed like two dozen shirts of bright white, ecru, cornsilk, oxford blue, and men's pink. There were shirts with stripes on stripes, in various colors too. Mother insisted that they all be washed to get the store-bought stiffness out, so Auntee soaked the shirts in fluffy suds, then rinsed and rinsed until the water was clear again. Standing in the backyard's knee-high grass, she hung the shirts by their tails, and when they were dry, Gina and I took them from the lines. We hugged the sun-warmed shirts against our faces, then dropped the clothespins, their hinges rusted from the rain, into the faded canvas bag hanging from the splintered post. It seemed that Auntee washed and ironed the whole two weeks before Uncle Jr. went away, dragging the ironing board on to the screened-in porch each afternoon, just before *Search for Tomorrow* came on television. After stretching lengths and lengths of extension cord from out of the living room, and rolling the television to the threshold of the door, Auntee stood there on the side porch in one of her dusters that snapped down the front, one eye on the television, the other on the shirts. Each time Auntee lifted the iron and pushed it back and forth along a sleeve or pointed collar of the pastel-colored shirts, or the creases of the khaki slacks, the veins in her hand rose up like welts and droplets of sweat collected on her nose.

When the shirts had all been ironed and folded and packed into the suitcases, along with the newly fitted sport coats, silk neckties, and the dark, dark socks with gold bands around the toe, Auntee busied herself with preparations for the going away party, to be held in Mother's backyard, after church, the last Sunday in August. Papa had cut the grass and raked the mulberries that had rained down on the ground. Gina and I unfurled bright yellow crepe paper streamers from the pendant branches of the mulberry tree over Mother's rosebushes, then wrapped more around the splintered post propping up the clothesline. I made the sign on poster board while Mother spelled out "Bon Voyage Dr. Williams." Uncle Jr. wasn't a doctor yet, I said to Mother, so why was she calling him one? He would be a doctor soon, she answered.

Having Uncle Jr. must have been like starting all over again, burying all the painful reminders of her past with Daddy Frank, down to the children she had borne in their brief, tormented time together. He would be the first and only one of her three children to finally make her proud. She thought Daddy had dreams but lacked the necessary ambition to bring them to fruition. He did not apply himself, she said. That's why he was stuck at the Pipe Shop, just as Auntee was stuck in Miss Carroll's kitchen. Uncle Jr. was going to be a doctor, though, the only doctor in the family. And he looked the part. He was six foot four, and in his healthy years weighed well over two hundred pounds. He projected a sturdy, solid presence when he strode into a room. Like he was somebody. He had a military bearing and a commanding baritone voice that bade you listen, and so I had no trouble whatsoever imagining him in a crisp white lab coat, a stethoscope hanging from his neck, striding through the halls of some hospital on his rounds, just like the white men in *General Hospital* or *Dr. Ben Casey*.

Although everybody knew that Auntee had actually raised Uncle Jr., had practically mothered him, Mother managed all the outward doting symbols of the role. She took his first shoes to be bronzed, then displayed the blunt-toed lace-ups prominently on the mantel. And through the years, his awards and certificates for outstanding Boy Scout patrol leader, member of the Honor Society, excellence in the Paul Laurence Dunbar High School Marching Band were framed, one by one, and hung at eye level all around the living room. Someone had donated used instruments to the band, but Mother thought Uncle Jr. should have his own trumpet, so on his birthday, one April ninth, she gave it to him in a compact leather carrying case lined in royal blue velvet.

He wore expensive clothes and took expensive trips. He went on the citizenship tour that the Bessemer Negro Voters League organized every year. Uncle Jr. took the two-week bus tour, along with the few students from Bessemer area schools whose parents could spare the money or whose churches sold fried chicken dinners to send them to historic sites in Virginia, Washington, D.C., Philadelphia, and New York City.

When Uncle Jr. returned, Mother pulled out her company china and threw one of her special Sunday dinners. Reverend Clifton, the minister who preceded Reverend Lockhart, his wife, and their two children came, and the presiding elder drove up from Tuscaloosa, all to hear about the trip. I proudly showed them the snow globe of the Washington Monument he had brought me as a souvenir. For years I kept it, mesmerized by the snow that swirled, then drifted, to the bottom of the sparkling glass globe. When we passed snapshots around the table, Reverend Clifton had trouble picking Uncle Jr. out of the bunch of students posed with their chaperons in front of the nation's capitol building. "Here he is," I said, and pointed. I knew him right away by his black-framed glasses and the tam slanted on his head.

Wide-eyed and awestruck, I listened as Uncle Jr. told stories of the trip. They had gone to Monticello and, I vaguely remember, the University of Virginia too, or did I only dream that Uncle Jr. posed in front of bright white columns, the life-sized statue of Thomas Jefferson and the building, looming in the background, with a large white dome on top? I'm certain they went to Radio City Music Hall by subway to see an Easter program, and to the Statue of Liberty by boat. To the Empire State Building and the United Nations. Yes, they had visited the White House and the Library of Congress. Seen the changing of the guard at the Tomb of the Unknown Soldier. Eaten lunch at the Supreme Court Building. Met the Negro congressmen and had even interviewed Justice Hugo Black, but what impressed Uncle Jr. more than all of these was Howard University. He had set his sights on going there ever since that trip.

Papa thought he should stay at home. Miles College, right there in Birmingham, provided an excellent education, and besides, it was a church school. But Uncle Jr. protested and finally got his way. The announcement that he was going to Howard ran in the *Birmingham World,* along with the news that he had won the only four-year scholarship awarded by the Voter's League that year. I'll never know if it was true, but when word got out that Uncle Jr. was that year's winner, Miss Byrdie Rembert, who had thought her son Boyd would win, began to spread the rumor that Mother had actually browbeaten the league into awarding the scholarship to Uncle Jr. Mother said it was a bald-faced lie for which Miss Byrdie would surely burn in hell. Uncle Jr. had won that scholarship fair and square. After all, he was one of the top five honor students in his class, was president of the Biology Club, the French Club, a member of the marching band and the junior choir at church. What more did they want? Boyd was a good student, but he lacked Uncle Jr.'s charm, his well-rounded qualities.

The Sunday of the party, all of Uncle Jr.'s friends from high school came, including Boyd. Church members and neighbors came too. The whole backyard was so crowded that people spilled over into Miss Wilson's yard next door, trampling down her dahlias. I can taste the lemonade that Papa made in a brand-new galvanized tub, see Auntee's plates of deviled eggs, heaping bowls of potato salad, and platters of fried chicken stretched from end to end on coarse pine picnic tables. Papa made his famous lemon pound cake too, and homemade ice cream from a new hand-cranked freezer that we bought with S & H green stamps, especially for this occasion. I proudly announced to Uncle Jr. that I had pasted all the stamps in the squares of the redemption books. And he was glad. Then came the presents. A Bulova watch from The Friendly Twelve, a Bible from the Sunday School. A pen and pencil set. A shaving kit. Bottles of Old Spice and many other items that filled two "Parisian" shopping bags to the brim.

As we picked up all the ribbons and the manly wrapping paper that blew across the yard, we were hit with the surprise that almost split Mother and Papa officially apart. Over the tumult of party favors, high-pitched and throaty laughter, and passing transfer trucks, we heard the horn. Heard it before we saw the car that rolled to a stop at the mouth of the driveway, Mother seated behind the wheel. Uncle Jr.'s face lit up like the torchlights at Woodward Furnace Field the night the Woodward Iron Men beat the undefeated U.S. Pipe Men. This was long before my memory, but Papa told the story so many, many times that, in time, it came to seem that I was there, the torchlights glaring in my face.

Uncle Jr. would not have to ride the Greyhound bus to Howard, but he would drive there in his own brand-new sleek black Chevrolet Impala with cherry red interior. Papa had not known about the car, which Mother had bought at Long-Lewis Chevrolet, then hidden in Auntee Garrett's garage four blocks away. Only she and Auntee Garrett knew. Stella would later confess that she also knew, but that Mother had sworn her to secrecy. Papa would never have agreed to the car, especially since Mother bought it instead of paying down on a cottage at Carver Colony.

Incorporated exclusively for Negroes, George Washington Carver Colony was a cottage development at Guntersville Lake. We had always used Miss Moss's Candy Cane Cottage at Springville Lake, but Papa and Mother had decided that we should have our own cottage and had driven Gina and me to Carver Colony to see the plats of this idyllic place southeast of Scottsboro, on the south side of the Tennessee River. Papa would be able to fish and Gina could swim, and we might even have the annual Sunday School picnic there one day. But we never got the cottage. Uncle Jr. got the car instead.

In turns, we piled into the backseat and Uncle Jr. drove a few blocks down the highway and U-turned round the other side, looped in back of Canaan Church, and headed home again. When the rides were over, Mother took pictures. In one, Gina and I stand on either side of Uncle Jr., who flashes his gap-toothed grin. My face is out of focus, but Gina says no one could miss me with my knobby knees.

The party was almost over when Mother asked, "Where's Wiley?" We had all come directly from church—Mama, with Bumbiddle still in her arms, Reggie, Grandma, and Daddy Les. Daddy had not gone to church, but before we left that morning, he said he'd meet us at Mother's house. I guess, because the party was so crowded and so raucous, that at first we didn't know Daddy wasn't there. But when the crowd had thinned and we began to clear the leavings from the table, that's when we noticed that he was missing. Mother tried to call him, but got no answer at our house. No, Mama had no idea where he might be.

As dusk descended on the party's end, it brought with it a pall that spread throughout the evening. As she stacked leftovers in the refrigerator, Mother kept shaking her head and saying, "I just can't believe Wiley would miss his own brother's going-away party." Papa said he bet anything that Auntee had told Daddy about the car, just out of spite, and so he had stayed away, but when Mama told the story as the years lapped by, she speculated that Daddy had stayed away that day because he could not bear the sight of all the other signs that he was not the favorite son.

Over the years there were other summer parties and dinners at Mother's house on Sunday afternoons when we made faces in the china as the grown folks clinked the glasses with the beaded rims, and the breezes made wind chimes of the pendants hanging from the chandelier. But there was never another party quite like the one the day before Uncle Jr. went away, and I will always remember that Sunday afternoon as the last day of laughter at Mother's house.

Perhaps I so remember (though through a later prism) because Uncle Jr.'s leaving fell in the last year in the decade of my birth, and the decade that took its place left little room for laughter. The world has well noted and shall long remember Medgar Evers, the Kennedys, and Martin Luther King Jr., Carole Robertson, Denise McNair, Addie Mae Collins, and Cynthia Wesley, Goodman, Cheney, Schwerner, Liuzzo, but just before this lengthening chain of corpses stretched from one end of the sixties to the other, there was the anonymous white girl at Christmastime, 1959, splayed at the foot of the Bessemer Super Highway bridge, killed in a traffic accident. Before they pull the blanket over her face, the rain beats down. Her father pleads to let them touch her. Mama tries to hide my face in the folds of her brown wool skirt, but I have already seen the girl, seen her horror-stricken eyes, seen the blood and the blue bruises and the tips of her feet peeking from underneath the blanket.

"Is she dead, Mama? Is she dead?"

I was eight years old. Although it was the first death that I remember, others came quickly in its wake, and soon there would be another, even more frightening for me—that of our neighbor Little Lizzie Durr on a snowy day in Pipe Shop, just before the Lincoln/Douglass Birthday Banquet, February 1960.

PART
THREE

Fire and Snow

Two inches of snow can paralyze Bessemer. Banks close, stores close, but, most important for a nine-year-old, schools close. No child with a day off from school could possibly stay inside, not even to color or gaze dreamily on the tiny frosted doilies before they melted from the windowpanes. Especially not on a day when a house is burning.

The story goes that Miss Eartha Mae Tubbs first saw the blaze creeping up the side of Miss Hazel's kitchen window. Since she didn't have a phone, Miss Eartha Mae ran next door, leaving zigzagged footprints in the snow, and pounded on first the front door, then the back door, then the window of Miss Hazel's and Mr. Saul's bedroom. When nobody answered, she ran the three blocks to Blankenship's to call the fire department, but it was too late by then. The flames had already engulfed the house. I remember being frightened by the piercing sirens that brought bodies, swaddled in quilts and blankets, to their front porches up and down the block.

When there was a fire in our neighborhood, everybody's greatest fear was that it would spread to the next house if the fire trucks didn't arrive in time. Seeing that the fire showed no signs of dying down, Grandma decided it was time to wrap us all up—Reggie, Bumbiddle, and me—and take refuge at Mama Lucy's.

Mama Lucy's was the last place I wanted to go, because her crowded house always stank of camphor and liniment and other strong medicines that old folks used. She dipped snuff, and her spit cup was an empty Trellis Peas can, which she kept by the side of her bed. On the way to the store or some Sundays after church, I accompanied Grandma Edie to Mama Lucy's to help her carry dishes of food, greenish-purple leaves of pokeweed, and, in the winter, chunks of kindling.

Whenever Grandma Edie issued the order, "Go get my sun hat and my parasol," that was one of the surest signs that we were bound for Mama Lucy's.

"Why do we always have to go to Mama Lucy's house?"

"Because we have to look after anybody that ain't got no people and living by theirselves."

And so without fully understanding these biweekly missions, I tripped alongside Grandma to Mama Lucy's and obeyed her orders to "Set still, you hear?" Who could do anything else? Every which way you budged in that little shotgun house with the tar-paper shingles, you were bound to rattle the tin chifforobe or bump into a rickety table and knock over the plastic roses stuffed down in empty Coca-Cola bottles wrapped in aluminum foil.

Mama Lucy had suffered from diabetes for many years, and the sore on her right foot, always swollen and oozing with pus, made my stomach turn. She lived alone in that three-room house, every inch of wall and ceiling covered with newsprint. She amused herself by making sculptures from old newspapers and aluminum foil—crosses, trees, snowflakes—that she would then give away or pin to the wall behind her bed. Every time I unwrapped the Goo Goo Clusters that were rotting my teeth, Grandma would remind me to save the silver paper for Mama Lucy.

I was determined not to go to Mama Lucy's the morning of the fire. I wanted to see the spectacle, to stand with the others—the women who pressed infants to their chests or tightly gripped the hands of toddlers, the children home from school, and all the other grown folks—who had thronged into the street in front of Miss Hazel's to watch her house burn down.

"I don't want to go to Mama Lucy's," I pleaded, "I want to go see the fire."

"Well, you ain't gon' see no fire," she scolded, then ordered me to put on my old green corduroy coat with the quilted lining that Mama had made. Since I could not find my cap, she pulled her old, dusty, frumpy, dimpled felt hat down on my head, nearly covering my eyes.

"I don't want to wear this old hat," I complained. "It's a hat for old folks."

Grandma scowled at me and said, "Put that hat on, gal," then growled, "I can't have you catchin' your death-of-cold."

While she smothered Bumbiddle in his snowsuit, I sprang out the back door and through the opening in the fence to catch the excitement of the fire. I was hypnotized by the flames that melted the tar shingles and the smoke that blackened the sky, soon leaving the house nothing but a charred stump standing pathetically in the middle of the block. As we shivered in the icy morning air, shifting in the slush from foot to foot, the question of where Miss Hazel was ran throughout the crowd. And where was Mr. Saul? Off on disability from the mines, he did little pickup jobs of carpentry for white folks out in Hueytown, so maybe he was there.

As the questions and the speculations filtered through the crowd, someone spotted Miss Hazel at the corner with a bag of groceries in her arms, Mr. Saul's green army coat flapping around her legs. Seeing it was her house on fire, she dropped the bag and ran screaming down the street, "My baby, my baby; did anybody get my baby?"

I don't know what stunned and shocked me more, Miss Hazel's piercing screams or Grandma's backhand upside my head. "You gon' have your way, do what you wanta' do anyway ain't you, Little Miss? Your head is harder than Bimbo's butt." (I never knew who Bimbo was, just that his behind was hard). "Well, a hard head makes a soft behind. I tole you to wait while I put Bumbiddle on his clothes, but nothing do you but act like you grown folks, like you ain't got to mind nobody." The words rang out to the rhythm of the licks on my arms, my legs, around my shoulders. But Grandma stopped beating me when somebody yelled, "Hazel is trying to get in that house." It took all of Mr. Whitman's strength to hold Miss Hazel back. For months after the fire I could hear her screaming in my sleep, "My baby, my baby, oh my God, my baby's in that house."

Well, we didn't get to Mama Lucy's that day, because the fire didn't spread. The neighborhood was in somber mourning for Little Lizzie Durr, barely eight months old. It was around that time that Grandma Edie became both feared and respected, because she had actually prophesied that Little Lizzie would not be long for this world.

"That child is too pretty," Grandma volunteered when Little Lizzie had lost that generic baby look and her face had acquired its own distinctive stamp. "She don't even look real. Look at her," neighbors marveled. Little Lizzie was the envy of every woman who had ever had a baby in the history of Pipe Shop. Anybody could see that she was going to be "bright," that is, light-skinned. Grandma used to say that the telltale sign was the baby's ears. If the outer rim hadn't turned dark by a certain month, then the child was sure to be fair-skinned and marked for success and the pain and satisfactions of others' envy.

Lizzie was the only baby that Miss Hazel had carried to term, and so everybody understood why she worshiped the child and spent every penny of her ironing income on little outfits—sparkling diapers fastened with pink-tipped safety pins, booties with satin ties, panties with rows of ruffles on the seat, pink dresses smocked and embroidered, and dainty crocheted sweaters ornamented with rosettes. Oh, how she would wheel Lizzie around the neighborhood in a carriage she found at the secondhand store. Mama had helped her to fix it up, scrounging through the scraps of fabric left over from somebody's outfit or upholstered chair until she found a piece of navy canvas to re-cover the ripped and faded carriage top.

One day, as Miss Hazel passed by our house, Grandma Edie called to her from her lookout on the porch, "Come here, Daughter." "Daughter" was the name Grandma gave many women younger than herself whom she favored with a motherly caring and concern. Miss Hazel trundled the carriage through the gate and lifted the baby out. Grandma met her at the top of the steps and, nestling the baby in her arms, launched into great mirations over Little Lizzie—cootchie-coos and bless-him-little-bones-es. They sat down side-by-side in the glider and settled into baby talk.

"When did you take the belly band off?" Grandma asked as she peeked under the baby's undershirt. Grandma had made some belly bands for Little Lizzie from flour sacks that she cut and bleached, then hemstitched all around by hand. Some women looked on the practice as old-fashioned, but those of Grandma Edie's generation insisted that belly bands be worn for at least three months to strengthen the baby's back. "She's strong too," Grandma added. "Look at how tight she got a holt of my finger." They talked a little while longer and Miss Hazel, motioning to leave, nestled the baby gently in the stroller. Her eyelids drooping, Grandma's face wore a grave expression equal to her words. "Daughter, seems like you look on this child too much. The Lord done seen fit to open up your womb and give you this child, but he don't intend for you to put it before him. You know the Bible speaks against worshiping other gods. It's the first commandment: 'Thou shalt have no other gods before me.' So, don't make this child your God. You know I don't mean you no harm in saying this." Miss Hazel replied with a simple, respectful, "Yes, ma'am, Miss Edie."

Because everyone knew how much Little Lizzie was Miss Hazel's heart, nobody could figure out just how or why she could leave the child in that house all by herself. By nightfall there were at least a dozen conflicting accounts of what had sparked the fire. Someone said a stovepipe had fallen across the bed where the baby was sleeping and set the room afire. Others said a kerosene stove had exploded and set the house ablaze, but we never really found out for sure just what had happened.

The evening of the day of the fire people flocked into our living room for Mama's club meeting. Mama had started to set the refreshments out when Minnie B. Vicks said, "I can't believe Kitty Burns would pass up a chance to eat." Miss Burns was the only member missing from the group, but no sooner had Miss Minnie spoken than a knock rang out. It was Miss Kitty with her husband at her side. "I knew she wouldn't miss no food," said Miss Minnie under her breath, as Mama ushered them in. Mr. Hezekiah accompanied his wife everywhere, including club meetings, because she claimed to have epileptic seizures that no one had ever witnessed. He helped her ease into the big blue claw-footed chair and then the talk resumed.

Miss Georgia, who sold bootleg whiskey, started in:

"I know the people's been saying that Hazel came and asked me to watch the baby while she went to Cox and Autry to get some milk, but that's a lie. She could'na no way and no how, 'cause I left home 'fore day this morning and Cox and Autry don't open that early. I left to catch a ride to Cippico with Eugene. He said they might be doing some hiring at the plant, and we wanted to get out there as soon as we could, so we could be up toward the front of the line." I wondered why Miss Georgia went, because they didn't hire women at Cippico. Mama later told me it was so she could fill out the forms for Mr. Gene, who could barely read and write.

"I heard Hazel left Saul in the house to watch the baby, but Old Man Garvin came by and asked him if he wanted a day's work laying some Sheetrock." That was Mr. Hezekiah, who droned on, pausing at suspenseful moments to puff on his pipe. "Since Hazel only went to get some milk and a few odds and ends, Saul thought the baby would be all right till she got back. Mr. Garvin was in a hurry to get started, 'cause his wife was trying to fix up the house. They was having company and he only had three days to finish the room." Mama interrupted him, I guess because she always used to say that Mr. Hezekiah belonged to the iron butt school of storytelling. You had to have an iron butt to sit long enough for him to finish. And don't let him reach into his shirt pocket for that red can of Prince Albert tobacco. That was a sure sign that he was settling in for one of his epics.

While the others talked, Miss Sadie Madison sat still, her dress pulled down over her knees, her face tilted to the side to hide the bluish gray birthmark that covered her right cheek. She drew on her cigarette and blew the smoke in my direction, unmindful of my presence at the table in the corner. "Now I can't say who told me, but somebody said they saw Saul up by the ball diamond this morning, and y'all know who lives over there."

Mama, who had no patience for gossip, tried to change the subject but Miss Sadie rattled on. "The truth is the truth and it shines in the dark," countered Miss Sadie. "And if a man care more about his outside woman than he do his own flesh and blood, then ain't nobody 'sposed to cloak him in his sin. Like I always say, if you don't want me to see it, don't show it to me." When Miss Sadie's loose and judging tongue broke its silence, I no longer pretended to be tracing the boot of Italy and penciling in its pastel cities for geography class. Just why I, a girl of eight, was so fascinated by talk of a husband and his "woman," I don't know, but I do remember finding this turn in the conversation so arresting that I stopped and did what no child in Pipe Shop was allowed to do: look grown folks in the face while they were having "grown folks' conversation." Mama, forgetful of my presence in the corner, shouted, "You, go to bed, Little Miss."

There is no irritation, no injustice like that of being ordered from the room just when a conversation has taken an exciting turn. And she had no business calling me "Little Miss." Papa had named me "Miss Priss," he said, because I was always prancing and being prissy. When Papa called me "Miss Priss," though, it was always with a loving tone of voice. The rest of the family and most of the substitute mothers in the neighborhood vulgarized and nastied up Papa's own special name for me. "Little Miss" was derogatory and associated with everything punitive.

"I gave your Little Miss a few licks for you," said Miss Ophelia as she led me by the hand up the front steps where Mama sat on the porch shelling crowder peas. "What was she doing this time?" Mama asked. "Mouthing off again?" Miss Ophelia nodded her head and strained to keep a straight face. "Were you sassing Miss Ophelia?" Mama asked. I answered, tears of public humiliation welling up, "Cleophus Diggins was bothering me, so I told him his mama had one titty and she carried it in a holster." "Where did you learn this kind of talk?" Mama wanted to know, fighting to suppress the laughter rising in her voice. But I couldn't answer her, because I didn't know. I guess it was something I had picked up in the lunch line.

Although I didn't like the name "Little Miss," I could take it as long as it wasn't preceded by the epithet for every verbal female child of the South: "womanish." "You are a womanish Little Miss," Grandma Edie used to say with that deep guttural sound that she would summon for mention of anything distasteful. It almost sounded like she was expectorating when she said it, and I was reminded of gagging on the cod liver oil she made us take to "flush out," as she put it. Every spring, Grandma would line up three drams of cod liver oil and three orange wedges at the end of the kitchen table for my brothers and me. To distract me from the tang of the cod liver oil, I concentrated on the wringer washer in the corner, then gulped down the oil and reached for the orange wedge just before I vomited it all back up. "Don't you vomick it up. If you vomick it up, I'll just have to give you some more."

Grandma Edie insisted I was womanish and would certainly come to a bad end for giving sass and listening to "reels" like "If Loving You Is Wrong" and "Who's Making Love to Your Old Lady," and "Steal Away," not to be confused with the spiritual of the same name.

I had always discounted Grandma's prophecies and dismissed them as the superstitions of an old lady grown more feeble-minded by the day, but when her prophecy of Lizzie's death came to pass, I started to believe her. Before the fire I would grumble and complain when she asked me to read to her the Ninetieth Psalm; after the fire, I would take that well-thumbed Bible from the mantel where Grandma said it had to rest, just to the right of a picture of the Last Supper, and handling with care its aged, cracked-leather backing, I would begin in the most sonorous and reverent tone my childhood voice could muster, "Lord, thou hast been our dwelling place in all generations." Before the fire I thought she forced me to read First Corinthians, Thirteen, to teach me my place in a world dominated and controlled by grown folks, but after the fire, I didn't question her. I simply read with slow precision, "When I was a child, I spake as a child, I understood as a child, I thought as a child. . . ."

When Mr. Saul laid a new foundation to rebuild the house in the very same spot where the old one had stood, Grandma prophesied that that would drive Miss Hazel completely mad. It did. From that point on she remained confined within the walls of her own skull. On summer evenings she stalked the streets of Pipe Shop, mumbling to herself, flaps of a dirty diaper hanging from her head. Reggie said he often saw her tearing notebook paper into tiny shreds. Nowadays, her face comes back to me burnt to a horrible sienna, almost as if the match she used to clench between her teeth has set her face aflame.

After the fire I still dreaded the trips to Mama Lucy's, but I dared not let on to Grandma Edie. Even when deep down inside myself I wanted to color or play jacks or make scrapbooks from the Sears Roebuck catalogue, I walked the blocks with Grandma Edie and served my apprenticeship to this witchy good Samaritan who had marked me with her mole. I sat stock-still in the corner beside Mama Lucy's metal chifforobe, the picture of Jesus Christ on the cross looking down on me as I held my breath to block the stench of Sloan's liniment.

Emancipation Day

The initiation into the arts of reading that I received at Grandma Edie's knee served me well when I reached the age of ten and graduated to the intermediate level of recitations held at Macedonia Church. These programs were arranged by a serial band of stout, chesty women wearing stiff, wide-brimmed hats adorned with artificial flowers. Because of the brassy, orange-colored dye that set their heads aglow, we called them the sweet-potato ladies. The recitations were held every Sunday, promptly at 3:30. Before a dinner of fried chicken, icebox rolls, and creamed corn had made its sluggish passage through the stages of digestion, we reassembled at church to begin the round of readings that the sweet-potato ladies had assigned the week before. Night after night, after dinner, after dishes, after homework, we memorized and rehearsed passage after passage of a Sunday piece.

According to the mistresses of ceremony, the recitations taught discipline and fought the eternal battle to stamp out the legendary slack tongue and lazy drawl of Southerners. This drawl, a stigma right up there with the myth of dirt-eating, was presumed to be the unmistakable sign of Southern ignorance and backwardness, and could only be erased if we learned lengthy "inspirational" readings or important historical addresses. But this was just a front. I will always believe that these recitations were actually a covert and primitive form of birth control, inasmuch as one of these big-bosomed, orange-haired women knew your whereabouts every Sunday afternoon and could appear from around any corner just when you thought you had escaped her eagle eyes.

Once I sneaked to the basement to share a Coca-Cola with Timmy, Reverend Lockhart's son. The bottle had barely thudded to the end of the metal chute when we heard the *clip-clop-clop* of blunt-heel shoes and Miss Harvey's barking voice.

"What are you doing down here? Upstairs, this minute."

"But what about my drink?"

"Leave it down here."

"But I'm not through drinking it."

"You should have thought about that before you bought it. You had no business buying a drink so close to service time anyway." There could be no protest, no argument, when an adult spoke. And when she gave orders, whoever she was—and it was always a she on Sunday afternoons—you simply obeyed.

Shoving his half-finished bottle in the slanted rack bolted to the red machine, Timmy tore off like buckshots were exploding in his pants, clutching his skinny little clip-on necktie. I followed behind Miss Harvey, rebelling by scraping the soles of my shoes against the gritty basement floor.

"And pick up your feet."

I smoldered throughout the service, cutting my eyes first at Miss Harvey, then at Timmy, who had beaten such a fast retreat out of the basement. When it came my turn to deliver Kipling's "If," I let my eyes rest long and hard on Miss Harvey when I reached the line, "If you can keep your head when others are losing theirs and blaming it on you."

In another era, Miss Harvey might have had a stage career—probably at directing—but she swallowed her ambitions and accepted the measure of status she enjoyed as the primly respectable wife of a local high school principal. The recitations she selected were always long and dramatic pieces or those that offered oratorical or choreographical possibilities that she was adept at coaxing from her pupils. She had a fondness for Tennyson and Blake (especially "The Little Black Boy"), but of all the selections she assigned me, Lincoln's "Gettysburg Address" became my signature piece, which I was first slated to deliver at the annual Lincoln/Douglass Birthday Banquet in February 1963.

Miss Harvey had been coaching me for weeks. "Remember now, President Lincoln was dedicating a cemetery. This was a solemn, lofty occasion. Don't go galloping through the words like you are on a racehorse. Start off slowly, somberly. Listen to me: 'Four score and seven years ago, our fathers.' See?" As instructed, I clasped my hands together just underneath my breast. "Speak from your diaphragm. Stand up a little straighter, and lift your shoulders. Be sure to enunciate 'continent,' 'dedicate,' 'consecrate,' 'tuh.' All right?"

"Yes, ma'am." And with all due gravity and with practiced emphasis, I recited, "Four score and seven years ago our fathers brought forth upon this continent a new nation, conceived in Liberty, and dedicated to the proposition that all men are created equal."

The Lincoln/Douglass Birthday Banquet of 1963 would fall just before my twelfth birthday, in March. Sponsored by the Bessemer Voters League, the banquet was held near every Valentine's Day in the basement of the church. Local clergymen speechified for hours, and students of all ages competed in oratorical contests. Although the Lincoln/Douglass Banquet was a significant event, the Centennial Celebration of the Emancipation Proclamation was the banner occasion of 1963, and thus I was upset to learn that Reverend Lockhart's daughter, Wanda Glen, had been chosen to deliver "Gettysburg" at that more august occasion.

For months, schools and churches throughout the Birmingham area had been preparing for the ceremony. To no one's surprise, Alabama was among those states denying official recognition to the celebrations occurring nationwide, but that did not dampen the enthusiasm that electrified the city. The *Birmingham World* headlined speakers, and black radio stations broadcast a veritable "Who's Who" of Civil Rights personalities, who flowed in and out of Birmingham throughout 1963.

Mama chastised me for admitting that I wanted to be center stage, to see my name in the paper in the very spot where Wanda Glen's was printed. "Don't try to be Miss Biggity. I'm glad you've won a few speaking contests, but don't go getting the Big Head." This was the injunction given anyone who appeared to be too flagrantly self-seeking and self-regarding.

The day of the big event, a royal blue banner billowed on the church's front facade, and you could see the gold lettering, EMANCIPATION—100 YEARS, all the way from the Bessemer Super Highway. The women of the Deaconess Society cooked all day for the event, and the girls of the junior choir helped to serve the collard greens, mustard-yellow scoops of potato salad, fried chicken, corn bread, and sweet-potato pie.

Swept up in the excitement of the celebration that New Bethlehem's choir had sparked, I forgot all about the limelight that would soon be Wanda Glen's. But when Miss Harvey announced that Wanda Glen was bedridden with the flu, and that I would have to take her place, I was suddenly frightened and no longer wanted center stage. I wasn't ready to deliver "The Gettysburg Address," had not practiced enough, I explained to Miss Harvey. I didn't yet have the curtsies down.

Reverend Manfred McKinley, a famed voting rights organizer and master orator, was the featured speaker for the Centennial Celebration. A long-time friend of our minister, Reverend Lockhart, he had preached several sermons at our church. On church business in Chicago, Reverend McKinley was returning to Alabama especially for the occasion, but he was running late. Every few minutes, Reverend Lockhart approached the pulpit and urged patience on the congregation. Reverend McKinley was making a special trip from Chicago just for us. When word finally came that Reverend McKinley was within minutes of Macedonia, Reverend Lockhart nodded to Miss Harvey, the mistress of ceremonies, to begin the preliminary portion of the program, after which she introduced my speech.

"Ladies and gentlemen, as is indicated on your programs, Reverend McKinley's sermon is titled 'Finishing the Unfinished Task of Abraham Lincoln.' What better warm-up could we have for him than a rendition of Lincoln's most famous speech presented by our very own little Miss. . . ."

With all eyes on me, I trudged up to the pulpit. Just as I had been coached, I found a spot on the back wall on which to focus and began the speech that I can still recite almost verbatim now, thirty-plus years hence. I had practiced it over and over again—in the basement with Miss Harvey, in the kitchen at home—but none of the rehearsals had prepared me for the overwhelming emotion I felt that evening in the basement as the candles flickered on the paper-covered tables and the room grew very still. There on the stage I stood in rapt communion with Lincoln's words:

> *we here highly resolve that these dead shall not have died in vain; that this nation shall have a new birth of freedom; and that this government of the people, by the people, for the people, shall not perish from the earth.*

As the amens resounded throughout the rafters, I bowed quickly and rushed toward the steps, embarrassed for the first time by all the applause. Reverend McKinley, who was ascending the pulpit from the other side, boomed, "Wait," his tone so thunderous that I jumped. "Wait, don't go, young lady. You stay right up here in the pulpit, so you can get used to sitting on platforms." I slunk back and dropped down into one of the three high-backed blue-red velvet chairs, mesmerized by Reverend McKinley's cadences.

He reeled off the requisite acknowledgments to the pastor, assistant pastor, mistress of ceremonies, platform guests, sisters and brothers of this congregation, and visiting friends. "I bring you greetings from Sherman Temple A.M.E. Zion Church in Demopolis, Merengo County, where we are fighting the good fight for first-class citizenship. Not second-class, not third-class, but first-class citizenship. Can I get a witness?

"I am always thankful to be inside Macedonia's walls, because, as some of you know, Reverend Lockhart and I go back a long, long way. As boys we fished for crawdads in the creek together in Chehaw, Alabama, nothing but a whistle-stop on the road to someplace else. We've been traveling together ever since. Gripping identical cardboard suitcases, we boarded the same bus to Montgomery, the cradle of the Confederacy, to enroll at Alabama

State College. When we both committed ourselves to the service of our Lord and Savior Jesus Christ, we commenced our training together at Hood Theological Seminary. We continue to follow in each other's footsteps, just on different parts of a well-worn path. I am honored to share this platform with him and these other distinguished leaders of the Bessemer community.

"I don't need to tell you that this is an historic occasion: the one hundredth anniversary of the Emancipation Proclamation. Sounds good, doesn't it? I don't need to tell you that the Emancipation is unfinished, that the business that Lincoln began remains to this day incomplete, that this government 'of the people . . .'" He paused, then turned to lock his eyes on me. "Speak it for me, young lady."

"This government by the people, for the people, shall not perish from the earth."

"That's it. That's good. Now this government, this ship of state, is at risk of sinking. Or let me put it a different way, the entire fabric of our society is fraying at every edge. It is fraying because people have been frightened into submission by gradualism."

"Go 'head."

"By Boswelling, poll taxes, literacy test bills, gerrymandering. Our people have been bombed into submission by the White Citizens Council and all their minions."

"Preach."

"It has been nearly nine years since the Supreme Court, the highest court in this land, decreed that segregation in the public schools is unconstitutional. But right here, right now, all over Alabama, our children still file into segregated classrooms and leaf through yesterday's dog-eared books. Meanwhile, the headlines read: 'Colored Children Kept from School,' 'School Jim Crow in Alabama,' 'Governor George Wallace Blocks Court-Ordered Plea to Integrate Public Schools,' 'Twelve Denied Entry to White Schools,' 'Virginia Fights Desegregation—Closes Schools.'"

"Preach the word."

"I'm here to tell you this evening, though, that this situation will not long abide."

"Not long."

"I say to you, this evening, church, that we stand before the wall of states' rights. Before the wall of Southern manifestos. Before the wall of interposition. But I assure you that all these walls will crumble like that great wall at Jericho."

"Preach."

"We will not be deterred because we know that states' rights have come to mean one thing and one thing only: the right to repress, the right to suppress, the right to dispossess the Negro. When Lincoln signed the Emancipation Proclamation one hundred years ago today, he abolished a centuries-long tradition of white possession of the Negro man. Oh, I can see him as he sat there in that executive office one hundred years ago, the cabinet members ringing round him. I want you to picture that afternoon with me.

"Oh, I wasn't there, but I imagine a bright blue sky and a sun beaming on the page. I wasn't there, but the historical record has left us with two important details about that day, and I want to refresh your memory: First, President Lincoln left a New Year's party to sign that historic document. Second, I want you to remember that he departed from one custom that day; he didn't abbreviate his first name. He signed 'Abraham Lincoln.' Not 'Abe Lincoln,' but 'Abraham Lincoln.' Now there's a message for us in that, and it is this: One—we must turn away from partying sometimes and get about the work of finishing the business of emancipation. It is unfinished, people. It is unfinished. Two—If we are to complete this business before the next centennial, then we cannot abbreviate the struggle. We must wage it on all fronts, enlisting every possible soldier—infantry, militia, all God's children, soldiers on the battlefield. The young, the old, and the in between. Everybody is needed. The M.D.'s, the Ph.D.'s, and the no D.'s. Dr. King can't fight this battle by himself."

"Speak it, speak it."

"Asbury Howard can't fight this battle by himself. Neither can Fred Shuttlesworth. Neither can Arthur Shores. Every last one of us has the battle marrow in his bones.

"People, I challenge you this evening to uphold a long and glorious legacy of the A.M.E. Zion Church. This was the church of Frederick Douglass. This was the church of Harriet Tubman. This was the church of Sojourner Truth. Let's reclaim that legacy in this emancipation year and rededicate ourselves to something more than looking good and standing pat.

"I have brought with me this evening leaflets from the voter registration/church participation program. I want every last member of this congregation to take some and distribute them in your neighborhoods, at your workplaces, in your barbershops, in your social and savings clubs, wherever you can plant them. I want you to attend the regular meetings of the Bessemer Voters League and commit to taking a nonvoter with you. And don't you leave the meeting unless that person's name is clearly on the rolls. The next time I visit Macedonia, I want you to report that you have so chinked the wall of segregation that all the king's horses and all the king's men cannot glue segregation together again."

By this time the roar of the audience was so loud that Reverend McKinley had to pause at several places for the roaring to subside.

"Let me close by encouraging you yet again to involve the youth in this struggle. Train them not up in the ways of fear, for if they are trained in that direction, that is the way they will always veer." He walked over to me again and, mopping the sweat that was striating his face, he said, "Stand up, young lady." Putting his sweat-dampened arm around my shoulders, he asked, "Who are your people?" and before I could answer, Papa gushed, "She's one of my grands, Reverend McKinley."

"I should have known that this was a child brought up with Zion in her blood. Brother and Sister Williams are two tireless servants. I have taken many a meal at their home and slept in their beds on many a night when I could not drive another mile. Where is Sister Williams? Is she here?" Mother stood up and smiled. "As we bring these services to a close, renewing our commitment to completing Abraham Lincoln's unfinished task, let us turn to the memory selection printed on the front of the bulletin. Come on read for us again, young lady.

> We wrestle not against flesh and blood, but against principalities, against powers, against the rulers of the darkness of this world, against spiritual wickedness in high places.
>
> —EPHESIANS 6:12

And then he swooped his arms up to bring the congregation to its feet and led us off in "Lift Every Voice and Sing," the Negro National Anthem:

> Lift every voice and sing
> Let our rejoicing rise
> High as the listening skies,
> Let it resound loud as the rolling sea.
> Sing a song full of the faith that the dark past has taught us.
> Sing a song full of the hope that the present has brought us.
> Face the rising sun of our new day begun.
> Let us march on till victory is won.

Easter Sunday

Spring was slow to start that year, as slow to arrive as Christmas to a child with hopes pinned on a brand-new electric-blue bicycle. It had been a soggy spring, but on Easter Sunday 1963 the sun was resplendent and the day warm enough for the Easter egg hunt. It was a sight to see children in their finery gathering outside the church, carrying Easter baskets crammed with chocolate rabbits and multicolored jelly beans. The girls fidgeted in their pastel dotted-swiss dresses, the nets of their tulle cancans peeking underneath, and stepped proudly in their patent-leather Buster Browns and white anklets edged in lace. The boys stood erect in sport coats and bow ties, their faces scrubbed clean for Easter.

I was still tired from staying up to rehearse my part as Mary Magdalene in the Easter pageant.

"Where is he? Who will roll away the stone for us from the entrance of the tomb?"

After all my practicing, Miss Harvey still said that I didn't have quite enough emphasis at the end of the question. "Raise your voice high," she had coached, but apparently I did not raise it high enough.

On Easter Sunday 1963 we had hairdos freshly done, but nobody had new outfits, except, that is, for Miss Annie Pearl Wilkes. The boycott had taken care of that. Although I didn't march in any of the demonstrations, I helped to letter signs reading DON'T BUY WHERE YOU CAN'T WORK.

Now everybody knows the boycott nearly brought Birmingham, Alabama, businesses to their knees. The Easter season was second only to Christmas, as far as profits were concerned, so local merchants were bending to the pressure of a selective buying campaign. Until they desegregated their eating counters, drinking fountains, rest rooms, sales forces, black folks weren't buying. From every pulpit in Bessemer came the call for pocketbook pride and the order forbidding black folks to shop where they couldn't work.

Martin Luther King Jr. was addressing random churches in the area, and when Papa learned that he was to speak at Shining Star Baptist in Muscoda, he piled Gina and me into the station wagon and drove to Macedonia, where we joined a caravan. Those without transportation stuffed into cars with vacant seats, and I ended up sitting on Miss Addie's lap, my knees pressing hollow circles in the blue vinyl of the backseat.

When we rounded the corner to Shining Star and saw all the cars, we knew there was no way we would even squeeze inside that tiny church, much less get a seat. We drove several blocks, past cars lining the shoulders of the road in both directions for as far as the eye could see, then walked back and stood with the masses in front of the white wooden church. The outside crowd mimicked the applause and the shouts thundering from inside the church, although nobody outside could have heard what Dr. King was saying.

The rally ended and we started to walk back down the road in pitch blackness, soon lighted by the headlights of oncoming cars. As we passed him, Mr. Jessie Pitts called out to Papa, "That was some speech, Brother Fred." "How did you get in, Jessie?" "Oh, we got down here around two o'clock and waited at the door. I wouldn't've missed this for nothing." I don't remember all that Mr. Jessie told us about the speech, but one thing has stuck in my mind, maybe because Papa always quoted it. King had declared, "We're going to take the heart out of Dixie." Well, come to find out, despite all the signs, rallies, and orders from radio stations, newspapers, and all the local pulpits, and all the ads from local newspapers, Miss Annie Pearl had still stolen into Loveman's through the alley, to get her Easter dress.

Then as now, a consuming woman with voracious appetites was figured as *the* impediment to black progress and revolutionary change, and so each week the Inter Citizens Committee ran ads in the *Birmingham World,* featuring pen-and-ink drawings of raffish matrons with bulging arms and legs, who hugged cavernous pocketbooks to their hefty bosoms. In one, two women in wide-brimmed hats and sleeveless dresses wear mink stoles draped around their shoulders as they stroll from the "Colored Exit" of a fashionable department store. Outside, a large thermometer registers 101 degrees above the caption: "I don't care what these folks say, you jest ain't nobody if you ain't got no mink."

So there it was, plainly. Miss Annie Pearl was wilfully impeding the march of progress by stealing into Loveman's for a banana yellow linen dress. Shamefaced, she would later claim that she was not burning to have a new dress as much as she was trying to save the one she had already in layaway that was paid nearly all the way off. She didn't have good money to throw away. I heard the grown folks say that she didn't have any money to throw away. It was Mr. Ivery Peters's hard-earned money from Tennessee Coal and Iron, which we called TCI. He was one of those men who asserted his manhood by paying women's clothing bills, and Miss Annie Pearl left no doubts in anybody's mind that he was a whole man. Grandma Edie thought that it was a plain disgrace and that she should lose no time in letting Miss Annie Pearl know she thought so. To this day nobody seems to know who spotted her first or how she got all the way to Birmingham in the middle of a transit strike. "Ivery probably took her," Miss Mae Walker said.

Anyway, news beat Miss Annie Pearl back, and the neighborhood was soon abuzz with rumors that she was a traitor to the cause. Word traveled from house to house on the plain black telephones with white rotary dialing panels. Miss Lizzie called Miss Mae Walker, who called Grandma, who then wanted to call Miss Annie Pearl, but, Mama talked her out of it.

"You don't like the telephone anyway, Miss Edie." It was true. I never knew anybody who could end a telephone conversation faster than Grandma. She would hold the receiver away from her ear and after a few, "You don't mean's," "Have mercies," and "Do Jesuses," she would clear her throat and speak her trademark closing line: "Well, I'll say bye now."

The next day at church Miss Annie Pearl had the nerve to strut down the aisle in the banana linen sheath and black patent leather shoes. I can see the saucy wide-brimmed straw-colored hat with black satin ribbon held down by a bunch of bright red plastic cherries. With her eyes hidden under the hat's broad brim, she avoided the judging gazes of the congregation as she strutted down front and sat at the end of the deaconesses' row. Her white gloves clutching the black-lace-and-lacquer fan like a flamenco dancer, she fanned herself to a fare-thee-well and looked straight at the preacher.

That day Reverend Lockhart announced that he was departing from custom. He would not take his text from the scriptures of the resurrection. "Church, I take my text from two passages of Matthew this morning. Open your Bibles to Matthew 7:25 to 28 and read along with me:

> *Therefore I say unto you, Take no thought for your life what ye shall eat, or what ye shall drink, nor yet for your body, what ye shall put on. Is not the life more than meat, and the body more than raiment?*
>
> *Behold the fowls of the air: for they sow not, neither do they reap, nor gather into barns; yet your heavenly Father feedeth them. Are ye not much better than they?*

Which of you by taking thought can add one cubit unto his stature?
And why take ye thought for raiment?

"Let me put this question to you again, church, why take ye thought of raiment? I want you to ponder that with me this morning. Why take ye thought of raiment?" I imagined that the church had turned to a thousand pairs of piercing eyes, nailing Miss Annie Pearl to the cross.

After the service the church members clustered as usual in the back of the main hall to greet the pastor and compliment him on the sermon. As Miss Annie Pearl neared the group, still fanning and hiding behind her hat brim, Grandma started loud-talking: "Reverend Lockhart, the Lord sho' spoke through you this morning. We needed that message. Some folks oughta know that a whole heap of things is more important than yellow dresses." Miss Annie Pearl rolled her eyes at Grandma and strutted out the door.

The next Sunday Miss Annie Pearl did not show up for church. When Grandma asked about her, Miss Ida Fletcher, her sister-in-law, said she was a little under the weather. Grandma raised her eyebrows in disbelief. It was just as well that Miss Annie Pearl wasn't there, because Reverend Lockhart devoted practically his entire sermon to thanking the congregation for helping to make the boycott a success. He waved a clipping from the *Birmingham News,* gloating as he said, "You know, the paper is blacking out news of the boycott and the demonstrations. Here even ole George Wallace is complaining that the sit-ins made the front page in Mississippi, but got buried inside the *Birmingham News.* How's that; he wants to advertise that Negroes have finally hit the white man where it hurts—in his pocketbook. Who would've thought that old George Wallace would end up on our side of the battlefield?"

On most Sundays, Reverend Lockhart stood in one spot, gripping the sturdy edges of the pulpit as if he might otherwise blow away. But that Sunday after Easter, he strode back and forth across the pulpit, waving newspaper clippings high above his head. From side to side, he weaved back and forth, chopping the air, his robes billowing behind him, the chain of his glasses clinking against the metal of his zipper.

"I feel good this morning. I say I feel good this morning, 'cause I see the dawning of a brand-new day. Church, it's a new day in Alabama when we got the Chamber of Commerce crying about the slowdown in Birmingham's economy. We got 'em eating their own words about segregation, eating their own words about where we can and cannot eat." He was warming up. "They got the nerve to tell us that Dr. King is an outside agitator.

Well, if he is, he's an outside agitator for the Lord. Can I get a witness? They think that if they just lock him up, they can shut him up. But we who are foot soldiers in this battle know the man upstairs has loosed his tongue, and the man upstairs will go his bond. My, my, how the mighty have fallen. You know, if you just hold on to God's unchanging hand, he will make a change. He will make you the victor, 'cause he's almighty. He'll bring the high low, because he's sitting high and looking low. Oh, if you just hold out, he will make your enemies your footstools."

From the missionary corner, handkerchiefs were waving like a bright cloud of white confetti suspended in the air. Lonnie answered Reverend Lockhart with crashing chords on the organ. And from the opposite corner, where the trustees sat, came Papa's "Preach! Preach, Lockhart!"

Reverend Lockhart was almost hyperventilating now. Sweat streamed from his temples and trickled down his collar, and foam collected in the corners of his mouth.

"We got ole man Loveman up on Second Avenue practically giving away his merchandise, but we ain't gone take it no matter how low he slashes the prices."

He put on his glasses, moving one of the clippings forward and backward until he reached an angle from which he could read. "Oh, Macedonia, tell me there ain't victory in this: 'Loveman's After-Easter Clearance Sale,' 'Advertised Savings Between 10 to 50 Percent,' 'Pay No Money Down,' 'Take Up to 24 Months to Pay,' 'Free Delivery Anywhere in Alabama.'" And in a parting shot of drama, seldom seen in Macedonia's walls, Reverend Lockhart ripped up the clipping and let the shreds of paper rain slowly to the floor, some landing on the toes of his wing-tipped shoes.

Pecans

"Where are the pecans?"

"There they are."

"Where?"

"Right there in the bag."

"I don't see them."

Gina leaned on her forearms, then pointed. "Right there, dummy."

"I still don't see them, Gina."

"There, right there."

"This brown paper bag?"

"Yeah, that bag."

"They never came in this kind of bag before."

"Papa got them at the farmers' market. I was with him when he bought them."

"When?"

"Yesterday."

"I know the pecans never came in this colored bag before."

"I'm telling you, Papa got them at the farmers' market and that's the kind of bag they put them in."

I was used to seeing pecans in see-through bags, like the ones that Irish potatoes came in, only smaller. Mother had asked me to arrange the Christmas bowl of oranges, waxed red apples, pecans, walnuts, nigger toes, and hard, sticky peppermint pillows.

I patted the bag, suspiciously, then drew back my hand.

"They don't feel like pecans."

"I'm telling you, stupid, it's pecans in that bag. Throw it up."

"Why?"

"Just throw it up."

I slowly lifted the heavy bag from the table and tossed it in the air. It burst. Country eggs fell out, cracking through brown-speckled shells, puddles and puddles of yellow yolks staining the blue-checkered tablecloth. The clear, slimy egg whites oozed like snot off the table's edge, down to the glossy floor that Auntee had just washed and waxed the day before.

Gina laughed that chilling cackle. "Uh-oh. Somebody's in trouble."

I started to cry. "Why did you make me do it? You made me do it."

Papa heard the noise and left the den, where he was reading his papers. I heard him shuffling toward the kitchen in his slippers, shouting on the way, "What's all this ruckus about?" He stopped at the threshold, still clutching the *Birmingham World,* then seeing the eggs that I was frantically scooping into the mixing bowl, he started fussing.

"Gina made me do it. Gina made me do it." I shuddered. "Mother told me to make the Christmas bowl and Gina said the pecans were in the bag. And I was looking for them, and Gina made me throw them up in the air. Gina made me do it, Papa, I swear she did."

"What did I tell you about swearing? And anyway, if Gina tells you to jump off the Empire State Building, you gon' do that? If Gina tells you to drink that bottle of ammonia over there on the sink, you gon' do that? When you gon' start to use your own head and quit following in behind Gina? You should've known better than to throw these eggs up in the air. You ain't no baby. You twelve years old. You old enough to know better."

I looked up to Gina. Then, I still saw her as my fearless older cousin. More like a big sister than a cousin, but a big sister who never adjusted to your arrival. By that point in our lives we had long since settled into the caricatures the family had drawn of both of us. I was the clumsy, homely bookworm with frowsy hair and knobby knees; Gina, the cute and shapely good-time girl, who had no mind for nor interest in memorizing speeches, but who quickly learned the latest dances and majorette routines. I envied her the attention she received from boys, and although it has taken me years to realize, she envied me the attention I garnered practically every Sunday afternoon, when I curtsied in the pulpit of Macedonia after reciting some long speech. Time out of mind, everybody had teased Gina about the morning she forgot her Easter speech. It was only one line, but she forgot it, and Mother had to whisper to her from the choir stand, "Christ is risen as he said."

Over the years, I laughed along with everybody else whenever Mother told the story of Gina and the Easter speech. Then it was just another funny story, for I truly believed that Gina was smarter than I would ever be at all the things in life that mattered, which is why I let her make a fool of me, time and time again.

The Christmas Eve I broke the eggs everything went wrong. The

Christmas tree was the first bad thing. That morning, Mother sent Papa out to pick a tree, and while he was gone, she climbed up into the crawl space for the box of ornaments and the green felt that skirted the Christmas tree. She lost her footing on the stepladder and sprained her ankle. Hours later Papa came back, not with the traditional evergreen, but with a boxed aluminum tree, complete with cobalt ornaments and a box of tinsel. Mother was furious. No fake tree would ever disgrace her living room. Wooden cardinals on aluminum fronds? Her gold-trimmed angel and Eastern star? No way. It saved money, Papa protested, and could be used again, year after year. Plus it wasn't a fire hazard. Mother shot him a withering glance and answered not a word. Removing the ice pack from her ankle, she ordered Gina and me to get our coats. We were going to get an evergreen tree.

Certain that she would find one, Mother flipped the backseat of the station wagon flat, so we could just slide the tree right on in. We three sat in the front seat and rumbled out Route 150 toward Muscoda, slowing down as we breasted the hill and spied the pink house at the crest, with reindeer on the roof, a nativity scene on the front lawn, and strings and strings of multicolored lights blinking in the ash gray afternoon. "There's no accounting for taste," Mother said snidely.

We drove on, passing roadside tree stands with SOLD OUT signs and others with the scraggly leavings of runt-sized trees. It was getting later and later in the afternoon and still no tree; I was hungry, and Mother's ankle was throbbing and swelling all the more. She whizzed the car homeward and set her face in a grimace that had hardened by the time she hobbled through the back door.

We had just hung our coats on the hallway hooks when Uncle Jr. called to say he wasn't coming home. Mother pleaded and cajoled to no avail, then took immediately to her bed, leaving us to create whatever Christmas Eve we could muster.

I drew the aluminum fronds from their cellophane casing and stuck them in the predrilled holes of the wooden column, then hung the fragile cobalt balls on its limbs. Auntee set the turkey giblets boiling in the kitchen, Papa read the Bible in the den, and Gina whispered to Forrest Jackson on the telephone. Mother had expressly told her to keep away from him, and thus presented with an opportunity to pay her back for making me break the eggs, I blared, "I'm gonna tell Mother."

Mother was propped up in bed, her red quilted satin bed jacket buttoned to the neck, her manicure case open on her lap. I was primed to tattle on Gina when Mother asked me to give her a manicure. As her long, spidery fingers soaked in the soapy water, she began to cry. Before that moment, I don't recall ever seeing Mother cry and, for some strange reason, it unsettled me.

"What's wrong, Mother? What's wrong?"

"Nothing. I just felt a little sad. That's all."

"How come you sad?"

"Oh, lots of reasons."

"Because Uncle Jr.'s not coming home?"

"That's some of it."

Since leaving in 1959 Uncle Jr. had come home precious few times and mainly just for weekends then. Even Mother's present that year of an RCA Victor stereo couldn't lure him back to Bessemer.

"I would give anything to see my Mama," Mother cried.

I had heard Auntee talk of Mother's early years in Sumter County, but Mother was generally tight-lipped about that part of her history. "The less said about Sumter County, Alabama, the better," she used to say. "That's in the past." That night was one of the few times that Mother dwelled more on herself than on whether I was staying on the path she'd laid out for me.

That night she talked about her mother, who had died when she was seven years old.

"How did she die, Mother?"

"It was after Uncle Sweetie was born. She went outside in the rain before the month was up. I don't remember too much about my mother. I just know she had thick, coal black hair and she used to sing to us. People used to say that she was a friendly woman, liked a lot of company, liked to laugh and joke. My brother, Sweetie, took after her that way. They said that's why she went up the road the day she took sick, because she was tired of being cooped up in the house. In those days, if a woman had a baby, she had to stay in the house until the baby was a month old. She couldn't take a tub bath or cook mustard greens or collard greens either before the month was up. Mama went outdoors and got caught in a rainstorm. Inside of three or four days, she had swollen up and died.

"Well, you see, my papa was farming and now he had three of us to look after—me, Huey, and Sweetie. And there was no way he could do it, especially with Sweetie being an arm baby and all. He held on for as long as he could, but then he had to make some other arrangements. I know how much he hated to split us up, but he had to. Huey was the oldest and he could help out at home, but I was too little to work and Sweetie was a baby. Papa's sister Maggie came and got Sweetie and took him to Bessemer, and his sister Dallas came and got me and I lived with her in Meridian. When

I first moved in with Aunt Dallas, I missed Mama so much I wished I could die, and all Aunt Dallas could do was fuss and drive, fuss and drive. 'Get that dreamy look off your face, and come in here and help me with this washing,' she would say, or, 'Quit moping around here, gal, that ain't gon' bring your mama back.'

"She was some kind of mean, Aunt Dallas. I tell you, she was mean as a rattlesnake. Nothing I did ever suited her. Look like she would just whip on me because she took a notion to. One day she beat me so bad, and for no other reason than that I asked her for a piece of pork chop. And do you know she didn't give it to me? Wouldn't give me a piece. That was the very day I made up my mind to run away. Her husband, Uncle Peter, must have felt sorry for me, because he talked her into letting me visit Sweetie in Bessemer. Huey had picked up and come to Bessemer by then, too, not long after our papa took sick and died. Once I got up here, I knew I wasn't going back. I didn't know how I would stay or where, I just knew I wasn't going back to be mistreated. And I didn't, either. Huey was married by this time, working at the rolling mill, so I bunked with him and his wife and Miss Lula, his mother-in-law, until I met and married Frank McDowell.

"Huey used to tease me and say that I came all the way to Bessemer for a pork chop. I came because I thought I would have a better life up here. And in many ways I have, but sometimes I wonder what would have happened if Mama had lived and we had stayed down in Epps. To this day, I can't forget that picture of Aunt Dallas and Uncle Peter sitting at the table right in front of me, eating pork chops and wouldn't even offer me so much as a slice of the fat. But I was determined that if the good Lord blessed me with breath in my body, one day I would have as many pork chops as I pleased."

After I had filed her nails and the pink translucent polish had hardened to a sheen, I started to leave the room, but Mother patted the bed and asked me to sit down again. She caught my hand in hers, then looked searchingly into my eyes.

I felt the love game coming. I had played the game with Mother for as far back as I can remember. Out of the blue Mother would spring the question, "You know that Mother loves you, don't you?" And I would always answer, "Yes, Mother." That was her cue to ask, "Do you love Mother?" And of course, I would answer, "Yes, Mother." Then would come, "How much?" Sometimes I answered, "I love you miles and miles, or oceans and oceans, Mother," or, "Deeper than the deep blue sea," or, "Taller than the tallest tree," vaguely intuiting that she was desperate for some expression of fathomless immensity.

From listening to the records Auntee played, day in, day out, I was fast becoming a junkie for the cry-in-your-beer songs that she favored. Though I barely understood the lyrics, I committed them to memory and ladled them out to Mother in exchange for ice pops that dyed my teeth turquoise, orange, and purple. Mingled with the ice pop's aftertaste was the disquieting echo of Mother's question and the memory of the wells of doubt and disappointment that filled her eyes. I doubt that Mother ever felt secure in the knowledge of anyone's love, except perhaps for Papa's, but when the wells of insecurity run as deeply as they did in her, the loving one must be rejected or be the fount of endless reassurances, none ever quite sufficient.

The next morning, Mother perked up when everybody converged at 1404—Daddy and Mama, Grandma and Daddy Les, Reggie and Bumbiddle. We all had several presents under the tree, many of them from Mother, including my first pair of roller skates. I am reminded of this Christmas whenever I teach Robert Hayden's *A Ballad of Remembrance* and read aloud the last two lines of his poem, "Those Winter Sundays":

What did I know, what did I know
of love's austere and lonely offices?

I was a child. I only knew what other children know at Christmas: that apples and oranges, pecans and red-striped candy pillows overflow the crystal bowl, and dolls and choo-choo trains, paints and crayons, bright blue bicycles and roller skates, majorette boots and clarinets pile underneath the silver tree.

Reverend Lockhart

We heard the screen door slam just as we pulled up to the house and Papa braked the station wagon at the mouth of the garage. And before we could unload the picnic cooler and hang our wet bathing suits and towels on the line, Auntee met us at the top of the steps and shocked us with the news that Reverend Lockhart had been murdered.

"Murdered?" Papa shouted, loud enough to shake his jowls. And then a second time, more softly, "Murdered," a cross between a disbelieving question and a cry. To this day the murderers have not been found, and for all I know, there may have been only one. Most blamed Reverend Lockhart's murder on his civil rights activities, while others whispered rumors that he was killed by the goons of a loan shark who financed the reverend's gambling debts. Some even said he shared a mistress with a white man, who paid to have him killed.

The presiding elder broke the news to Auntee. He had called from Tuscaloosa to say that the body had been found buried in a shallow grave in Chehaw, near the church Reverend Lockhart had pastored since leaving Macedonia. I vaguely remember that Auntee clutched a glinting butcher knife, fish scales clinging to the blade. Or maybe it was a fish. I do remember that when we stepped into the kitchen, the room was heavy with the scent of hand-sized reddish fish mounded in the sink, pairs and pairs of gelid eyes clamping mine in fright.

It was the summer of bright white tennis shoes and the Ben Casey vogue. The girls had all worn the white side-buttoned doctors' tunics to the Sunday School picnic that day at Paradise Lake, on the old Tuscaloosa Highway. I think of the shirt only because mine was a bit too small and, as Auntee recounted the gory details of the murder, the buttons seemed to tighten like a noose around my neck.

"Oh, Mr. Fred. I can't believe it. The presiding elder said they found the hand first. He was still wearing his wedding ring. Then they found one arm and then another one. And then the head. They had plucked out all his hair, every last strand of it, by the roots. Now you know that had to be somebody stone-cold crazy." I couldn't bear to hear the rest and left the room holding my hands over both my ears. Auntee and Papa were glued to the telephone all that night, and the radio on the night table could not muffle the fragments of horror that seeped through the door of Mother's room, where I lay facedown on the quilted bedspread.

When Papa finally reached Mrs. Lockhart later in the evening, more details emerged. Two men were taking a shortcut through an open field when one stepped on the hand. The crunch beneath his feet compelled the man to look beneath the thin layer of pine needles, brush, and debris. And there they found his naked parts, bathed in blood and pierced with stab wounds too numerous to count.

Sick of absorbing each new version of the horror, Gina came in to play dominoes. As usual, she got the first move. As usual, she called "Domino!" leaving me staring vacantly at the black rectangles abutting end to end. I never really liked this game; besides, who could concentrate on dominoes at a time like this? The white dotted tiles turned into so many arms and legs and rib bones strewn in an open field.

Reverend Lockhart had last been seen at his church three days before by the church treasurer, who had left him standing as straight as a Georgia pine on the wooden steps of the white clapboard church, his arm extended, waving the man along. Reverend Lockhart had walked the two miles from his home to the meeting at the church set far back in the woods. The treasurer had offered him a ride, but he had declined; the spirit moved him to work on his sermon. "Well, then, I'll come back and pick you up, Reverend; you just tell me about what time, and I'll be back here to get you," the man had said. "Oh, that's all right, Brother Lucas, I need to stretch my legs."

After twenty years in Philadelphia, Reverend Timothy Lockhart had remigrated to Alabama and lit sticks of dynamite under Macedonia's slumberous pews. In later years, Papa would remember that Reverend Lockhart's first sermon at Macedonia was so rousing that Miss Rachel Minnifee registered her satisfaction by throwing her patent-leather pocketbook in the direction of the pulpit. One by one, other women followed suit that day, and thus began a tradition that, in its first few months, seemed meant to spur this biscuit-colored wonder with coal black lustrous hair on to flights of sermonic brilliance. With each passing month, however, the gesture grew more ambiguous: Was it an alternate amen or a rude obstruction of a message they could not bear to hear?

Whenever Papa recalled the preacher's whirlwind two-year stay in Bessemer, he would mention that first sermon when Reverend Lockhart's baritone rattled Macedonia's stained-glass windows and shook the memorial plaques. "Lockhart was a stone preacher, now," Papa would say. "He could preach the horns off a billy goat."

Immediately upon his return to Alabama, Reverend Lockhart was swept up in the rush of a swiftly turning social tide. He joined ranks with other local ministers, leaders, and ordinary citizens like Mother and Papa committed to desegregation and first-class citizenship. He and his wife were fixtures at Mother's dinner table on Sunday afternoons and at the meetings of the Bessemer Voters League that sometimes followed. Central to the voter registration/church participation project, he had helped to establish and operate more than two dozen registration clinics throughout the city, hanging the project's placards all around the basement's wall and in the church's vestibule:

BALLOTS AND BUCKS ARE WEAPONS FOR FIRST-CLASS CITIZENSHIP
USE AND SPEND BOTH WISELY

He had used his pulpit to denounce the beating and jailing of Mr. Asbury Howard, following with an editorial to the *Birmingham World* indicting all those who thought silence in the matter a defensible response. Anyone who quaked and quivered in the face of change should take Asbury Howard's place on the chain gang, busting rocks along the edges of the Bessemer Super Highway. Howard's only "crime," he said, was making a simple sign:

VOTE TODAY FOR A BETTER TOMORROW

Theirs, on the other hand, was the crime of silence, puny self-interest, and smug self-satisfaction. His sermons and his editorials garnered invitations for Reverend Lockhart to speak throughout the city, but his new-found popularity did not endear him to those who demanded that *their* minister be always at their beck and call. It wasn't right for his assistant to serve communion wine to someone's sick-and-shut-in relative who had tithed to Macedonia all her life; that was the pastor's job.

As the superintendent of the Sunday School and himself a longtime, trusted member of the church, Papa became something of a confidant for those members grown progressively ambivalent about their new pastor. He pacified them with reassurances that the pastor's occasional absences were the price they had to pay for long-awaited justice. At the dinner table, Papa prayed for the pastor's safety. Ever since Reverend Lockhart's car tires had been slashed and his windshield shattered, Papa worried that his life might be in danger, which meant that our lives might be in danger too, since the reverend's dark blue Ford Fairlane was parked so often at 1404 Ninth Avenue. These were the days when Mother insisted that we no longer sleep with the doors wide open and that we search underneath the bed and in the closets whenever we had been out all day. When the Sixteenth Street Baptist Church was bombed in Birmingham, blasting the face of Christ out of the lone surviving stained-glass window, no one's fears could be assuaged. The explosion that buried the bodies of Carole Robertson, Denise McNair, Addie Mae Collins, and Cynthia Wesley occurred on Mama's birthday, September 15, 1963.

As Macedonia's honeymoon with Reverend Timothy Lockhart hastened to an end, members no longer scrambled to outdo each other in the charms of Southern hospitality. Those who had always temporized in the face of segregation's tumultuous decline—and long before Reverend Lockhart graced the pulpit—continued to voice their discontent in usher board meetings, at choir rehearsals, and even openly, before the morning processional of "Holy, Holy, Holy."

Mrs. Lockhart dared to say at Sunday dinner one afternoon at Mother's house that Macedonia was of several minds about the sluggish changes in Birmingham. Despite their pronouncements, there were those members who only wanted a taste of freedom, only wanted to sample it as they might some unfamiliar food like sturgeon or hard-boiled eggs in aspic. They had said they wanted movement, but most of their feet were cemented solidly to the ground. Of course, none would admit to being comfortable with what Martin Luther King Jr. had called the "horse and buggy" pace of change in his famous "Letter from Birmingham Jail." Rather, they blamed their discomfiture and creeping dissatisfaction with this lanky new firebrand in their midst on such nebulous reasons as "his funny ways."

He might have been born in Alabama, they averred, but he had acquired distinctly "Northern" ways. Those who deigned to grant him the benefit of the doubt reckoned that he was not the problem, but his wife. She was a trace peculiar, many thought, and showed how truthful was the axiom that "A little learning is a dangerous thing." She was college educated—had a master's degree—which must explain why "No one could tell her anything; she was Miss Know-It-All." And then there was the fact that she was born in Philadelphia and had lived there all her life and thus did not understand how things were done here, down home.

They first criticized her for not having enough meat on her bones and for declining second helpings of the Sunday dinners they had slaved to make all Saturday afternoon. She did not eat much meat, she said, and did not favor ham at all. She earned yet more strikes for ignoring the custom of wearing saucy, wide-brimmed hats and white cotton gloves to church. Then for going bare-legged during the week in the summertime. For wearing pedal pushers at the grocery store. And how dare she show up in the broad-open daylight in that deep midnight blue taffeta dress, exposing her collar bones? Whereas others came to the annual Mother's Day luncheon sporting the customary two-piece suits of white piqué or eyelet or sable linen and silk shantung, she rustled around the basement in this strange "getup," weaving between the luncheon tables she had not helped to set.

They might have eventually forgiven all her sartorial transgressions and, perhaps in time, even her habit of smoking Winstons openly on the steps of the parsonage, but her "ways" of raising children were beyond the pale. She doted too much on Timmy and Wanda Glen and gave them too much rope. They were practically little heathens because she was so lax. The women of Macedonia gave themselves permission to step into the breach until Mrs. Lockhart made it politely but pointedly clear that these were *her* children; no one else had permission to discipline them. She saw no harm in their chewing gum in Sunday School and did not accept their explanation that "it wouldn't look just right" for Timmy to play Joseph in the Christmas pageant. After all, he was the pastor's son, and it might look like they were playing favorites. Fine, Mrs. Lockhart answered, but she would not force him to be either a shepherd or one of the Magi. That finished her in the minds of many, whose jaws tightened and whose arms folded underneath their heavy bosoms in that unmistakably defiant stance. "We'll see," their bodies seemed to say, "who is the stouter woman in this standoff."

The standoff was foreshortened. When the annual conference of the A.M.E. Zion Church rolled around in November 1963, Reverend Lockhart was reassigned, and by January 1964, he was gone. The bishop had dispatched him farther south to Chehaw, Alabama, where he had been born and bred, and the aftershocks of the decision reverberated for several weeks. "The man has barely unpacked his bags and is already booted out of town? It's nothing but petty, Negro mess," Mother insisted when she heard the news. She never bought the story that he had asked to be transferred, in order to be near his eighty-year-old mother, now ailing and alone.

Whatever the reasons for his transfer, Reverend Lockhart moved back to Chehaw, the little whistle-stop outside Tuskegee, and, without delay, continued the fight for the black franchise. This struggle had been waging since

1957, when Negro voters were fenced out of the city of Tuskegee by a statute that redrew the city's boundaries. This remapping removed nearly every Negro voter from within the limits of a city in which they outnumbered whites by over five to one. The move to make Tuskegee a territory of Alabama and a colony of the state legislature was in plain defiance of the federal court order of 1954. The Supreme Court had to issue yet another decree that the State of Alabama could not abolish a whole county or introduce any other measure to disenfranchise black citizens, that colonialism could not be restored in America; it had ended with the Revolutionary War.

Reverend Lockhart was a casualty to a latter-day Revolutionary War; so Reverend McKinley concluded in his eulogy for his longtime friend.

Mother made us late for the funeral. At first, she had not planned to go; said she couldn't bear it, but she changed her mind the hour before we had planned to leave, and called for Auntee to fill two flagons of water and piece together a funeral ensemble. Papa protested about having to drive miles out of the way to Mountain Brook to pick her up when he had just taken her back there the day before. Mother rushed to the door in her nurse's uniform and ordered us to wait in the car while she changed into her navy blue suit and white crepe bow-tied blouse. Pressed for time—she had to work that day—Auntee had forgotten to pack a hat, and as Papa turned the car around and pointed it through the wrought-iron gates of the Bergers' estate, Mother complained about going bareheaded to a funeral. "I never go to church without a hat on."

Permitting himself a rare and brief reproof, Papa snapped, "Miss Vi, why didn't you just stay home yesterday? That way you could have seen to your own clothes."

"I told you, Fred. I didn't think I could stand to go to the funeral and see Alberta and those poor little children all broken up."

Unable to tolerate conflict for very long, Papa turned to joshing. "You know that's not the real reason. You were just scared I would give Miss Campbell a ride." Miss Campbell had called the day before to hitch a ride to the funeral, and without so much as a stammer, Mother, who had answered the phone, allowed as there was no room in her car for another body. Papa couldn't believe his ears.

"Why did you tell Miss Campbell that? It's just the four of us riding in that big ole station wagon."

"If it wasn't for these women at Macedonia, Reverend Lockhart might still be alive. They stirred up this mess that got him moved in the first place, so you can better bet your last dollar that it'll be a cold day in hell before any one of them will be skinning back her gums and plopping her fat ass in my car."

"That's not a Christian attitude, Miss Vi, plus it's not the truth, and you know it. Lots of women worked hard in this church for the pastor. You can't let one or two people spoil the whole bunch of apples."

"Damn a Christian attitude."

"All right, Miss Vi, that's enough. Don't go talking in front of these children this way. You have to set an example."

I didn't want to go to the funeral, and had hoped that, at the very last minute, Papa would relent and let me stay at home. I had spent the days since Reverend Lockhart's murder holed up in Mother's room. And at night, in bed with Gina, I insisted that the ceiling lights stay on. While I had known people to die, no one I knew had ever been murdered. To that point, murder existed for me only as some anonymous headline in the *Birmingham World* or on the Wild West set of *Paladin*.

The day of the funeral was stiff and windless, and it seemed that we would never get to Chehaw. Papa hurtled down limitless stretches of deserted country road, passing crude signs on crucifixes prophesying: JESUS IS COMING SOON. As I fought a rising wave of nausea, Mother turned around and said, "Did Estella give you your Dramamine?" I shook my head no. Throughout my childhood, I suffered from dreadful bouts of motion sickness, which ruined nearly every family outing. But this was no ordinary outing, and maybe retching up my guts could purge the awful taste of death. After we spotted a store and stopped for ginger ale, I drank it and dozed off and on, waking to hear Mother and Papa still reminiscing about the times they had spent with the Lockharts. Just months before, they had taken the bus tour sponsored by Reverend McKinley's church, tracing the shrines and monuments that formed the highlights of Lincoln's life. Auntee still has the snapshot of the four of them—Mother and Papa, Reverend and Mrs. Lockhart lined up in a row inside the rough-hewn cabin of Lincoln's birth.

I woke again to hear Mother scolding Papa for not remembering to bring a map.

"I have directions."

"What kind of directions are these? You can't find your way to the corner with these directions." We stopped at one roadside store after another with rusted Coca-Cola signs hammered to weathered boards and tar-paper shingles. After many twists and turns, we finally stumbled on the sign pointing to Chehaw; then through an opening in a thicket of trees and underbrush, we spied the squat white church with belfry that backed up on a woods at the far end of a sandy stretch of road. Parking behind the train of empty four-door cars, we plodded down the road, each step stirring up clouds of dust that reddened our shoes all over.

Reverend McKinley was in the middle of the eulogy when we eased open the heavy wooden door with a black broadcloth bow drooping from a center hook. Although we tried to walk noiselessly, on tiptoe, our footsteps fell like horses' hooves on the wavy wooden floorboards of this spartan, rustic church with bare oak benches and clear glass windowpanes.

An eight-by-ten picture of Reverend Lockhart in his stiff white cleric's collar, black shirt, and silver cross hanging from his neck, rested on top of the steel gray coffin banked all around with heart-shaped wreaths of carnations and gladiolus attached to stands with long, thin metal legs. Reverend McKinley paused and nodded to us, then resumed the eulogy that he delivered with calm control. "When Alberta called me with the news that the death angel had come for Timothy, I cried in disbelief. Then she asked me if I would deliver the eulogy, which struck me right then as too heavy a cross to bear. But when I thought of the cross that Timothy bore through the stations of this barren land, I knew that I must bear this cross today, heavy though it be. In truth, I stand here not just to eulogize my friend, but to substitute for him, to deliver the Sunday sermon he would have given tomorrow. Some of you know that he stayed behind last week to prepare that sermon, and thus he speaks to you through me this afternoon. I am become his tongue, his lips, his mouthpiece.

"Let me read to you the last words he scribbled in his tablet. It was a favorite scripture of his:"

We wrestle not against flesh and blood, but against principalities, against powers, against the rulers of the darkness of this world, against spiritual wickedness in high places.

Reverend McKinley could not continue. He sobbed loudly, slumped across the pulpit, his forearms resting on the open bible. Those packed inside the tiny church answered his sobs with theirs. He collected himself and went on: "'I need to stretch my legs.' These were the last words Brother Lucas Shaw heard him utter. And hoods, no doubt shrouded in white sheets hiding in the bushes and waiting to ambush, chopped off those legs just like they were butchering meat. But I'll have you know, they can't chop off the legs of this movement; the legs of this movement are sturdy and strong and they will carry us on to freedom, with all deliberate speed.

"Many of you know that, as boys in short pants, Timothy and I walked the dusty back roads here in Chehaw with nothing in our pockets save balls of lint, but our talk was rich with 'somedays' and 'whens' and 'soons.'" When Reverend McKinley broke down a second time, another minister in the pulpit stood up and ushered him gently to the bare-seated, steep-backed chair, then began to speak for him. All that I remember of this man's words was some vague reference to Ezekiel. "When we recommit his body to the dust in this churchyard, here in his humble birthplace, we do so prophesying that his bones will rise up again."

The rest of this day comes back to me in fragments that still visit me at night: the clangor of the mournful bell, the flap of the mortician's black frock coat, Mrs. Lockhart's black net veil, Wanda Glen's runny mascara, two girls in red-flocked dresses and dusty white socks, the double colon-nades of black flannel legs and white-gloved hands of the pallbearers. Gina snags her stockings on the bark of a tree. Square, sunken letters on oval tombstones. The casket lowers to the grave at the edge of the churchyard, the woods shrouding it in darkness. A spear of light bounces off the hearse's fin. We rush toward the car as the raindrops fall. Clear plastic accordion rain scarves cover Gina's head and mine. A woman turns to Mother and, noticing her freshly pressed hair, politely asks: "Do you want some newspaper?" She reaches inside the back window of a car. Papa strides on, bareheaded, just in front of us; sheets of the *Montgomery Advertiser* form a tent over Mother's head.

rousing rendition of "Long As I Got King Jesus Don't Need Nobody Else," I waved my arms along with all the rest, thinking this must surely be the joyful noise that we at Macedonia could only read about in Psalms.

Soon after his arrival, Reverend Davis made it clear that he did not approve of the more gospel-like directions in which Lonnie, the organist, was taking the senior choir. Reverend Davis dropped in on one evening's choir rehearsal, determined to supervise, but Lonnie let the reverend know in not-so-subtle ways that he resented the intrusion. Before the rehearsal was over, Lonnie had stormed out of the church, never to be seen again.

Now temporarily without an organist, Reverend Davis asked me to play, just until they found a replacement for Lonnie, someone who would understand that Macedonia was not a Pentecostal but a Methodist church—A.M.E. Zion, to be exact—and thus the music should be more dignified and stately, absent tambourines and drums. Although I did not agree with Reverend Davis's restrictions, I obeyed them nonetheless, playing, without a mumbling word, all the hymns and anthems he selected. It was harder to find a replacement for Lonnie than anyone anticipated, and so I played for several weeks without one cent of pay.

The final chord resounding, I continued to turn sentences around in my head again, settling on, "Reverend Davis, I hate to bother you, but I need my paycheck. I have to buy something for school."

Any mention of school was bound to win attention, and the good reverend didn't have to know that the "thing" I needed for school was not actually in the service of the scholastic. No cobalt bottle of Schaeffer's blue-black ink, required for all English compositions; no spiral notebook; no packet of construction paper or bottle of mucilage glue to squeeze through the slit of its rubber nipple to make a scrapbook for Negro History Week or a decoration for the bulletin board. No new book, no new pair of gym shoes, not even money for a field trip to Vulcan. No, the "thing" I needed for school was a mohair sweater.

It was 1965 and girls were still closing ranks with uniforms. Those in our group—Tommye Hinton, Linda Bankhead, Elizabeth Clark, Vera Hayes, Carolyn Oliver, and Carole Dobbs—had been dressing alike, or nearly alike, since the start of that school year, when we founded The Dignitarians, the private club and fragile nucleus we formed when it was clear that the other cliques wouldn't accept us because we were too bookish. Not to be outdone, we organized one weekend and showed up at the end of the next week wearing red flannel "tight" skirts and black sweatshirts with red satin letters, D-I-G-N-I-T-A-R-I-A-N-S, emblazoned on the backs.

Blue Mohair

As I lingered over the last chord of "Yield Not to Temptation," I rehearsed my lines: "Reverend Davis, I wonder when I will be getting paid? I've played several straight Sundays without a check."

Reverend Davis broke into my thoughts, calling for "one more chorus of this wonderful hymn."

And obligingly I repeated: "Ask the savior to help you, comfort, strengthen, and keep you, he is willing to save you. He will carry you through."

"How many of you know that Jesus will carry you through?" Heads nodded and a few hands waved, but the tepid response to Reverend Davis's question left no doubt that he lacked the power to fire the congregation in the way that Reverend Lockhart had.

Following Reverend Lockhart's whirlwind tour of duty at Macedonia, the church reclaimed its age-old reputation as a sleeper. As we members of the junior choir used to say, it would have been more aptly named the Church of the Frigidaire. When Reverend Davis was assigned to Macedonia as Reverend Lockhart's replacement, the service actually became even more leaden and pretentious. Now, for the first time, we had altar boys in crimson skirts and matching droopy bows pinned to starched white cotton robes. The choir sang still more anthems in largo, leaving fully two-thirds of the heads bowed in the congregation long after the morning prayer. Many was the day I fanned myself, then twisted on the pew before finally drifting off to the choir's soporific strains of "Lift Up Ye Heads O Ye Gates" or "Peace Be Still."

When I discovered that our choir's version of "Peace Be Still" differed so dramatically from New Bethlehem's, I wanted to know why, but Mother only answered, with a whiff of contempt, "It's 'cause they're Baptist." Baptist or not, nobody could ever fall asleep inside New Bethlehem's walls. The fifty-member gospel choir rocked and swayed down the aisle in the morning processional, their long, flamboyant burgundy robes billowing out from spit-shined wing tips or patent-leather pumps. And when they sent up their

When I asked Reverend Davis for the money, he sputtered before offering a string of homilies like "It's a privilege and a duty to serve the Lord" and "Working for the Lord is its own reward" and suchlike. Nevertheless, he promised to take my request to the church treasurer before the start of the eleven o'clock service. Although I'll never know whether he did or not, I've always suspected that Reverend Davis went straight to Papa and told him that I had done the unseemly thing of asking the church for pay. Given the tightrope all children had to walk in this gerontocratic community in the South, it's likely that he did tell Papa first.

It seemed lost on everybody but me that I had earned this money. Every Saturday morning I had trekked across the Bessemer Super Highway bridge for music lessons, had endured Miss Pigrom's humiliating glances when I sounded a lumbering arpeggio, had risen early every single Sunday morning, ironed my choir robe, polished my shoes, and trotted to Macedonia A.M.E. Zion Church, still rubbing sleep from my eyes.

I knew something was gravely wrong when Papa shot me a reproving glance. He had just finished his standard morning prayer—two verses of "Just As I Am Without One Plea"—but did not remain on his knees at the altar as he usually did. Instead he stood straight up and looked in my direction, and his head trembled from side to side. The way it shook the time I darted in front of a car that almost hit me. The way it shook when, in a fit of jealousy, I came home to tattle that Gina and Joyce were over at the construction site dancing for the white men under the red-striped tent. The way it shook when he found out that Bumbiddle and Butch stole Milky Ways from Mr. Paul's store. (Bumbiddle maintains to this very day that it was a false accusation.) Yes, this was that unmistakable Papa headshake; it held no ambiguity, it said, "Your butt belongs to me."

We rode home from church in silence. I was afraid to read the road signs and carry on my customary chatter. On most Sundays, if Mother was not home, Papa just dropped us off and hastened on to Mountain Brook. But today, he pulled the station wagon in front of our house and killed the engine. Inside he found Daddy stretched out on the sofa watching the World Series and, wasting no time, he unloaded, "Miss Priss taken to begging in church."

"Begging for what?"

"Asked Reverend Davis to pay her for these few little piddling songs she plays for the Sunday School service." I interrupted, "But I worked for that money." I could have predicted that I would be ordered to shut up, and I was. Obligated to take Papa's side, Daddy began to question me.

"What you need money for? You hungry? You barefoot? Unless you hungry and need shoes, ain't no reason for you to be begging for money."

"But I wasn't begging," I protested, "I was asking for what was mine. I worked for it."

"You watch your mouth."

"But Daddy—"

"Shut up."

When I started to cry Daddy snapped, "And stop your sniveling or I'll give you something to cry about."

"She told Reverend Davis that she needed something for school."

Daddy now turned to me with the first softening sign since Papa had interrupted his game, and by this time, Daddy's shouting had drifted to the kitchen and brought Mama to the living room.

"What do you need for school?" Mama asked. "You didn't bring a note home from the teacher."

I would have preferred to keep this to myself, but there was no such thing as "privacy" at home. What could a fourteen-year-old have to hide? I had no room of my own, so what need had I for thoughts of my own? Hoping to end this merciless arraignment, I finally confessed that I wanted the money for nothing that furthered education, properly speaking. I wanted the money to pay down on a mohair sweater. All the girls were planning to wear them at Homecoming. I pictured myself in fuchsia or magenta, pulled down long over a box-pleated skirt. Valada, Reverend Davis's daughter, already had hers—soft, pink, and V-necked—that she wore with a burgundy wool flannel A-line skirt and black suede penny loafers.

"Asking for money was bad enough," Daddy scolded, "but asking for money to buy a sweater? I don't believe it. As hard as I work to keep you in clothes? I could see it if you needed a book or some school supplies, but a sweater? I'm ashamed of you."

Later in the afternoon, Daddy went to Blankenship's and brought me back a stage plank. He came into the room where I was reading.

"I brought you something."

I took the package from his hand and laid it, unopened, on the desk blotter.

"Don't you still like stage planks?"

"Yeah," I pretended. "I'm just not hungry right this minute." I didn't have the heart to tell him that I had graduated from these squares of frosted gingerbread when I abandoned paper dolls.

"If you wanted a sweater," Daddy continued, by way of an apology, "why didn't you ask me, and we could have seen about getting it for you?"

"I did ask you, Daddy. Remember? Two weeks ago."

*   *   *

I started my brief stint of domestic work for the sake of a mohair sweater. Auntee, who cleaned for Mrs. Carroll, said she could use some extra help with the ironing. Mrs. Carroll was planning some big family gathering or social event, which meant silver had to be polished and linens starched and ironed. I never saw so many sheets or understood just why they had to be ironed.

I stayed over on Friday night at Mother's and rode the seven-thirty bus with Auntee to Five Points West. Auntee pulled on the cord and the bus dropped us off two blocks from the house. We walked down a street shaded with trees and then unhitched the latch on the low-slung wooden gate, walking up the graveled path to the redbrick house with forest green shutters, surrounded by a fortress of pine trees.

The house was dark, quiet, cool. My eyes surveyed the living room, resting on an overstuffed chair with matching ottoman, upholstered in glazed chintz—a bouqueted pattern of large pink peonies, lavender tulips, and clusters of grapes against an ecru background. A piano stood by the window, covered with photographs in ornate frames: a young girl on a pony, a young girl on Santa Claus's knee, a teenage girl in a cheerleading outfit—a gray felt poodle skirt, turtleneck sweater, oxfords, and bobby socks. She smiled to reveal the faintest outline of her braces. In another, the same girl wore a scoop-necked black dress and a strand of pearls, her blond hair loose below her shoulders. Auntee said that she was Mrs. Carroll's daughter, now off at college in Sweetbriar, Virginia.

I followed Auntee through the house, pausing before what must have been the girl's room before she left. It was decorated in light pink gingham with white trim. On a ledge that ran the length of one wall perched a row of dolls and stuffed animals. There were even more on a window seat in the corner. Pink gingham draperies matched the cornices, and the bedskirt and white eyelet pillow shams were piled against the headboard.

While Auntee scrubbed and vacuumed, removing all signs of mildew from the bathroom tile with Clorox and a toothbrush, I ironed sheets, cocktail napkins, luncheon napkins, dinner napkins, table runners, hand towels—all damask—working the point of the iron around the thickness of the monogram.

Just after lunch Mrs. Carroll came home, calling out to Auntee as she entered the house. "Stella, Estella," she called, as she *clip-clopped* down the hall. Pausing just inside the door of the room where I was ironing, she looked surprised at first, then I guess she remembered that I was Auntee's niece. She was an ordinary-looking woman, without the aristocratic bearing I had imagined her to have. I was still uneasy in her presence, and I quickly told her that Auntee was in the upstairs bathroom. She cast her eyes on the stacks of linen and asked if I had ironed all that. When I nodded yes, she said, "That's wonderful." Or maybe she said, "How wonderful," then asked me what grade I was in at school and what my favorite subjects were.

"I like English class and history," I answered, and she finally went on her way. I did not like the line of questioning, did not like being in the house with her. Although she never came right out and asked me, I felt that she wanted to know of my availability for domestic work. Neither Mama nor Auntee (we hid it all from Daddy) had liked the idea of my going to Mrs. Carroll's in the first place, but even if they had approved, I knew that very morning that this was just a temporary thing for me, a means to a mohair sweater. I could tolerate the discomfort I felt in the house that day and abide the anger at the knowledge that there were so few jobs for black teenagers in 1960s Bessemer.

Although I know that, for a time, domestic work was the only work around for Auntee, a part of me still detested the very idea of her scrubbing, scouring, bleaching, and buffing, while her "boss lady" went for her Saturday manicure. I was glad when she found a job cooking in the cafeteria of a local school, glad, not just because the job paid her a little more money, but more because it ended her submissive posture—on her hands and knees.

For ironing from about eight-thirty in the morning until three in the afternoon, I earned $6.50. Though fatigued, I insisted that Auntee and I get off the bus downtown so I could finally lay away my sweater. We walked in first one store and then another, finally ending up at Momart's Discount Store. Just that week the *Bessemer Sun* had tucked a flyer advertising "Momart Value Days" inside the fold—Women's cotton briefs, six for $1.00, Men's Ban-Lon sweaters, $6.99. Women's mohair sweaters, $15.99. A variety of colors and sizes. Shop early, quantities limited.

Inside Momart's double plate-glass window, prices on cardboard placards were propped against the feet of pearly pink mannequins in misshapen wigs. We entered the store, where two small dressing rooms with mirrors on the door broke the monotony of stark white walls. Several round racks displayed the cheap garments that sagged on clear plastic hangers, but from rack to rack, I found nothing to suit me. Like Mama, Auntee was never a patient shopper, and hurriedly plucked sweater after sweater from the rack. "This is a nice one. Don't you think this is a nice one?" And then, in exasperation, "Won't this one do?" Bubble-gum pink was much too loud, so I settled for the only other option in my size: powder blue.

The V-necked sweater was hip length, with two rows of cable knitting down the front and another row down the side of each sleeve. The hanger had left stretch marks just below each shoulder line, which gave the sweater a shopworn look. I paid the $5.00 down and sulked all the way home while wondering what gave powder blue its name. After all, who wore blue powder? Maybe it referred to the color of powder rooms, but how would I know? I associated powder rooms with scenes in movies, in which blond actresses in black crepe cocktail sheaths with plunging necklines signaled their need to escape from the clutches of a boring date with, "Excuse me while I go to the powder room."

After two more weeks of work, with still no pay from the church's coffers, I took the bus to retrieve my sweater from layaway. It was near closing on Saturday afternoon, and the sickening smell of Evening in Paris cologne met me at the door. The clerk seemed dressed for a party, and for some reason, my eyes fastened on her white patent-leather shoes with a twist of braided ribbon on the side. It was long after Labor Day and she was still wearing white shoes. Mother had said that nothing bright white should ever be worn after Labor Day. The bell-sleeved red taffeta dress, pleated from the tiny waist, reminded me of one of those Tennessee Valley Authority poles that lined I-65. They looked like oversized, broad-shouldered, stick-figured sculptures, chopped off at the neck.

Seeming impatient to leave, the clerk asked me a second time, "Can I help you," in that unmistakably contemptuous manner Southern white women can affect on cue.

"I'm here to pick up a layaway."

"Name?"

I gave her my name—first, middle, and last, slowly, precisely, each syllable sharply sounded.

"Do you have your card?"

I fished in my wallet for the card that showed the $8.00 balance due and laid it on the counter without a word, the bills folded on the top. Stamping "Paid in Full" on the card, she stacked the money in the register, then whisked off to the back room, returning with an oatmeal-colored box, my last name written in bold black letters on the side. She plunked the box down on the counter, and before I snatched it up I shot her a hostile glance, then hoisted the box under my arm and strutted out of the store, planning my outfit for Homecoming in my mind. The navy blue box-pleated skirt would be a good match.

I had hitched a ride to Bessemer Stadium with Melissa and her brother, but before they even blew the horn, strands of mohair were sticking to my skirt like a million furry spores of dandelions. This was only the beginning of a disastrous evening. Brighton was losing the game by thirty points, and when Abrams scored yet another touchdown, ending this humiliating game, someone stumbled behind me in the bleachers, spilling a cup of Coca-Cola down the side of my sleeve.

After that evening, I could never bring myself to wear that sweater again and swore that I would no longer be manipulated by fashion trends, but when the rage turned to bell-bottomed hip-huggers and multicolored crocheted vests cropped just above the waist, I boarded the No. 2 bus and yanked the cord at Momart's once again.

Steal Away

When Baybro came south from Brooklyn the summer of 1966, all the fifteen-year-old girls in Pipe Shop took bets on who would be the first to give him tongue. Girls more brazen than I would ever be took bets on who would give him cherry, but I drew the line at tongue. Heaven only knows why I thought I could be in the running to give him anything, since I had this thick, unruly mass of hair and knobby knees that knocked together when I walked. Most important, I had no titties, no hair on my spindly legs, and never seemed to find much to say in the presence of a boy. Baybro was paper-sack brown with curly hair and cat eyes and wore a scowl on his face just like Daddy Frank.

For a time, the Pipe Shop boys aped Baybro's cool mannerisms, pulling on imaginary goatees and speaking in whispers. That summer, we flocked to the community center for Friday evening dances. The girls had usually arrived when the Pipe Shop boys herded in, sporting their Ban-Lon sweaters, faking Baybro's bop and sway. One night Larry Kirkland and Joe Nathan Carter step-slided over to where a few of us girls were propped against the wall. Larry extended his arm toward me and whispered, "Do one of y'all want to dance?" We threw our heads back and howled in his face.

When the boys eventually accepted that they would never be more than weak, lame imitations of Baybro, they decided to hang on to adolescence a wee bit longer. They resumed those silly rituals and pastimes that made them look so stupid and even less attractive to the Pipe Shop girls: tying inflated balloons to the spokes of their bicycle wheels and riding in packs through the neighborhood, creating a hullabaloo that you could hear from blocks away. But worst of all, they tattooed themselves with the tips of erasers. One of them, I believe it was Mickey Hackworth, even had to go to the doctor for a shot when he came down with lockjaw. It's a wonder they didn't all get lockjaw. I watched Calvin Barnes sit on our front porch and score his initials, C-A-B, on his forearm, and it made my flesh crawl.

He rubbed and rubbed away at the top layer of skin, then left it to fester and scab over. When he scraped the scab away a few weeks later, there were his initials, engraved in a lighter shade of brown.

I can't explain just what this fascination was with the sight of their initials, but the boys in Pipe Shop wore them as proudly as they did the hickies on their necks and their water waves. After plastering their hair down with a pomade of Vaseline and water, they strutted around in stocking caps, fashioned from their mothers' or sisters' cast-off nylons, and waited impatiently for the tiny waves that hugged their heads to stiffen.

These were the respectable boys our parents and elders expected us to marry when their capering days were done. They were known. Their families, who worked hard and went to church and watched their children closely, lived either in the neighborhood or somewhere nearby. And if they slipped up on occasion and got a girl "in the family way," they shouldered their manhood and married her.

The Baybros were another matter: sluggards who loitered on every corner, who disrespected grown folks and left scores of big-bellied girls to bear their shame and degradation all alone. The Baybros were strictly off-limits for good, churchgoing girls like myself, who were being groomed and programmed for a different life.

When Baybro came to Pipe Shop, I lost all interest in that program. The Sunday afternoon recitations were now a trial and a bore, which was fully evident in my performances, Mrs. Harvey said. She was right. Instead of rehearsing "Invictus," I spun long, narrative fantasies about Baybro. He was so different from the boys who went to church—a renegade, mysterious and scary. He wore his wrinkled shirts cut off at the biceps and open far down on his chest. And when no grown-ups were about, he grabbed his crotch in front of the blossoming girls who swooned, giggled at his nastiness, and gamely quarreled with each over which one of us he loved the best.

Baybro, short for Baby Brother, was the youngest of five children born to Mr. Moses McClendon's only daughter, Vivian. He was the only one of her five children born in Brooklyn, where she rushed off to after quitting her job at Cox & Autry. The bell clappers of the neighborhood allowed as how she never should have left Pipe Shop. She wasn't used to city life. And why in the world would anybody in their right mind follow behind Jimmie Lee Witherspoon? She wasn't following behind Jimmie Lee, any such thing, Miss Classie corrected the busybodies who found reason to pass the time so frequently in her front yard. And if anybody knew what was going on, she did. Vivian was her own daughter. Vivian had moved to Brooklyn hoping to find one of the jobs that the Colored Labor Employment Agency advertised in the *Birmingham World*. She would get more money in Brooklyn than she could possibly earn anywhere in Bessemer.

Though Miss Classie tried to set the record straight, the neighborhood women remained convinced that Vivian had foolishly trailed behind Jimmie Lee Witherspoon, nothing but a plain old roughneck, to a place where none of her people lived. It was no wonder that her luck turned sour. All four of her older children—except for Carl, who enlisted in the army, where he learned a trade—had ended up on heroin. She feared that Baybro would be next. He was going wild—staying out late, missing school, and cursing out the teachers when he did show up. Since Vivian had to work and couldn't watch him every minute of the day, her last resort was to send Baybro back home to Bessemer for the slower pace and the stricter discipline for which the South was famous. If her mama and daddy couldn't straighten him out, nobody could. All these rumors and speculations, most already embroidered, circulated at Ophelia's, where all the greedy gossips waited our turns for the bouffant hairdos the Supremes had swept into style.

Somebody said that it was already too late for Baybro, who was using dope cigarettes on a regular basis. Marijuana had not yet filtered into Pipe Shop, or at least not that anybody knew of, so it was not in our lexicon; "dope cigarettes" was the only terminology the community had for it. In our adolescent minds, dope was right up there with "doing the nasty"—nice girls did neither, especially if they wanted to go to college and marry nice men.

Since his grandfolks lived right next door to us, I saw a lot of Baybro the summer he moved to Pipe Shop. It was July and I had just come back from Mother's house. Gina was gone again to Washington, D.C., to visit Uncle Jr., and I had returned to the drudgery of helping Grandma out with Daddy Les, now in the final stages of senility. At first, I just watched Baybro obsessively as he walked back and forth down the street. It seems that's all he did that summer—lope up and down Eighteenth Street with a cigarette dangling from the corner of his mouth, the red bill of his khaki-colored baseball cap turned defiantly around at a slant in back.

Flouting the Southern custom of speaking to neighbors rocking in their gliders up and down the block, Baybro passed by without a word, staring straight down the tar-on-gravel road that bent slightly, then vanished behind a field of overgrown trees and brambles. He refused to cut the grass or go to church or take any interest in the other neighborhood boys who played sandlot basketball at the community center; he just trudged up and down Eighteenth Street with the flat-footed determination of a burdened hiker hoping to reach camp by sundown.

I had a perfect perch from which to observe him. Separating the short distance between our two yards was a row of flower planters hand-hewn from automobile tires. Cut in a zigzag design around the top, the tires were filled with red and yellow zinnias and marigolds that Mama and Miss Classie planted together every spring. The job of tending the flowers generally fell to Miss Classie, because Mama was so busy with her sewing. That summer, I was glad to take over, watering the flowers so often that the roots began to rot. If I spotted Baybro down the block a piece, I would fly off the porch, screw the nozzle to the hydrant, and spray for dear life. One day he actually dipped and swayed over to me, fondling his goatee as he whispered, "Don't you ever do nothing besides water flowers?" I stumbled, then dropped my head, and my tongue skulked quickly into hiding like a lizard through a crannied wall. We had similar encounters throughout the next few weeks, that crackled with sexual excitement. One day Baybro asked if I did the nasty with Calvin. I was embarrassed and walked away.

Because Daddy had been switched back again to the day shift, I still don't know how he found out that Baybro was hanging around and whispering illicit questions in my ears. Perhaps Miss Evaline had seen us from her kitchen window, but in the summertime the fig tree screened that side of her house. Anyway, one night at the dinner table, without warning, Daddy announced that Baybro was too old for me to talk to. "Too old? You're older than Baybro, and I talk to you—every day, so why can't I talk to him? What's wrong with talking to him?"

"You better hush your wisecracking, or I'll give you something to talk about." It made no sense, just another commandment that only other grown folks could understand, because they held the code. Besides, what Daddy didn't know was that I wasn't talking to Baybro anyway, just watching him with increasing fascination.

Our group of Pipe Shop girls frittered away the summer in Melissa's room, where we watched *The Days of Our Lives* or swapped tattered copies of *Bronze Thrills, True Confessions,* and comic books of Archie and Veronica. Unlike the rest of us, Melissa had a television in her own private room in a house in Washington Place, a brand-new development of split-level houses that sprang up in the late 1950s at the far western edge of Pipe Shop. Before many houses in the development flooded and we found out they had been built over Valley Creek, everyone was jealous of the residents of Washington Place. We contemptuously dubbed it Brick City, just because all the houses were constructed of red brick with matching walkways, and barbecue pits. No weeds sprouted between the bricks of the walkways and the grass was never high.

Girls who had first gone home with Melissa returned with stories about the large picture windows that never smudged, crushed-velvet sofas covered in plastic that ran the length of the living-room wall, twelve feet across. And the bedrooms all had matching furniture—French Provincial in Melissa's room. All this, plus a wardrobe purchased every season from Sokol's, Parisian, and Pizitz made Melissa the envy of the girls from the eastern end of Pipe Shop. Most shunned her and flung idle "who-she-think-she-is?" insults "at no one in particular" when we hustled through the lunch line just before music class. But when her family joined Macedonia, Melissa and I became friends during rehearsals for the youth day pageant. After then, all the other girls slotted to "make something" of themselves cut her in, one by one.

We strained hard to keep our envy to ourselves, because Melissa was slowly introducing us to knowledge forbidden all good girls. Her four older brothers funneled juicy tidbits to their baby sister, who then passed them down to us. We learned why boys thought girls with hairy legs were sexy, and how a hard-on felt, and why boys did not like rubbers and knew how to pull their pee-wees out just before the white-hot come exploded and made a baby. I was eager to feel a boy tracing circles round my breasts, the wetness of his tongue slithering down my throat. What did it taste like? And didn't it make you gag? I asked Melissa, who laughed and shook her head. Sooner than I expected, I got my chance to experience some of these sensations, not with Calvin but with Baybro.

I was in the backyard hanging out the wash. Over the top of the clothesline, I spotted him seated on the edge of his grandfolks' back porch, the rays of midafternoon sun streaking his face. He didn't say anything to me, just sat there drawing on a cigarette and blowing out the curls of smoke. Hugging the damp folds to my chest lest they drag on the ground, I sang along to "Steal Away," one of the summer's hottest records, blasting from the radio perched in the kitchen window. I didn't even hear him coming. When I glanced up from the basket, there he was, standing on the heels of his Converse tennis shoes, a pack of Camels peeking from his shirt pocket. My eyes traveled from the hairs of his goatee to those below his chest and then back up again.

"What you doing?"

That was the beginning of our first real conversation. After long minutes of silence, I finally found the courage to ask him questions about Brooklyn.

"Can you see the Statue of Liberty in Brooklyn? Is it far from here? How long was the bus ride to Bessemer?"

"Why you want to know so much about Brooklyn?"

"I might want to go and live there one day."

"You don't want to live in Brooklyn."

"Why not? Is it because of dope, like they say?"

"Like who say?"

"They say your mama sent you here because of dope, because you take dope."

"Is that what they say?"

He neither confirmed nor denied, and his silence hooked me deeper to this cat-eyed seventeen-year-old incorrigible manchild who impressed me merely with the revelation that he had taken a bus all the way from Brooklyn to Bessemer by himself. With the stealth of a panther, Baybro padded into the backyard a few more times, and we stood behind the fig tree. His broad, calloused hand under my T-shirt, he stroked my budding breasts. Just as Melissa had instructed me, I pretended I wanted him to stop. He didn't. I didn't want him to. I liked the wavy feeling rising and swelling in my stomach.

"What y'all doing?" It was Mama. Baybro jumped and disappeared through a break in the fence. "Well, your daddy will hear about this, Little Miss." I never expected to be caught, especially not by Mama. I knew that there was no ass burning like the one I would get—first for disobeying, then for acting like an alley cat. Mama kept her promise and dropped the news on Daddy as soon as he came home from work. Much to my surprise, he didn't scold me, not at first. He tried to talk, but his words were faltering and oblique—all about the dangers of "getting in the family way." His eyes were worried, and the tremor in his voice was far more frightening than any whipping or its threat.

When Daddy walked next door to talk to Mr. Moses and Miss Classie, I knew the end had come. I was right. Baybro did not sneak into the yard again. Daddy worsened my disappointment by announcing that he had made up his mind: I would not be receiving company that summer. I had to wait until I turned sixteen. My behavior had left no doubt that I was not mature enough. Later that summer, he consented to nylon stockings, but that was nothing compared to what Melissa was allowed. Her mother had bought her a pair of high-heeled patent-leather pumps and permitted her to wear a trace of pastel lipstick ordered from the Avon catalog.

But Daddy vetoed all of this for me, especially the lipstick, with the irrational pronouncement that it was distracting and not ladylike. I wore the lipstick anyway, sneaking the bullet-sized white plastic sample tubes out of the house. Safely out of Daddy's sight, I smeared my lips with carnation pink, and just before I switched into the house, I wiped it off again.

It took me a while, but near the end of that summer I came to understand why Daddy was so irrational: It was all because of Martha Faye. Seven years had passed since she had gone, and suddenly, almost in a flash, what had mystified me as an eight-year-old was coming to the light. I had been kept in almost total ignorance about why she left Pipe Shop in such a hurry, but the summer when Baybro came and went, I cobbled together an explanation for myself. It came late one night soon after Baybro was warned away and fragments of my parents' bedtime conversation drifted through the kitchen to the back room: "Martha Faye," "shame," "disgrace," "sent off," "no good," "baby," "adoption," "Troy Winfield." Then it hit me; he was her boyfriend, who brought me bags of Big Moon cookies, her date to the prom she did not attend. After graduation that next month, Troy moved to Cleveland to build bridges and never came back to Pipe Shop except to visit his mother, who always asked after Martha Faye.

Daddy knew from hard experience that seventeen-year-old hands that pulled on goatees and loitered on street corners long past dark held only danger for barely fifteen-year-old girls. But I was too young to truly comprehend this wisdom, and my desire too strong to be snuffed out.

Rehearsals for the piano recital broke some of the summer's tension. Mama poured herself into making my first formal gown, yellow crepe georgette, which we bought at Goldstein's. I had chosen the color because it reminded me of Martha Faye's yellow satin strapless gown with layered flounces that ended up inside the Goodwill bin.

In between practicing my pieces, I imitated the rhythm and blues hits the deejays spun all afternoon. I learned to play several by ear that summer, and could belt out their lyrics from start to finish. Grandma shook her head and said the devil had caught me in his grip. Why else would I be plunking "reels" right there in the living room, the front door gaped wide open for every passing soul to hear? Any piece of music that did not conform to standard Wesleyan hymn meter was a "reel" in Grandma's eyes, but that day I ignored her preaching and sang my song.

The first sting of the belt was shocking. I hopped up from the piano bench, lost my footing, and stumbled against the coffee table. The belt raised high above his head, Daddy was standing in front of me, bellowing, "You gon' steal away, huh? You gon' steal away? Well, you won't do it under this roof. As long as you under this roof, you won't be stealing nowhere. And if you grown enough to steal away, you go right on and do it, but you'll have to do it somewhere else."

Mama said, "Wiley, that's enough."

That Friday night we ate our fish in silence with no mention of Baybro.

In fact, after that day, neither Mama nor Daddy nor even Grandma Edie ever mouthed another word about "Steal Away" or Baybro or the backyard tonguing episode. We stored the incident away like the evening's dinner dishes behind the white tin kitchen cabinet, like the dark green Wurlitzer music book underneath the piano bench.

I was still distracted by the time the recital rolled around. I was to play two pieces: the *Moonlight* Sonata and "Moon River," one classical, one popular. I had waited a long time to play the *Moonlight* Sonata; I could read the piece, Miss Pigrom said, but I didn't have the maturity of feeling to play it. I persuaded her that I did. Over and over again I practiced the piece, obeying Miss Pigrom's coaching: "Don't plunk the keys. This ain't honky-tonk. Move over. Let me show you how it's done. Softly. Pianissimo. This is a melancholy sound." After several weeks, I had mastered all that Miss Pigrom had drilled into my ears, but by the time I reached Jerusalem Baptist Church at five o'clock that Sunday afternoon, the *Moonlight* Sonata had vanished from my memory and I sat at the stool, my frozen hands suspended above the keyboard, until Miss Pigrom gently ushered me to the basement. To this day, I don't know what happened, but the embarrassment brought an end to my piano lessons and triggered days and days of grief.

Mama and Daddy showered me with books, which had always been my refuge, but I found no interest in anything they brought home that summer. Not the weekly turquoise-colored volumes of *Understanding Science,* purchased from the A & P, nor the full set of *Funk and Wagnall's Encyclopedia,* bought from a salesman traveling through the neighborhood. Lined up in their own finely crafted two-shelf wooden case, these volumes eventually drew to our house most of the Pipe Shop teenagers, who tromped in after school and sometimes stayed through dinner to complete assignments.

Near the end of the summer, to Mama's relief, I pulled the burgundy volumes with gilt-edged pages from the dusty shelf almost every day, but she had no way to know I wasn't really reading them. After Baybro, *Funk and Wagnall's* became my "plain brown wrapper" for the appetizing soft porn that snaked its way through the virginal underground of Pipe Shop: *Candy, The Seduction of Demby Martin, Mandingo,* and *Peyton Place.* The two Lindas, Earline, Melissa, and I piled on those remaining dog day afternoons in the air-conditioned seclusion of Melissa's room.

I recently checked the library's holdings for *Candy* and found a well-circulated copy in the stacks. There, in the shadowy corridors, I was transported back to the butter-colored room, where I giggled as I read, emphatically, lengthy passages to my adolescent friends: "With a few whimpering sounds of surprise, the gardener had held her kiss and was reaching into her dress now for her breast while his other hand had plunged between her legs." And she "contented herself for the moment with the giving of her left breast, to which his mouth was fastened in desperate sucking."

One day we lost ourselves and forgot to load more forty-fives on the record player to muffle the soft-porn lines I was reading aloud, and were jolted out of fantasies when Melissa's mother pounded on the door and ordered us all home. As we slunk sheepishly down the hall, she flung epithets in our path—"womanish," "gut-bucket"—and ordered us to "keep these nasty, trashy books out of my house." Fearing that she would call my parents, I walked the streets of Pipe Shop until pangs of hunger drove me home. Nothing seemed amiss: Mama was making dinner and Daddy on the porch, sketching Miss Hattie's house. I chatted with Mama as I made a bologna sandwich, then retreated to the side of my bed, feet in flip-flops propped on the cedar chest. With *The Seduction of Demby Martin* snugly between the covers of "Carthusians–Cockcroft," I read, my ears pricked for any footsteps, poised to shove the pages, now worked loose from their spine, underneath the bed. Though puzzled by my newfound fascination with *Funk and Wagnall's,* Mama and Daddy praised my industriousness, and I laughed at the knowledge that I had finally accomplished something that had escaped their vigilant eyes.

Just before the start of school, Baybro went back to Brooklyn and I turned to writing the book reports that I had neglected to the very end. All who were members of the College-Bound Society and required to take the course of college prep had to complete them by the first English class. Unlike Melissa, I was too chicken to crib from Cliff's Notes, which meant that I was reading day and night, dozing off repeatedly on *Walden.* And, I confess, although I read *Les Miserables* through and through, I skipped some pages in *Oliver Twist* and *Pride and Prejudice,* but Miss Bowman didn't notice.

With Miss Harvey's encouragement, I joined the Thespian Society, where we wrote plays of our own and acted in others. My first play was titled *Steal Away.* Set in a backyard with scruffy grass and a large fig tree, it opens with a girl and boy who stand behind bright white sheets softly flapping in the summer breeze. I carried the play in a three-ring binder, secreted like a diary, the handwritten pages that rendered into melodrama those bittersweet July meetings with Baybro. I never showed the play to anybody, not even to Melissa. Only I need remember the furtive pleasures of that feverish summer, when much more than the "C" volume of *Funk and Wagnall's* kept me company there in the back room, where I sat scrunched between the bed and the powder blue wall.

A Very Ancient Grief

We had to go right straight back to get Daddy Les from the old folks' home. In all, he had been there sixteen hours and we had been awake almost the whole time. Even when Daddy finally persuaded Grandma that we should all go to bed and think about what to do tomorrow, there still was no sleeping, what with Grandma pacing, slamming dresser drawers, and praying out loud, stabbing the hush of morning.

> *Father, I stretch my hands to thee; no other help I know. If thou withdraw thy help from me oh whither shall I go? I come before you this morning, Lord, knee bent and body bowed. So low down this morning and heavy in my heart. I give my promise to stay with Les in sickness and in health till death would take one of us from the other, but he done just got to be too much for me to handle. And there is Frank. Paralyzed. Can't do nothing for his self. And Wiley and Jim, well they got they own burdens. Got they own to look after. I just ain't got the strength to see after Les when they ain't here. I know you didn't send your only son, Jesus, down here to bear the cross alone, and I know you said you wouldn't put no more on me than I could bear. . . .*

It went on in that vein, then closed with the line that ended all of Grandma's predawn prayers: "And do Lord, if it is thy holy will, please keep me clothed in my right mind. Amen."

At the first sign of daylight, she announced for all to hear: "Wiley, get up, we got to go get Les. I can't rest if I leave him in that place."

"And nobody else will rest either," I muttered under my breath. I was in tenth grade and now very serious about my studies, staying up often until 2:00 A.M., long after everybody else had been asleep for hours. It was barely 6:00, and Grandma Edie was rousing us, disturbing the one last hour I had to rest before I dressed to catch the bus for school in front of Blankenship's.

I sat rocking on the porch reading *Silas Marner* when they returned from Riverdale. Daddy and Mama struggled to pull Daddy Les's six-two frame from the backseat of the car. His eyes were wild and frightful, and he gripped the upholstery with fingernails sharp, long, and hard, like the back of a terrapin. He would fight anyone who tried to trim them. Inside, Daddy settled him in bed, leaving Grandma peering through a black-framed magnifying glass at the Twenty-third Psalm. As Mama cooked dinner, Daddy and I went back outdoors and sat in somber silence on the porch. For reasons not yet clear to me, Daddy and I were growing apart and finding it hard to talk and play with one another the way we used to do. To break the awkward silences that often passed between us, Daddy would generally order me to do something, which is what he did the day Daddy Les came back from Riverdale. Reaching in his pocket, he pulled out two quarters and said, "Run to Blankenship's and get me a Goody headache powder. Buy yourself something with the rest."

Because Daddy Les was sometimes lucid, Grandma vacillated between believing that he was faking it all to accepting that he couldn't help it, that he was, in fact, no longer clothed in his right mind. When his daughter, Dorothy, drove from Tuscaloosa on Sunday afternoons, along with her husband, Sandy, her daughter, son-in-law, and great-grandson, Orrin, Daddy Les didn't recognize any of them. Insisting that he was just being contrary, Grandma would light in: "Les, how can you act like you don't know your own kin people? Here, they done drove all the way up from Tuscaloosa and brought you these nice new pajamas, and you acting mean and ornery."

He had to be faking, she maintained, because when Dorothy led us all in his favorite song, Daddy Les would join right in with "When I Can Read My Title Clear," remembering all the verses. Or when she turned the Bible to his favorite psalm and commanded him to read, Daddy Les would begin in that deep, stentorian baritone that lent itself so perfectly to the utterance of his stately name, "The Earth is the Lord and the fullness thereof." That settled it: Daddy Les had to be faking. How could he remember a psalm when he couldn't even recognize his own great-grandson? One Sunday, in the throes of frustration, Grandma stood behind eight-year-old Orrin, on whom Daddy Les had doted all his life, and hounded him: "Who is this, Les? You know you know who this is." Daddy Les grinned, baring his gums, now too shrunken to hold either his top or bottom plate, and answered, "Emory."

Emory had become his imaginary companion, the person he called for all the time. Sometimes, of an afternoon, while Grandma was off at Mama Lucy's, I'd sit with Daddy Les, wondering what he could be thinking as he stared intently at the closet where Grandma kept her quilts, insurance policies, and the bottles of whiskey that she sneaked nips from when Miss Mae Walker came to visit. One day I watched while he sat quietly in his brown Naugahyde platform rocker, his feet resting on top of his house slippers. Suddenly he sprang up like a jack-in-the-box and shuffled over to the closet. He opened the door just slightly, discreetly, like someone peeping through the curtains of a neighbor's house at midnight. Then, cocking his ear toward the closet, he whispered, "Emory, Emory, I know you're in there, Emory." Three Emorys, then the look of anguish followed by the despair that Emory had not answered. Grandma said Emory was Daddy Les's boyhood cousin whom he had tried to save from drowning, but he had had to let him go or be pulled right along with him down to the bottom of the Black Warrior River where they had gone to fish.

When Grandma didn't think Daddy Les was spiteful and contrary, she decided he was just plain old nasty, and only acting crazy as an excuse to cover up his nature, rising once again in his eighty-ninth year. Auntee, who never muffled talk of sex in my presence, laughed at the idea that Daddy Les was getting horny at his age. But Grandma swore up and down that he was. Why else would he come into the room naked as a jaybird only when company came? Someone from the church would have arrived to give Daddy Les communion, and he'd come out first fully clad, his shirt sleeves fastened, his collar buttoned tightly against his neck, just as Daddy had dressed him. Then he would disappear and blunder back into the room, a shriveled, ashen, slumping column of blue-veined flesh dotted with liver spots, wisps of silver hanging limply on the edges of his ears.

Grandma ignored, then fought these signs that Daddy Les had completely lost all grip on sanity, but she began to ease her way into acceptance the day the bumblebees nearly ate him up. She and I were home alone, sitting on the front porch. We thought he was sleeping, but when I went around to the backyard to pick some figs, I noticed him seated on the ground, propped against the back of the tin shed, the front side of his body scorched by the blazing sun. I yelled for Grandma when I saw his head bobbing to one side and his eyes, walled way back in his head, dazed and stricken at the same time. His lips were swollen and blistered, and the folds of his stomach draped softly down on his penis, which grazed the ground. First, Grandma looked hard at me and said, "Turn your head"; then, "Run get Mr. Virge." Mr. Virgil Johnson came running and hefted Daddy Les into the house. As he helped Grandma dress him, I felt ashamed for Daddy Les, who had always been so proudly independent. Dr. Terrell rushed him into the clinic and wrote out a prescription for the bee stings. On the way back home from the drugstore, Grandma talked out loud, preparing herself for the inevitable. Daddy Les would have to go back to Riverdale.

Home from work when we returned, Daddy and Mama were relieved to know that Daddy Les was all right, yet worried about what was in the offing. None of us wanted to abandon Daddy Les to that place that reeked of urine and Lysol, wanted to see him strapped down again and sedated in that stark room with fluorescent lighting overhead that cast a sickly yellow dinginess on everything. Daddy drew a loud sigh and squeezed Grandma on her shoulder: "Don't worry," he said, "I promise you, Mama, we won't take him back to the home, no matter what." And somehow, his words made me feel safe again.

Mr. Virge dropped by later in the week to say that he had canvassed the men in the neighborhood, who volunteered to take turns bathing Daddy Les. They kept their word. And when he wandered from the house, no matter how vigilant we thought we were, Charles Blackman, Ophelia's nephew, walked him back. With his arm wrapped around Daddy Les's rounded shoulders, Charles talked to him lovingly, like the baby he had become again. Daddy Les languished for two more years, then died in his sleep, three months after Daddy Frank, in the iron bed with white-chipped paint.

We had the funeral at Macedonia. Mr. Herbie Young sang "When I Can Read My Title Clear," and Miss Averhart, "It Is Well with My Soul." Mr. V. G. spoke as a neighbor, Mr. Clinton Hearns as a fellow class leader, and Brother Ishmael Mitchell, who was paired with him for years at U.S. Pipe, spoke as a friend. Miss Hester German, the church secretary, read sympathy cards, and the congregation filed up to view the remains. I had already seen Daddy Les laid out at home in brand-new white cotton pajamas, his face cleanly shaven, his hands neatly composed across his torso. I wondered why Daddy had pared his fingernails and toenails, since his feet would be covered. And, according to standard burial practices, his hands would also be encased in bright white cotton gloves just like the ushers wore. We buried him in Tuscaloosa, in a family plot where his mother, first wife, and Emory were buried too.

That night we drove the hour back to Bessemer, and I think it was the first time in my memory that Grandma didn't tell Daddy to slow down the car. In fact, she didn't say much of anything, all the way home. I kept chattering because I could not bear the silence. Wasn't it nice that so many people in Tuscaloosa turned out for the burial? And didn't they lay out a nice spread for Daddy Les? After all, he hadn't lived in Tuscaloosa in a long time. Daddy finally asked me to be quiet so he could concentrate on his driving, and I settled sulkily into the wordless semidarkness of the car, lit intermittently by the high beams of transfer trucks approaching from the rear.

Life returned to normal. We ate the food that neighbors had stuffed into the refrigerator, from vegetable drawer to freezer, all week long. The next morning Mama and Daddy returned to work and Reggie and Bumbiddle to school. Suffering terrible cramps, I was allowed to stay at home, which gave me a chance to comfort Grandma Edie too. I made Cream of Wheat—her favorite breakfast food—and offered to read her the Ninetieth Psalm. The untouched Cream of Wheat hardened in the bowl, and she refused the scripture.

We rocked in silence on the porch until we saw Miss Mae Walker at a distance down the road, red parasol aloft. "Here come Mae Walker," Grandma muttered listlessly. She and Miss Mae Walker had been friends for many years, though neither would say how many. Now in their early eighties, they had reclaimed that quality of forgetfulness that only children seem to have. They constantly fought—over the best way to can tomatoes, the best moment to spread jelly between the layers of Grandma's famous jelly cake. They even fought over which directions the stitches should run when they were finishing the wedding band quilt. But much like children, they always resolved their conflicts by visit's end, just in time to share a dip of Garrett snuff.

Miss Mae Walker strolled at her typical unhurried pace, her hands crisscrossed behind her back. As she neared the gate and folded up her parasol, I could see the familiar look of sober contemplation stenciled in the furrows of her face. Although it was seventy-five degrees, she was clad in her trademark brown cotton stockings, black lace-ups just like Grandma Edie's, and black cardigan sweater buttoned down over the front of a gingham dress. Winded after hauling herself up the steps, she paused to catch her breath and placed her wide-brimmed sun hat on the brick pillar. Then, wrapping one arm around Grandma, she said quietly, "I know you all tore up over Les now, but remember, E, He don't put no more on you than you can stand. You know he took B.D. and she was my only child. Let that nasty cancer eat her up. Felt like I wanted him to take me right long with her, but he didn't. Wasn't ready for me, and if he ain't ready for you, you can't go." Grandma nodded her head and kept on rocking, so Miss Mae Walker sunk slowly down into the slatback rocker. As she tightened the knot just below the knee to secure her stockings, the salmon-colored knee-length panties peeking from the hem of her skirt, she turned to me and asked, "You still keeping company with that Thedford boy?"

"No, ma'am, Calvin Barnes."

"Barnes, Barnes. Ain't them the people live up there behind the ball diamond?"

"Yes, ma'am."

"Chile. Don't you know that that boy's mama *and* her mama both been in the sanitarium?"

"No, ma'am."

"Well, they have. Craziness runs all through that family." Maybe that was why Calvin lived with his grandmother on his daddy's side and got upset when Cleophus asked him in the lunch line if it was true about his mother, and the white man, and the magazines. She had supposedly ordered more than a dozen magazines from a white man traveling door-to-door through the neighborhood—*McCall's, Life, Look, Ladies Home Journal,* even *Road and Track.* And when the man came to collect, she swore up and down that she couldn't have ordered any magazines, especially not in May, because she was still in the crazy house in May.

Recounting that story, Miss Mae Walker kept up, "If you marry that Barnes boy, all y'all's chilren liable to end up in the crazy house too."

"I'm not studying about marrying him."

"Then why you keeping company with him?"

Grandma finally spoke up and said, "Mae Walker, hush your mouth; leave the gal alone. It's craziness or something in everybody's family."

Not to be outdone, Miss Mae Walker shot back, "But not like the craziness of them Barnes folks. Every one of them is crazy as road lizards." Grandma did not return the volley, so Miss Mae Walker sucked on her tooth, took a dip of Garrett snuff from the tin in her apron pocket, then offered it to Grandma, who declined to dip. Miss Mae Walker squirted snuff juice in the yard, missing the edge of the porch a few times. After a while, she stood up to leave, then made her way tentatively down the steps, steadying herself on the point of her umbrella. "I'll see you tomorrow, ole 'oman," she flung over her shoulder, "I'm gon' cut through the alley."

After her almost day-long silence, Grandma began to speak.

"Crockett didn't come to Les's funeral."

"But Grandma, did you really want him to come? Plus, you know he's been feeling pretty low."

"He still could've paid his respects to Les."

I had been hearing the story of Crockett's leaving for as long as I could remember. It took its place in the family annals along with other stories of tragedies and celebrations and turning points. But why did she want to revisit this very ancient grief the day after burying the man she had been married to for the past twenty years?

"He didn't take no more than he could get into the suitcase I bought that time I went down home to visit Fang. I can see him right now, just as clear, just like it was yesterday. We lived in the Pipe Shop quarters then, up around Twentieth Street. I was back in the kitchen putting up peach jelly. I had been canning all that week. I was through with my tomatoes; then I did my okra. All I had left was the jelly. I heard him call me. He said, 'Edie, come in here a minute.' I told him, 'I'll be there directly.' The jelly had started boiling and I wanted to skim off the foam first. I did that and wiped my hands on the dishrag. When I got to the living room he was standing next to the davenport. Now, I want you to know, if you had told me that very minute that Crockett was fixin' to tell me what he did, I wouldn't've believed you. It would have been easier to believe that somebody would walk through my front door and hand me a million dollars.

"He said, 'Edie,' it was soft-like, but I heard him just as plain. 'Edie, I want to separate.' It shocked me so much at first, that it liked to knock the wind out of me, like Saul on the road to Damascus. But when I come to myself I asked him. I said, 'Crockett, why you gon' leave me after all these years? We been married soon will be thirty years.' I have you to know that he couldn't give me no better reason than he didn't want me no more. That's all he could say before he told me I was black and my hands was big. When he turned his back and closed the door and left out of that house that day, I wasn't good for nothing. I left that jelly on the stove all day, never did get it in the Mason jars. Didn't matter anyway, 'cause I was making it for Crockett. He favored peach jelly. I ended up just throwing it out in the alley.

"Different ones said I oughta try to get back, not give up on the thing, but what could I do but let him go? You know you can't hold on to nobody when they ready to go. It'll kill both of you. Dead as you can die. If they wanna go, you got to let 'em go."

That's all she said for the longest time, and I knew I should be quiet too. I was just sixteen and had no way to understand how Grandma could still be carrying Crockett in her heart. Even two marriages hadn't killed the feelings she harbored for this man, who fathered her only child to live past infancy.

Soon after moving to Bessemer in 1905, Grandma Edie had a family portrait done of her, Crockett, and Daddy Frank. At once like a photograph and a drawing, it hung over her mantel at 1805 Long Eighteenth Street for as far back as I can remember. Crockett is on the far right. Broad-shouldered in suit and striped tie, his thick moustache and hair, with hints of gray, are neatly trimmed. His worried eyes sink down in the folds of his plump cheeks. Daddy Frank is on the right, looking much older than his tender years. His face is already haggard, his eyes listless and dull, his lips disappearing into his face. Grandma Edie's coarse mass of hair is sectioned and knotted, one knot prominently atop her head, and, with eyes like searchlights, she stares piercingly at the viewer. Almost no one fails to notice that Crockett, the patriarch, isn't at the center of the frame. Grandma Edie is. A head taller than Crockett and Daddy Frank, just as she was in life, she is firmly at the apex of the triangle their bodies form. The portrait now hangs over the mantel in my house, and each day I pass it on my way out of the door, her ancient eyes meet mine again with that unblinking stare I learned to know and fear so well throughout my childhood. It was the way she stared at me that day, after we buried Daddy Les. I finally broke the silence. "What did you do, Grandma?" In all the times I'd heard the story of his leaving, I knew little of what happened in its wake—no more than talk of hardscrabble times.

"Well, quite naturally, I had it tough, scrimping and saving and scraping by. And some days I couldn't see no farther than my two eyes could behold, and that was from the front gate to the back fence. But you know I always had some kind of garden, and I could get day work to keep something on the table for us to eat. One day I was taking the streetcar to Birmingham, and another day walking way out Arlington Avenue. It helped out that, for a while, we stayed in the church parsonage—me and Stella and your daddy, because it didn't go to suit Reverend Wells. And different ones helped 'cause a whole heap of women was without men for one reason or another—most of 'em widow-women—so we helped each other out.

"When he left Pipe Shop, he moved down around Virginia Mine. He even switched to being a Baptist and started going to Rising Star. I didn't used to see him too much, but folks would bring me word when they saw him in different places. I guess he had been gone long 'bout a year the first time I laid eyes on him again. I was up at Bruno's butcher shop buying meat. I was already standing at the meat counter when I made out that it was them coming through the door. I guess they had been somewhere nice or was going somewhere nice 'cause they was both dressed up. He had on a nice suit and tie, shoes shined and all. Used to be that I couldn't get him to get dressed up and take me nowhere, but that day, I bound you, you could see your face in them shoes and his pants was creased stiff as a ironing board.

"I was shame to let them see me looking the way I was. I had been working all that morning at Miss Beasley's house and walked from there way out Arlington Avenue back to First Avenue. I had one of my old wash dresses on. Used to be that if I had to get groceries on Saturday, I would clean myself up a little bit, but after Crockett left me, I didn't have a great mind to do things like that no more. But when I saw her standing all back in her legs looking like Miss Biggity, I wished I had at least took off my head rag. She was a stout 'oman, put me in the mind of Cake Pie, tall and heavyset. Light complected, and that day she had on the beautifullest dress and her hair looked like somebody had just fixed it. It had a nice style, waved and combed all off to the side."

No matter how many times Grandma told this story, she would never utter the name of Miss Winnie Phillips, nor were we allowed to. It had long been understood that Grandma thought that to speak her name amounted to unleashing an evil spirit in the house, which could take possession of us all. I had never really known Miss Winnie, but Mama had pointed her out to me one time on the No. 2 bus, with hushed tones and a "don't-look-now" admonition.

"I was so shamed. I knew I had sweated in my kitchen and that it had turned all the way back. I don't reckon they wanted to see me either, but we tried to make nice to one another anyway. Somebody talked about the good price on meat—maybe it was Crockett, maybe her. I don't remember. I didn't think the price of meat was good. I had just made a few dollars to last me the whole week, unless somebody called me to do another day's work. I went there to get a pound or two of neckbones or maybe some oxtails to make a stew and a piece of streak o'lean, but 'cause they was just standing there looking like they was the best thing since sugar, I wanted to make like I was just as able as they was to buy meat and not think twice 'bout what it cost. I asked the man to cut me a slab of ribs. Don't ask me why I did it. I guess there was something in me that didn't want her and Crockett to see me low. Don't never let no man see you low, 'cause then he'll sho'nuff try to walk all over you, and sometimes, you can't get up from it.

"But you know, he got his payback. The Lord saw fit to make him reap just what he had sowed. Made him too shame to go out of his house."

Crockett had had a colostomy a few years before, and Grandma was convinced that it was a sign of God exacting retribution. Miss Winnie had not planned to tell anybody about the operation, but when it seemed that Crockett might not survive it, she felt she had to call Daddy Frank, at least. After all, he was Crockett's only child. The story goes that Grandma tracked Daddy Frank to Georgia's shot house, where he was passed out on the floor. She shook his jaws awake, crammed his shirttails in his pants, and off they went to Bessemer General Hospital, where Crockett lay in semiconsciousness. After the visit, Grandma announced, "Crockett's bad off, but the Lord ain't ready for him yet." I don't know how she knew this, but she predicted that he would survive this illness, and he did, in fact, for several years.

Grandma cleared her throat. "You know, he begged my pardon."

"Crockett?"

"Yeah. That last time in the hospital when I went with Frank to see him. He couldn't talk; they had them tubes going all down his throat, up his arms—every whichaway, but he told me."

"How did he tell you if he couldn't talk?"

"He begged my pardon with his eyes."

Grandma smoothed her dress down over her knees and rocked back and forth. I watched her stern face, her snuff-colored eyes nearly squinted shut against the glare of the westering sun, her thinning gray hair, the liver spots speckling her cheekbones, the mole, in the same spot as mine. Her hands were clasped together, resting on her lap. I studied them long and hard. They didn't look that big to me, just bony and knotted at the joints from rheumatism. After a while she bestirred herself again and turning to me, whispered, "Go get the Bible and read me the Ninetieth Psalm."

PART
FOUR

The Wedding

When word spread that Auntee was getting married, everyone was shocked. Shocked, in the first place, because nobody believed that she would ever leave her mother's house; shocked, in the second place, because nobody believed that she would ever break off with Mr. Lige, not to mention to marry a man almost twice her age. Perhaps Auntee had decided that when Julie London started sticking in the record's grooves, it was time to make a change.

I picture her now, lying on the white camelbacked sofa, swishing the liquor in one of Mother's monogrammed old-fashioneds, the torchère's soft glow illuminating her face, Julie London wailing mournfully, "Cry me a river, cry me a river, I cried a river over you." It was Mr. Elijah Honeycutt who made her cry, always around the major holidays. While he might show up on the Fourth of July to eat a barbecue sandwich and sip a can of beer or on Labor Day just long enough to run a Boston at bid whist, his black Buick—waxed always to perfection, mirroring the silky, deep blue-black of his face—was scarce at Thanksgiving and Christmas. These were family days.

Mother was completely unsympathetic. I distinctly remember one day when she was home from Mountain Brook, lingering just long enough to pick up fresh nurse's uniforms, bleach her shoelaces, and scold Auntee for taking up with a married man. "What did you expect? What man will buy the cow when he can pump the milk for free? Once a man keeps company with an alley cat, you can be sure that prowling is all he's got on his mind. You can just forget marriage, put it out of your mind for good." The barrage of insults escalated, with Mother pulling other metaphors from her arsenal, including, "No man wants to drink from a soiled cup. And let me make it clear. If you don't have a marriage license, you can't lay up in *my* house with *any* man. If I catch you doing it or hear of you doing it, I will put you out with nothing but the clothes on your back." Auntee did not flinch; she just walked away, leaving Mother in the middle of the kitchen, hurling invectives on the air.

Because I felt sorry for Auntee and ached for her whenever I remembered Mother's fusillade, I didn't have the heart to answer when she pumped me with questions about Mr. Lige. Had he set foot in her house? When? What did they do? Silently siding with Auntee, I always pled ignorance, never letting on that not only had Mr. Lige set foot in her house, but he had also left stubs of his Prince Albert cigars in her ashtrays, had slept in her gleaming four-poster mahogany bed, on her fine-gauged vanilla sheets edged with scallops, greasing her pillow slips with Royal Crown hair pomade.

Gina and I were always shooed out of the house or bribed with quarters for candy or potato chips, but if we had to pee, we had to pass the door of Auntee's bedroom, always left slightly ajar, and see Mr. Lige's coal black shoulders peeking from above the satiny sheets. Sometimes they dressed and left together, Mr. Lige always in his sleek black pants and white shirt opened peek-a-boo at the neck, exposing the scoop of his Fruit of the Loom tank. In summer he always wore a beige straw hat with a black band around the crown. On the Saturdays I saw him in the winter, he sported a gray fedora with a high roll on the side brim. Hats were his trademark. Mr. Lige seemed to worship them as much as he did his Buick. I guess that's why he lined them up in the back window of his car.

Once when I came down from music lessons, I recognized Mr. Lige's car, with the four chrome side eyes and the gleaming whitewall tires, parked just outside the door of Miss Pigrom's studio, and I concluded rightly that he had been sent to pick me up. Seeing that he wasn't in the car, I climbed into the backseat and picked up the dark brown hat, its brim bound in matching grosgrain ribbon. I was brushing my fingers across the felt when he startled me with, "Put that down. Don't ever put your greasy little hands on my hats." I trembled all the way back to Mother's.

When Auntee left with Mr. Lige, she was always dressed in something flashy, adorned with glittering brooches or her famous rhinestone pins. She wore them on the black chemise that time they snapped her picture at the Madison Night Spot. For a while, the picture hung out front in a display case shaped like a triptych mounted on cast-iron legs. Posters of coming attractions were thumbtacked to the center case, and on either side were photo collages of regular patrons, smiling at each other or hamming for the camera. Auntee was among the gallery of partygoers and, when the case got crowded, the manager, who was always sweet on her, gave Auntee the picture of herself, which he had framed.

She is standing on a stage, elevated just a bit above the floor. The rhinestones are clipped to the squared corners of the dress's neckline. Both of her arms are high above her head. One hand holds a shot glass and the other strikes a finger-snapping pose. Standing next to her is a man in an iridescent smoking jacket, a guitar hanging from the shoulder strap. His hair is processed like Chuck Berry's and Fats Domino's, and he stands gape-legged and grins in Auntee's direction, his gold tooth gleaming like his hair, his jacket, his sweaty face. One of the many musicians looking for a break, he billed himself as the second B. B. King, naming his guitar Stella. That was why he posed with Auntee that evening on the stage; she was the only Stella in the club.

Most of the time, Mr. Lige departed 1404 Ninth Avenue by himself, leaving Auntee standing in the driveway in her duster as the Buick hastened south down the Bessemer Super Highway, then U-turned beyond the railroad crossing, past the billboard of the Marlboro man, and proceeded up the other side. Her back turned to the house, Auntee kicked circles in the gravel until she could see the car line up briefly with the driveway on the other side of the road. He would honk the horn and she would wave, then slowly walk away. The evenings after he had left must have been the hardest, because Auntee peck-peck-pecked at Gina and me until she went to bed: The television was too loud, the dishes weren't clean, and dominoes should never be left scattered on the coffee table and Chinese checkers on the floor.

As one year blurred into another, and it became clear to everybody that Mr. Lige was gone and was not coming back, Auntee got really desperate. Desperate about her prospects for marriage to another man. Desperate about the weight she had gained. Desperate because she was almost forty and had never left her mother's house. Desperate to act as if all was well, as if she was still the gay-popping, brazen hussy who could close the Madison Night Spot after drinking all her running buddies under the table. But we knew that something had cracked in Auntee and could not be mended no matter how hard she pretended otherwise.

At Christmastime, she ceased pretending and just let Jack Daniel's and Dinah Washington rock her right to sleep. Sounding for all the world like she too was weeping drunk, Dinah sang, and Auntee belted out the words right along with her; and in time, so did I.

Somewhere along the line, you met this heart of mine
Wooed it and won it, now you would shun it. Over a glass of wine-i-i-i-ine
Friends knew it all the time, that no wedding bells would chime
I was just a young dreamer, no match for a schemer
Yours was a lover's crime.

For a time, Auntee quit showing up for work at Mrs. Carroll's and spent her days dressed only in her duster, stacking LP's of Gloria Lynne and Billie Holiday bewailing the loss of a man. On the Saturdays I was there for music lessons, she enlisted me to stack the records, plastic pressing plastic. As the needle edged to the end of the very last cut and the arm lifted itself to plop the second record down, Auntee poured another drink. When Mother was summoned home, she only exacerbated the situation.

"Stella, get up. Are you trying to kill youself?"

Auntee said she was. She even gave everybody but Mother a scare by threatening to jump off Shades Mountain. And in a parting shot that I can still remember, she said to Mother, "Then, I guess you'll have to come back and take care of your own house and husband."

Auntee's drinking worsened. When she tripped on the front steps, gashing her forehead, Papa began his own crusade to save her. First he urged Jesus as a cure for her despondency. But the ever-practical Mother urged something much more concrete: the newly widowed and much older Mr. Jethro Strickland. Since she had never cottoned to religion, Auntee chose Mr. Strickland in its place.

Earlier in the year, Mother had hired Mr. Strickland to remodel the house. He was to remove the green-and-white-striped awnings, add a bathroom, and enlarge the living room by shaving off part of the side porch. A contractor for several years, Mr. Strickland had a face that had assumed the hue and texture of sawdust; even his glasses were so flecked and sandy that we wondered how he could see. Whenever Mother came home to inspect the job, she allowed as how he didn't see, at least judging from the way he was botching up her house. She harped constantly about the renovations. "You get what you pay for. I told Fred, you buy cheap, you get cheap." She complained about the drop cloth, spattered with paint from jobs long past. It was an eyesore in the living room, she said. Then she complained about the paintbrushes soaked in linseed oil that stinked up the house.

Gina and I used to say that Mr. Strickland couldn't hear either, or maybe he was on perpetual delayed response. Somewhere in the course of this endless job—as we picked our way over stacks of Sheetrock, piles of tools, and inhaled the gray dust that powdered the entire house, Gina stepped on a nail and had to go to the doctor for a lockjaw shot. Mother threatened to fire him then, but Papa persuaded her to keep her cool. Plus he must have known that by this time, Mr. Strickland had hopes of marrying Auntee.

As he wormed his way into the family's favor, Mother began to tick off and total Mr. Strickland's assets. He had built his own house in West Highlands, complete with a big glass picture window in the living room, a bedroom outfitted in antique white-and-gold French Provincial, a bathroom done up in light blue honeycombed tile, a freestanding water fountain (of all things) in the hallway, and a bricked-in barbecue pit in the backyard. Mother cared nothing for the decorations, but it was a house, paid for clean and clear.

Mr. Strickland had even remodeled Macedonia. True, now everybody complained that he had converted it from a church to a dance hall, down to the mirrored altar. It was tacky and had no place in a sanctuary. You could barely read the lettering:

THIS DO IN REMEMBRANCE OF ME

And yes, the steps were a bit too steep for pallbearers and the elderly to climb. But his labor was reasonable, and he was frugal besides, except where Auntee was concerned. While Mother did not approve, in Auntee's mind, Mr. Strickland's stock shot way up when he outfitted her for Cake Pie's funeral, gave her money for gas, then wired her more money for a bus ticket home when Mother's blue station wagon broke down on the way from Demopolis.

Mr. Strickland had started remodeling Mother's house in late July 1965, and two weeks before Christmas it remained unfinished. Mother came down from Mountain Brook and faced off with Mr. Strickland, threatening, once again, to fire him on the spot. And once more, Papa prevailed. "Miss Vi, you just can't fire the man after all these months. Plus, he's already got half the money."

Mother then demanded to know when she could expect her house to be finished, whereupon Mr. Strickland removed his cigar and muttered affectlessly, "Miz Williams, I'm gon' try to get you ready by Christmas." As he shuffled away, his hammer dangling from the side hip of his paint-stained overalls, Mother shouted, "I'm not the one who has to be gotten ready; my house does. And I don't want you to *try* to get it ready, Mr. Strickland. It *must* be ready by Christmas. My son is coming home."

I thought Mr. Strickland was dragging the job out in order to see more and more of Auntee, who had not the vaguest interest in returning his affections. He was just a sugar daddy. A week before Christmas, it was clear that the job would not be completed, but at least the living room would be finished, as soon as he added the chair-rail molding and painted the walls.

Mr. Strickland finally finished the house in March, just before my birthday, almost eight months after he had begun the task. As the project neared its end, he asked permission to marry Auntee, and Mother lost no time consenting and pressing Auntee to accept. She even pretended to have grown fond of Mr. Strickland, reasoning, I suppose, that if he married her daughter, it would more than compensate for his slapdash carpentry.

They married in August 1966, a few weeks shy of Auntee's thirty-ninth birthday. They stood up together in Mother's living room just in front of the sofa, next to the torchère lamp. Mr. Strickland had been to the barbershop for a fresh haircut, but his face was shadowed with the fuzz his razor never fully cleaned. He looked so awkward in his stiff new suit of midnight blue that seemed cut for someone twice his size. The sleeves of the jacket hung almost to his knuckles, and the cuffs sagged over his shoes. About the only piece of clothing that seemed at home on his frail body was the navy blue tie, sprinkled with tiny pin dots of gold. Beads of sweat covered Auntee's nose and trickled down the sides of her face, which she mopped again and again with a small white handkerchief trimmed in lace and stained with face powder. Half-moons of wetness darkened the underarms of her navy blue silk shantung. The shantung was Mother's idea, as was the borrowed strand of cultured pearls. The outfit was far from Auntee's style, but I figured that she had no need of a shiny, slithering chemise with rhinestone clips since she wasn't marrying Mr. Lige.

"Who giveth this woman away?"

"I do," said Papa, then he looked soberly on the ceremony from the wing-backed chair in the corner, his face half-hidden by a fluted lampshade.

As Auntee solemnly took the wedding vows—pledging to love, honor, and obey—she fidgeted, lifting her heel in and out of the blue-and-white spectators that pinched her toes. When Reverend Mays intoned, "What God hath joined together let no man put asunder" and pronounced them man and wife, Auntee planted a brief, obligatory kiss on Mr. Strickland's lips.

Mother scurried back and forth from living room to kitchen, setting out bowls of Spanish peanuts and tiny sandwiches spread with Cheez Whiz, cut in the shapes of circles, squares, and stars. She set thin slices of the white wedding cake with pink sugared rosettes down on her elegant gold-rimmed plates. The handful of neighbors, friends, and family wished the couple well, nibbled on the sculpted sandwiches, and sipped lime-sherbet frappé from Mother's cut-glass cups. Then came the pictures: of Auntee and Mr. Strickland posed behind the table, feeding each other wedding cake, then more as Auntee opened her presents, offering feeble thanks and affectations of excitement over sheets, towels, an iron, an electric mixer, and plates for every-day. She tucked the folded money in her bosom and stacked the wedding cards with silver bells on the marble-topped table, then made a paperweight of Uncle Jr.'s bronzed high-top shoes. Back in the bedroom, a pearl-pink negligee spread out on the four-poster bed, Gina and I unhooked Auntee's Playtex long-line bra so she could breathe again.

Hush Now,
Don't Explain

Everything changed at Mother's house when Auntee married Mr. Strickland, and she and Gina moved with him to West Highlands. Though only six miles away from Mother's, Auntee still came back to 1404 Ninth Avenue almost every day. Adjusting to her life as a newly married (and unhappy) woman was difficult for her, and so, as often as she could, Auntee escaped from the redbrick bungalow at the crest of the hill, just beyond the rock quarry. She blamed her restlessness on Gina, who was lonesome for her friends at J. S. Abrams High, but the truth of the matter was that Auntee hated West Highlands. There was no life out there, she said, just a bunch of old retired and sickly people sitting on the porch.

As 1404 Ninth Avenue emptied out after Auntee's marriage, I spent scarcely any weekends there. Meanwhile, we were adjusting poorly to our own changes at 1805 Eighteenth Street. With both Daddy Les and Daddy Frank now dead, Grandma Edie passed weeks on end with her relatives in Greensboro and Demopolis, and in her absence the family seemed to splinter, as everyone went their separate ways. Although we honored some of our cherished rituals— especially the Friday night games and snacks— something was missing, and it took a while to determine what it was.

When Auntee married Mr. Strickland, we inherited her hand-me-down stereo system, along with a few record albums forgotten inside its cabinet. These included a scratched and dusty Lou Rawls album featuring his soulful rendition of that old Billie Holiday standard "Don't Explain." Daddy played it over and over again, especially when he'd been out all day. Unmindful of the fact that everybody in the house was sleeping, he turned the volume way up so the sound would carry from the living room to the kitchen, where he scrambled eggs and fried bacon in a cast-iron skillet seasoned with oil.

I lay awake, listening for his footfall followed by the static of the needle before it found Lady Day's first plaintive note.

Hush now, don't explain.
Just say you'll remain.
I'm glad you're back
Don't explain.

I had been listening for Daddy's footfall since the days when he was switched to the night shift—three to eleven. During the week, I was always up, hunched over homework at the kitchen table, when he arrived home around midnight. In the late-night quiet, broken only by the vibration of the Westinghouse refrigerator, I could better concentrate on memorizing the dates and details of world history that might appear on one of Mr. Lacey's pop quizzes. Daddy would appear, his freshly showered skin still matte and ashen, and would place his black humpbacked lunch pail on the kitchen counter, then give me a noogie before asking about my schoolwork.

Daddy had maintained an interest in my schooling, ever since the early grades. He drilled me on my multiplication tables and was constantly exasperated that I could not (still can't) keep dates and numbers firmly in my head. History fascinated Daddy, and during one Negro History Week Mama teased him and asked if he was going back to school, when he absorbed himself in clipping pictures from the Negro History kit: P. B. S. Pinchback, Hiram Revels, and Blanche K. Bruce and all the other Radical Reconstructionists, which we pasted onto pages of black construction paper bound together with yellow yarn.

On Saturday mornings, Daddy would get dressed up and leave. I often watched him as he opened the door of the chifforobe. Would he wear the butterscotch shirt with pinstripes of sagebrush green? Or the white cotton one with cuff links that we had all given him one Father's Day? I had wrapped the box in a brown paper bag, and Reggie and Bumbiddle decorated it with Crayola sunbursts. Would he wear his favorite green silk necktie, the one that Mother gave him for his fortieth birthday? If he pulled the skinny tie from the wooden rack, that was the sign he would be wearing his dark brown worsted suit. When my girlfriends giggled behind their hands and said that he was handsome, I feigned embarrassment, but actually I was very proud that he was there to see me act my parts in Friday evening plays. Those were the days when he was always clean-shaven and well turned out, and beamed in my direction when my teachers reported on my progress. My English teachers always liked him and volunteered that I must have inherited my love of words from Daddy. I did.

From fifth grade until I left Pipe Shop Elementary for Brighton High, we studied vocabulary and were often required to make sentences or write stories using an ever changing list of words. Often Daddy would help me, and Mama would sometimes join the fun, generally tilting the exercise in a humorous direction. Perhaps I misremember, but I would swear that it was Daddy who suggested the compound sentence using "impeccable" and "managerial": "Mother has impeccable taste, but she is managerial."

Sometimes Daddy and I made sentences on those ritual Saturday mornings as he readied to leave. I would watch him shave, lathering his grizzled beard with a blond-bristled brush, plopping the blood-flecked foam into the washbowl. When Daddy uncapped the Old Spice and slapped it on his face and neck, that signaled the end of wordplay. I can still see the dreaded milk white bottles with blue-masted ships resting atop the dresser next to the jewelry box I made for Mama at Vacation Bible School. The clean, crisp, masculine scent of Old Spice, which saturated the room, always filled me with such sadness; it was the scent of departure, the certain sign that Daddy was going out and would likely be gone all day.

Just where these Saturday mornings took him, after he drove away in the brown secondhand Oldsmobile, remains a mystery to me. Although he often said he was headed for a union meeting at the C. I. O. hall, we knew that union meetings couldn't last from 10 A.M. of one morning until 3 A.M. of the next, but no one dared suggest this to Daddy or ask him where he had been so long. "Hush now, don't explain" brought a day of waiting to its end. The sound of that song gave me one more Saturday night's relief and secured me in the knowledge that Daddy was back in one piece, his iridescent suit intact, awaiting the next all-day excursion.

I know he never stayed out all night long—3:30 A.M. was the latest. I know because whenever I heard his footsteps, I would look at the luminescent hands on the face of Baby Ben, the squat, round alarm clock that Mother gave me so I could break the habit of oversleeping my music lessons. Three-thirty was the latest the blue hands ever glowed. On those nights when I was back at home in my bed, I tossed and turned with worry, but when I heard the slow, unsteady clomps from steps to porch to living room, I could stop worrying for one more week. With a mixture of relief and sadness, I greeted the refrigerator's dim wedge of light and the strains of "Don't Explain," and dreamed of the days when I would live in a sprawling house with soundproof rooms, far away from Pipe Shop.

The night that Daddy didn't make it home, I had finally drifted off to a full night's sleep as rain pounded against the roof with the violent force of a tropical storm. I woke to see the sun peeping through the gap where the shades didn't quite meet the windowsill. The smell of vanilla and the sound of butter sizzling in the skillet meant Mama was making pancakes. She stood over the stove, her watery eyes locked on the yellow pancake batter inside the red-striped bowl.

"What's wrong, Mama?"

"Nothing. Start getting ready for church."

I pulled out the ironing board from the corner, spread newspaper on the kitchen floor, and ironed my choir robe and pink whipped-cream dress.

"Can I wear your pearl necklace?"

"Yeah."

I stepped into her bedroom and walked over to the dresser, pausing before opening the jewelry box. I craned my head slightly to notice that there was no mound beneath the white bedsheet. Daddy always slept late on Sunday morning, covered from head to foot no matter how hot it was. It was then that I remembered, I had not heard his footsteps the night before.

I walked back into the kitchen. "Where's Daddy?"

"I don't know; he didn't come home last night."

I stood stock-still, certain that all my fears had finally come to pass. I had often worried that he would be killed—maybe even violently—in a head-on collision or fatally shot or stabbed at Duke's Place, which used to be a decent hangout until it became a haven for hotheaded drunks ever on the lookout for a fight. I had to pass Duke's on my way to music lessons on those Saturday mornings when this now dingy jook joint looked peaceful, but I knew that by midnight, it would jump to the deafening howls of Johnny "Guitar" Watson, Koko Taylor, and Clarence "Gatemouth" Brown.

As Mama fried rounds of Ziegler's sausage, I pressed her with questions, every last one of which she deflected, cutting me off to wake Reggie and Bumbiddle for Sunday School. They washed up, then stumbled into the kitchen, still rubbing their eyes, and sat down at either end of the table.

Not noticing that anything was amiss, Reggie and Bumbiddle chatted as Mama walked over to the door to have a smoke. I watched her, angling her face to blow tendrils through the back-door screen that gridded Miss Classie's clothes hanging since yesterday on the line.

Mr. Hearns tooted the horn and we scurried to the door for church. Mama followed us outside, yelled good morning and thank you to Mr. Hearns, then turned to me and whispered, "Don't you say a word to Mr. Fred about your daddy." And we left her there, standing on the front steps as the car barreled down the street.

I can't recall the songs I played that Sunday, nor anything else that happened before Papa dropped us off and sped on to Mountain Brook. I found

Mama on the phone, the directory open to the Yellow Pages on her lap. Her cigarette rested on the edge of the encyclopedia case, its ash about to sprinkle on the floor.

"Do you have a Wiley McDowell there?"

After a long pause, I heard, "You don't? Well, thank you."

Mama drew on her cigarette and returned the heavy black receiver to its cradle.

"You-all get out of your Sunday clothes."

Dinner wasn't ready, so after they changed their clothes, Reggie and Bumbiddle went outside to shoot marbles. I sat with Mama in the living room, noticing the weight of her breasts that curved her shoulders forward. Although she always tried to protect me from her sadness by pretending everything was fine, her eyes never lied, and they were scared that day.

"Daddy still didn't come back?"

"No."

"Who were you calling?"

"The jails and the hospitals."

"Daddy wouldn't do anything to get thrown in jail. Why are you calling the jails?"

"Sometimes they lock people up overnight for driving under the influence."

I followed Mama to the bedroom, where she pulled off her duster and I could see where her bra straps had dug narrow trenches in her shoulders. She pulled a yellow seersucker dress over her head and pivoted around for me to zip her up. I then trailed her into the kitchen, where she turned off the blue gas flames flickering underneath the pots, reached for her sandals beside the kitchen table, strapped them loosely around her heels, and said, "I'll be right back."

"Where are you going?"

"To see if I can find your daddy or find somebody who might have seen him or might know where he is."

"I'm going too."

I half expected her to stop me. The rules of "grown folks" generally demanded keeping secrets from children, especially about adult affairs. Mama looked long and hard at me and walked slowly toward the door. I walked behind her, waiting for the moment when she would order me to stay at home. She didn't. Maybe she figured that, at sixteen, I was now of an age to make acquaintance with the shifting seasons of emotion.

We passed O. K. Rubber Welders, where a large sign advertising 50 percent off creaked on its rusty hinges in the breeze. Mama quickened her pace, and I concentrated on matching the rhythm of my steps to hers. We rounded the corner to Miss Georgia's and climbed the three wooden steps to the shotgun house. It was a while before Miss Georgia heard us knocking over the boom of the stereo. She opened the door wearing her trademark black skirt, tangerine blouse, and black patent-leather sandals. Her strutting clothes, she called them in that husky voice of hers.

The shades of the house were tightly drawn, and the denseness of the smoke was suffocating. Mama and Miss Georgia bantered lightly and headed toward the back. I was right on their heels until Mama stated firmly, "Stay here." Standing in the doorway of the front room I followed them with my eyes the short distance to the kitchen. Since she had let me come this far, I didn't know why Mama would order me to stay back now. Anyway, I had already been in Miss Georgia's kitchen that time Auntee sent me inside to ask for Mr. Lige. I had knocked at the back door and thinking I had heard someone say Come in, I opened the door right into Miss Georgia's face and was startled momentarily by her bright magenta lipstick. Wearing a bright blouse that day too and black patent-leather high-heeled Joan Crawford "throw-me-down-and-fuck-me" shoes, she glowered at me and said in that hoarselike way, "What you doing in here? Who sent you in here?" I said I had come to see if Mr. Lige was there. "Well, you can see he ain't here," she shouted, "so you get your little butt on outta here. Go on home. You ain't got no business in this place." But before she shooed me out I spied a gape-legged man in two-toned shoes with a wet spot in the crotch of his charcoal trousers. And men and women with processed hair, guzzling clear liquid from shot glasses and whacking diamonds, hearts, and aces on the laminated table.

When Mama returned, I asked, "Was he back there?"

"No."

"Has anybody seen him?"

"Georgia saw him last night at Pearl Harbor, but she says he left there around eleven o'clock with Woodie."

We left Miss Georgia's, then walked to Mr. Woodie's, but finding no one there, we headed back to our house, taking the shortcut through the alley.

They were standing several feet in from the mouth of the alley, where the acrid smell of ripening garbage hung in the humid air. Their backs were turned to us, but even from the distance I could detect the lean outlines of Daddy's frame. He was still wearing the white cotton shirt from the day before, tucked neatly down into the brown pants that matched the brown iridescent suit. I couldn't make out who the woman was. She wore a sleeveless, tawny-colored floral shift and white shoes. I could not tell if they were sandals. Daddy's shirtsleeves were rolled up, and his sturdy right arm encircled her waist. Her body turned slightly toward his, and her left hand rested softly, possessively, securely on his right shoulder, as if it belonged there.

At first, Mama and I just stared at each other, eyeball to eyeball. Then I jerked my face away from hers as I heard her murmur lowly, "That's Baby Jean." For some odd reason, the first thought that popped into my mind was whether the skin at the back of her arms was still taut, not sagging. I followed at a slight distance on Mama's heels, but neither of us said a word.

Daddy finally appeared long after nightfall; after dinner; after Mama had ladled a plate of food for him and left it covered with aluminum foil on the stove; after I had washed the dishes and stacked them to drain in the red rubber rack on the sink; even after *Bonanza,* which he always watched on Sunday evenings. When he walked in, he headed straight for the kitchen and brought his plate into the living room where we were all watching some movie. Without a word, Mama stomped from the room, dragging the half-sleeping Bumbiddle by the arm, leaving Daddy, Reggie, and me sitting on the couch in the feather-gray glow of the television light.

One by one, we rose and went to bed, and before too long, I heard the rancorous voices now no longer confined to Saturday night and early Sunday morning. But the tones had traded places: Daddy's hisses could be heard in Mama's mouth that night, as she shouted out the question asked by every woman who has ever had to ponder why a man has left her for another woman: "What she got that I ain't got?" For once, I could not hear Daddy's answer, but I heard Mama's second sortie loud and clear:

"The Lord said for a woman to multiply and replenish the earth, and she can't do that with her mouth." Grandma came around to our side of the house and pleaded with them to hush, and the house soon settled into an ominous quiet that hung on through the following week. I knew that something serious had happened when I came home from choir rehearsal on Wednesday to find Mother there. She never left Mountain Brook in the middle of the week unless someone had died or something had gone awfully wrong. All of them—Mother and Papa, Grandma, Mama, and Daddy—huddled and whispered together around the kitchen table. Mama ordered us to the living room to watch television, another major oddity on a school night. I said I had to write a book report and needed to do it at my desk, in the back room, just a few steps off the kitchen, but Mama gave me the look that said, "Get outta here, this minute."

After a while, I walked back to the kitchen, announcing that I had come for more loose-leaf paper, and rummaged in my desk. I wanted to eavesdrop and not eavesdrop at the same time, but the swatch of what I heard next drove me fearfully back into the living room: "Why you got to leave now? Think of your children."

All that week, relatives with somber faces streamed in and out of the house, seated elbow to elbow around the kitchen table, averting their eyes whenever I searched them for signs that would explain the heaviness that engulfed the house. I finally pieced two and two together and concluded that Daddy was about to leave and that all the family had been summoned to make him change his mind. The pressure must have worked. Daddy didn't leave. At least not in the body, which was the hardest part to take. From that very moment, I felt that he had left without leaving, for whenever he was home, the air was supercharged with tension and Daddy sat in smoldering silence, burrowed down inside himself in some unreachable place, or snapped at everybody for any little thing. Since we had once been very close, I felt his distance keenly, and sometimes wished he'd go away. Absence, I told myself, would be a far sight easier to bear than this silence and the shadowy side of his face.

I have tried to quash the memory of that day we left them standing still, their backs to us, as we retreated slowly down the alley, but it will no more die than Grandma Edie's memory of the day that Crockett went away. Just when I think I've finally banished the scene and the finger-in-the-car-door throb it conjures up, everything comes rushing back unbidden to gnaw at me again. One day, years after graduate school, I stood in a bookstore leafing through a collection of Walker Evans's photographs, pausing inexplicably for a long, long time over "Couple at Coney Island." It was Daddy and Baby Jean all over again, except that Daddy had not worn suspenders, nor Baby Jean a backless dress. Shot in broad daylight, Walker Evans caught the couple in an intimate pose, just like the one Daddy struck with Baby Jean, behind her house, in the bright light of the rain-soaked alley where I stepped into a puddle, squishing the sludge between my toes.

College Bound

The incident with Baby Jean was yet another symptom of Daddy's growing distance from the family. Mama blamed everything on his unsteady
work. He was either laid off altogether or his hours cut way back. To compensate, he found odd jobs here and there, one as a security guard in a bank,
but he grew more and more bitter with passing years.

Although I cannot pinpoint just when things began to fray, the early
signs are still quite vivid in my mind. First we dropped the games. On Friday night and sometimes late Sunday afternoon, after church and recitations, we used to play Monopoly and dominoes, checkers and bingo for
multicolored jelly beans or Hershey's kisses.

Then Daddy and Mama no longer read the newspaper together or
played card games with their friends. In time, we ceased to go on any family outings. No more drive-in movies, no more yearly trips to the carnival,
where once all three of us—Reggie, Bumbiddle, and I—got sick on pink
cotton candy spun in big vats of stainless steel.

And then there was the Fourth of July. While Daddy still barbecued for
us and all the neighbors, still slow-cooked his secret piquant sauce in the
dented boiler, it all seemed so perfunctory—like he was simply perform-
ing a family ritual with all the fizz sucked out. Constantly irritable, the
least little thing touched Daddy off, and he no longer threw his head way
back and laughed from deep down in his throat.

Daddy abandoned all that used to bring him his deepest satisfaction.
The tailor's samples still arrived once a month like clockwork in the mail,
but Daddy no longer fantasized aloud about the shop that he would one
day own. He ceased to sketch the men in double-breasted jackets and high-
draped pants. But harder to bear than all these changes was the pride he
lost in his own appearance. He let his moustache grow scraggly and his
dress-up shoes get scuffed and down at the heels.

The only ritual he did not abandon was jazz radio on Sunday afternoon, but even that seemed observed more out of habit than out of pure delight. When we returned from church on Sundays, we often found him seated in the living room or, in summer, on the porch absorbed in the three-hour program while drinking beer. That's what he was doing—rocking on the porch and drinking beer—the day he busted Grandma Edie.

We could hear the music blasting before we even reached the porch. Daddy had leaned the radio in one window of the living room and turned the volume way, way up. As I recall, the entire program was dedicated to John Coltrane, who had died suddenly of a heart attack the week before at the youthful age of forty. That would have been 1967. Daddy and I shared a love of Coltrane's music, which Mama did not understand. "Give me B.B. and Aretha any day," she said. "This Coltrane music sounds just like screaming." And Daddy had once quipped, "It is."

We reached the top step just as the deejay was identifying the previous cuts and interjecting praise songs for the genius of 'Trane. Grandma Edie shouted over the announcer's mellow tones: "I don't believe you sitting here playing reels out loud on Sunday for everybody to hear."

Daddy slowly exhaled smoke and said, "Mama, I ain't in the mood for one of your sermons today."

"Well, you need to be. You needed to be at church, right up on the first pew, 'cause you done strayed clean away from the path of righteousness."

Daddy's silence just egged her on. "Wiley, how can you be drinking whiskey on Sunday? It's a scandless." Again, he didn't answer her, but she kept on nagging, provoking Daddy to speak the unspeakable: He allowed as how she had no room to condemn him for drinking, since she did the same herself and had even given her own son the drink that caused his death. Grandma stomped her black pin-pointed lace-ups on the floorboards and shouted, "You're a liar and the truth ain't in you. Beg pardon."

Daddy moved again to walk away, his eyes holding that familiar bloodshot glaze. He had already dared far more than custom granted a forty-four-year-old man to say to his eighty-one-year-old grandmother. Grandma followed on his heels, angrier than I think I ever saw her. By now, the noise had awakened Mama from her nap. She came outside and tried to hush them up, but Grandma paid her no mind and kept right on shouting, following Daddy all the way to the privet hedge.

"I 'clare 'fore God I'm not a whiskey drinker, and if I speak a word of a lie, may God strike me dead."

"Well, he might just do that," Daddy muttered, and this time Grandma's backhand struck him squarely in the face.

"Hush yo' mouf. How can you speak to your gray-headed grandma thisaway? I'm the one what changed your didies. And who you think looked after you when the very one that birthed you went off and left you, and your daddy was roaming from one shot house and honky tonk to another? And who gave you a roof over your head all these years? Helped you raise every last one of your children? And this the payback that I get? I never thought I would live to see the day when you would 'buke me like this, Wiley, after all I done for you. You beg my pardon now. I mean right now. Beg pardon." Daddy coughed up a half-hearted apology, but Grandma kept on scolding. "Wiley, look to me like you done gone and lost your mind, and turned your back on everything I tried to teach you."

Ironically, after that violent scene, things took a temporary upward turn, as if all that had been suctioned tight for years on end had been allowed to breathe. Luckily for Daddy and for all of us, he was called back to the Pipe Shop in mid-July. He took advantage of the opportunity to work double shifts. The constant working tired him out, but put him in a splurging mood in time to launch me off to college. He took me to the commissary, where I bought a three-piece set of Samsonite luggage in Hawaiian blue, a portable record player that we named the "Blue Goose," three pleated skirts, and two pairs of penny loafers, one black and one brown. I was Tuskegee-bound.

Mother's hand was heavy in the college preparations, and her generosity seemed to know no bounds. Following her strict instructions, Mama did the packing, after cross-stitching the labels of my name into the collars and waistbands of my clothes and at the far right edges of my towels. Daddy barbecued the day before I left, and neighbors came with dollar bills tied up in sweat-stained handkerchiefs, jars of pickled this and that, and advisory opinions that would put Polonius to shame.

The day before I left, Daddy tanked up the car and the next morning he was up at daybreak, checking and rechecking the oil and water in the battery, the air pressure in the tires, arranging and rearranging the luggage in the trunk. I was surprised when he handed me the Coltrane recording of "My Favorite Things." "I'm not giving it to you. I'm loaning it to you. It's a temporary *transfer*." When he put the emphasis on "transfer," I knew that he was remembering the spelling bee, way back when I was still at Pipe Shop Elementary. Daddy had coached me every evening as I washed the dinner dishes. Seated at the kitchen table while I stood at the sink, he called out the words. I had little trouble with the complex words; it was the simple ones that seemed to slip me up: "receipt," "relieve," "achieve," "brassiere." When I kept transposing the "e's" and "i's," one afternoon in the kitchen, Daddy said, "Turn the water off. Listen, you can spell every four-syllable word on this card, but you get too cocky with one-syllables. All you got to do is stop and think, the same way you do with the big words. Just stop and concentrate before you start spelling."

Since he was then working the eleven-to-seven shift, Daddy drove me to the spelling bee down in McCalla and coached me all the way there. "Remember what I told you. Just say the word. Stop and think before you spell."

I was defeated in the third round, when I added an "e" to "transfer." I cried all the way home. Daddy tried to comfort me, and whether it was true or not, he said he had lost a spelling bee one time.

"What word did you miss, Daddy?"

"Oh, I don't remember what it was. That was so long ago."

Daddy cheered me up when he stopped to buy me a Hula Hoop on the way home, and the humiliation of losing that afternoon receded with each round-the-world rotation of the purple hoop.

We had reconnected, or so I thought. Daddy seemed transformed by the experience of whooshing down East 150, then to the Old Montgomery Highway and on into Tuskegee, "the pride of the swift-growing South." When Mr. Gamble, my trigonometry teacher, had learned that I was headed for Tuskegee, he had taught me this from the first line of the school song, which he had sung with pride as a student there: "Remember," he had written in my yearbook, "you are bound for the 'pride of the swift-growing South.' Conduct yourself accordingly."

I was ecstatic to be going off to college. It was the first time I had been away from home and on my own. It was also the first time in several years that I actually felt weightless, blissfully free of the cares of Pipe Shop. And for the first month at Tuskegee I basked in this freedom and let myself block out all thoughts of Daddy's potential lay-offs, shutdowns, and long lines at the unemployment office. But while exhilarated, I also felt a crushing responsibility on my shoulders, especially from Mother. While her generosity was unstinting, it was not without a price. As always, although she was physically at a distance, Mother's presence was palpable and strong, and in all her letters was the subtle but insistent pressure to achieve, the constant reminders that I could not fail. All hopes for the family were now on me.

Parents' Weekend fell in late October and everybody came— Grandma Edie, Mother and Papa, Daddy and Mama, Reggie and Bumbiddle—and we had a great time, even though they could not stay the whole weekend. Daddy was beginning work the very next day at a brand-new part-time job. They arrived early on Friday morning and left at dusk, but we still managed to cram a good bit in. While the others took the campus tour and visited the George Washington Carver Museum, Daddy accompanied me to class, where he was treated to Dr. Gomillion's spellbinding rendition of the events leading up to the landmark case *Gomillion* vs. *Lightfoot.*

Afterward, Daddy actually wrote a short letter to say how much fun he'd had. He folded a five-dollar bill between the first page and the second blank piece of paper. But he wrote few letters after that, and I matched his silence with my own. When I called home on weekends, he was never there, and Mama was characteristically evasive concerning his whereabouts. It was Grandma Edie who finally told me that he had taken up with Baby Jean again and spending little time at home. At first, I continued to hold myself at a distance as a form of adolescent punishment, hoping that it would bring him back around. When it didn't, I wanted at least the satisfaction of "running him in the ground."

I tried to recruit Mama to my side, wanting her to hate him too. But in truth, I did not hate him, I only wanted to, thinking that it would protect me from the hurt. No matter how much I tried to get Mama to join with me in these attacks on Daddy, she never would, a stance I could not then understand. She had caught him with another woman, after all. Oddly enough, Mama never ceased defending Daddy. "This is a hard time for your daddy. The situation is getting worse at the plant and wants so much to shoulder his manhood. Try to understand. Whatever is going on between us is grown folks' business, not yours. No matter what happens, he's still your daddy." That meant the case was closed.

It was all so ironic. Daddy had taught me a love of words, he had even taken me to get my first library card, had been my coach for the spelling bee, but from my college days through to the end of his life, few words passed between us. Mama was often the conduit, relaying messages from him to me and back the other way. During those days, I had reduced Daddy to a pronoun and tried to banish him from my thoughts. I became miserly with references to him, which were confined to my own wants and needs. Would he be driving me back to Tuskegee? When would he be sending the money for my meal ticket? Why was the money late? I was already a week into the month. What time did I want him to pick me up? Did I have more stuff than would fit in the trunk of the car? Reggie and Bumbiddle might like to ride along. And on and on.

He was to pick me up for my first Thanksgiving away from home, the weekend when I would also get my portrait taken with the class of debutantes who would be "coming out" with me at Christmastime. At the last minute, however, Mama phoned to say he couldn't come; the car had broken down.

"Can't he get it fixed?"

"I guess not."

While I was disappointed that I would be riding the bus back home alone, this was yet further confirmation that Daddy could not be counted on.

Mrs. Kennedy, the dorm mother, gave me a ride to the Greyhound station. I was one of the last to leave the dorm that Wednesday afternoon.

"I was afraid you'd decided not to leave," Mrs. Kennedy said when I paused outside the doorway of the office. "Are you planning to come back?" she teased while surveying my very large Samsonite bag, the matching cosmetics case at its side.

"Yes, ma'am, I'm coming back."

"Then you must have lots of activities planned for these four days?"

"Yes, ma'am."

One never knew what my friends at home had in store, especially Clara Oliver or the wild and brazen Marguerite. Clara had phoned earlier in the week to remind me to bring a party dress, and I packed the "fancy" sheath that Mother had bought me in a flurry at Five Points West two days before I left for Tuskegee. When she called to say she was picking me up for a shopping trip, I said, "But, Mother, you've already bought me so many things for college."

"Those were just clothes for every day. You need some fancy things just in case an occasion should arise." So we purchased the requisite black cocktail dress; an emerald sheath, iridescent like the throats of pigeons; black pumps of *peau de soie;* and a tiny black beaded bag shaped like an Instamatic camera. Almost three months had passed without a "fancy" occasion, but one would surely emerge during the Christmas holidays.

Mrs. Kennedy reminded me a bit of Mother, with her French roll and her bangs. She sat in her glass-screened office, watching for boys sneaking in or girls sneaking out in midriff tops and miniskirts and hip-huggers with buckled wide leather belts. And I can still hear the mischief in her voice the night she activated the intercom to call my name and announce, as she must do for all the other women in the dorm, "You have a gentleman caller."

"Man on the hall. Man on the hall."

After that first Thanksgiving, Mrs. Kennedy gave me lifts to the Greyhound station whenever I made one of my infrequent trips back home. For a time, she'd ask, with a genuine note of motherly concern, why I was always the last to leave the building. I never said, and after a while, she stopped asking, just gracefully extended her offers, which I gratefully accepted. I could not find the words to say that I had finally discovered what a powerfully comforting and yet oppressively liberating thing distance can be.

Papa picked me up from the station that weekend and dropped me off at home, where everyone was gone but Daddy, who sat at the kitchen table poring over tailor's swatches. I passed my hand over the ridged edges of aluminum that trimmed the green marbleized table. The trim had long since lost its shine, as had the rickety tubular legs that needed propping up on chips of wood or folded matchbooks from the Dew Drop Inn.

"Where is everybody?"

"Your mama went to the grocery store. Reggie and Bumbiddle, I mean Roderick, went with her."

"Since when did you start calling Bumbiddle Roderick?"

"For about a month now he's been asking everybody to call him by his name."

"Bumbiddle *is* his name. I gave him that name."

That very first semester at Tuskegee, in English composition, we were first assigned to write a personal essay, and I wrote about Bumbiddle and how he got his name. Mrs. Alma Britten read it to the class. I knew from the very first day Mama brought him home from the hospital, swaddled in the blue-and-white receiving blanket that Mother had crocheted, that Bumbiddle should be his name. When Mama pulled back the blanket so we could see his face, he looked so small and scaly. I don't know why, but it seemed to my six-year-old eyes that he looked just like a baby chicken, or what we used to call a biddie.

When I was six I had gone with Mama to visit Mother's sister, Aunt Die, in Epps, Alabama. Every morning, she would let me feed the chickens and I'd imitate her calling: "Here chick, chick, chick. Here biddie, biddie, biddie."

I liked the sound and played with it. That's what I did on Bumbiddle's first day at home. I added the first syllable to "biddie," but I didn't like the way "bumbiddie" sounded, so I changed it to "bumbiddle," and it stuck.

As Daddy drew on his Winston, clouding the corner with smoke, I sat down and resolved to talk to him, despite our recent bout with silence. I asked questions about his swatches. What was the difference between worsted and flannel? They looked much the same to me. And where did herringbone get its name? He explained as he fingered the pinked-edged swatches glued to the side flaps of the glossy, bone-colored paper.

At the moment that I saw signs of relaxation on his face, I said, "I have something to show you." On the bus ride, I had turned things over again and again in my mind. Should I show him the paper? Written for classics of world literature, part one, the essay was on Shelley's "Ozymandias," and I had gotten a B+, my highest grade yet in that course, taught by a meek, petite white woman who had just finished a monograph on black poets of the 1960s, though none figured in the course.

On the other hand, maybe I shouldn't show it to him, unless I found him in a pleasant mood. His mood was pleasant enough, I decided, and so I pulled the essay from the leather fishnet bag we all carried back then, uncreasing the paper's stiff, vertical fold. I admired again the bright red B+ inscribed beneath barely legible comments about perceptive insights and encouragements to keep up the good work on the take-home exam, an analysis of Thomas De Quincey's "On the Knocking at the Gate in Macbeth."

As I moved to pass the essay to Daddy, he asked, just as I was placing it in his hand, "What grade did you get?"

"B plus."

"Well, that's pretty good, but you should try to get an A next time."

The tears rushed instantly to my eyes. "Did you make all A's when you were in school?" I asked with deliberate contempt.

"Oh, yeah. Lots of them—even in English, but I did even better in math and history. I was nobody's slouch when it came to school."

"Well, I'm not either. At least I made it to college."

As soon as the words escaped my mouth, I wanted to snatch them back. "I mean, I know it wasn't your fault and all, the reason you didn't go to college. I know you wanted to, but. . ."

"You don't know half of what you think you know, Miss Priss."

Tears always made Daddy uncomfortable, so he half-apologized and drew on his cigarette. "What did I tell you about popping off at the mouth? Once words come out of your mouth, you can't call 'em back. So think before you speak."

I pushed the chair back from the table and grabbed the essay, which lay atop the card of swatches at the table's edge. I had gotten as far as the doorway, headed toward the living room, when he called out to me: "So now you want to clamp your little mouth shut, huh, now that you finished popping off? Well, let me tell you a thing or three." Tradition forbade me to walk away when a grown person was addressing me, so I paused, leaning against the doorjamb with my back still facing Daddy. I did not want to listen as he shoveled through his compost of ancient resentments and disappointments, although these reflections never failed to tug at me.

"When I left school, I went to work in Lovett's Tailoring Shop up on

First Avenue. That was one of the happiest times of my life, but then I had to go into the army. I had just married your mama. They shipped me to Fort Lee, in Virginia, and from there to Germany. The best thing about the army was that I got to travel, got to see a little bit of the world. Folks used to think the army gave people opportunities for advancement, but it didn't give me any such thing.

"When I got my discharge papers I came home, but Mr. Lovett had died and the business had been sold to a man who didn't need another tailor. While I was trying to figure out what to do, I got a job with North Carolina Mutual, writing insurance policies. I was pretty good at it too. Sold all kinds of policies, not just life and burial. Ask Helen Fagan. To this day she thanks me for getting her to take out a college policy on her oldest daughter, Rosalyn."

I had heard this all before, and the more I heard it, the less I sympathized. "Your mama was making good at her sewing and working part-time with Dr. Davis. He was the only black dentist in the city at the time. He always said your mama was a good advertisement for business—because of her pearly white teeth. You and Bumbiddle get your teeth from my side of the family, but Reggie has your mama's teeth. Anyway, we were doing all right. Getting by. Doing more than getting by, but when you came along, we needed a little more money." I thought to myself, So now Daddy's thwarted dreams were my fault.

"I let Mother talk me into going out to the Wenonah trade school, and I did. Studied business—took courses in accounting and such, but, after that, I still couldn't get a job, so I went to work with Mr. Fred down at Pyne Mine. You have no idea what it's like to work in a mine. I couldn't stand it. Didn't last down there more than a few months. From there, I went out to the Pipe Shop, and been there ever since."

I knew Mother would eventually work her way into the conversation. When all else failed, everything could be blamed on Mother, the person who managed everybody's life. But I thought it was unfair to hold her responsible for everybody's failings.

"If I'd had a chance to get my own shop, I wouldn't have to be out there working in that hell-hot de Lavaud with no more chance to move up than I had in the army."

It seemed to me he was making excuses for himself and feeling sorry for himself. Now, I know he wasn't, at least not entirely.

The phone rang and I ran to grab it. It was Clara Oliver, at home from Barnard College. Within minutes, I had forgotten all about Daddy, as Clara and I were caught up in the evening's plans, the local gossip, and news about our college days. After more than half an hour, I ended the conversation and sauntered back into the kitchen to hear the rest of Daddy's story. I was surprised to find him sketching again—a long, tall man in a double-breasted peg-legged suit, a cigarette between his fingers.

Coming Out

The Friendly Twelve intend to sponsor you this year. For the Debutante's Ball."

I sighed and held the phone away from my ear.

"Are you there?"

"Yes, Mother."

"Miss Ravizee says you need to get your portrait taken at Lacey's when you come home for Thanksgiving. He's giving special rates and will have the pictures developed in time to run in the *World* and the *Bessemer Sun*."

"Okay, Mother."

Gina had come out three years before, and now it was my turn. Mama thought the ball was just a bunch of saddity folk putting on airs, not to mention a waste of money. But in the end, as always, she caved in to Mother's pressures, though not before making it absolutely clear that she would not contribute a single penny to the cause, "not one red cent," she insisted, pausing after each word. She didn't have to, Mother explained. I would be sponsored by The Friendly Twelve, Mother's social and savings club.

The Friendly Twelve was just one of such clubs scattered all over the Birmingham area. Announcements of their meetings often appeared weekly in the *Birmingham World* right alongside notices of meetings of the Bessemer Voters League and the voter registration/church participation meetings. Their names ran the gamut from the pretentious to the prosaic: Club Imperial, Club La Petite, Club Entre Amis, Club La Casa Loma, Club Elite, The Dew Drop Social and Savings Club, The Cinderella Thrift Club, The Friendly Matrons, The Thrifty Ten, The Helping Hand, The Watercolor Society, and countless others. They cohosted Christmas parties with the clubs their husbands joined: Gentlemen of Pleasure, The Cosmos Club, The Dauntless Club, The Friendly Brothers, and The Esquires.

The club members were a group of striving black women who lived in the wider Bessemer area, although they would all have sooner been caught dead without their face powder than called black. They were Negro women, had always been. They all attended Macedonia, sang in the choir, and served on the usher board or Missionary Society. They raised money at bake sales for the building fund, visited the sick and shut-in, and made sure "the pastor" had a proper appreciation day. Unlike some of the local and more prosperous Baptist churches, the club members were A.M.E. Zion, and they did not observe the custom of presenting their pastor with the latest model Buick or Cadillac or Lincoln Town Car, but they guaranteed him a hefty bonus and no shortage of fulsome praise.

Proud to be solidly middle class, the members of The Friendly Twelve bought U.S. Savings Bonds and made biweekly deposits to passbook accounts held at Birmingham Trust National Bank. Most were not extravagant, just comfortable, making sure that their husbands' salaries from Pyne Mine or TCI or Pullman Standard or U.S. Pipe and Foundry paid for modest homes—nothing fancy or palatial—but, as they were wont to say with smugness, "their own."

Whenever the meeting rotated to Mother's house, Gina and I prepared the refreshments: Cheez Whiz on Ritz crackers, salted peanuts still in their russet skins, and the little sculpted sandwiches like the ones we ate at Auntee's wedding. The Friendly Twelve drank no alcohol, at least not openly, just frappé, made by pouring ginger ale over half-gallon blocks of sherbet bought at the A & P. For years, The Friendly Twelve had been "sponsoring girls" in December at the end of their first semester of college. Next to their annual Red, White, and Blue Tea, which they hosted near the Fourth of July, and their Mother/Daughter Luncheon around Mother's Day, The Friendly Twelve were proudest of the annual Debutante's Ball they sponsored every year. Each December, the photographs of the latest group of debutantes appeared in the local newspapers along with information about what they were studying at their respective colleges.

Lacey and Sons photographed all the debs in my group. Tucked away at the end of a strip of businesses long since boarded up, Lacey's had hung on for years. Folks said the lone picture of Martin Luther King Jr. standing on an easel in the front window either brought luck to Mr. Lacey or warded off evildoers. No girl past puberty dared go to Lacey's by herself, because old man Lacey, who was most often on duty, had a habit of pinching her breasts or patting her behind. The Saturday after Thanksgiving, I went with Clara Oliver. We had not seen each other since September, when all of the college-bound graduates of Brighton High went to her going-away party and danced elbow to elbow in the blue-lit basement of her house on

Jaybird Road until the sun came up. That night, we drank punch spiked with Mogen-David wine, ate Ritz crackers slathered with pimiento cheese, and laughed nonstop when Clara changed her name. From that night on, she announced, she wanted to be called Clarissa. Clara was a country name she said, and she was headed for the city. Clara was the only one of our close-knit group to go so far away. "New York?" we marveled when she showed us her acceptance letter. Tuskegee, Montgomery, Talladega, Memphis, and Atlanta were as far as most of our eyes could see. But Clara was different, daring, and had set her sights on Barnard early on. Because you never knew what to expect from Clara, I was only partly shocked to see her wiry mass of hair when she met me at the door.

"Girl, what did you do to your hair?"

"It's an Afro."

"I know what it is, but are you gonna take your picture in it?"

"Yeah. What's wrong with it?"

"Nothing, I guess, but Miss Ravizee will have a hissy fit."

"Well, it can't be any worse than the one my mama threw when she met me at the airport. And she ain't let up yet. This morning she resorted to begging me to straighten my hair, just for the ceremony, 'just for one night, Clara.' She's mainly worried about her reputation as president of the PTA and what these old biddies will think."

"What did your daddy say?"

"Well, you know Daddy. With four women in this house—one of them Mama—he gave up having opinions long ago. All he said was, 'If you like it, it's all right by me.'"

Checking our names off an appointment book, Mr. Lacey ushered us into his large, dank studio.

"Who first?"

"I'll go," Clara answered.

"Take off your waist," he said in a voice that was part gargle and part growl. "You can leave your brassiere on." He handed her the black velvet drape and she ducked behind the curtain of the dressing room, coming out with cleavage showing and rhinestone earrings dangling almost to her shoulders.

"The other girls been wearing different ear bobs," said Mr. Lacey. "Something like hers," gesturing to the small pearl studs that Mother had given me for graduation.

"I'm gonna wear these," Clara stated flatly.

Later, as we waited to board the bus for Five Points West, Clara whispered, "I have a secret."

"What is it?"

"I'll tell you on the bus."

As the bus crept through the heavy holiday traffic, Clara reached into her bag and pulled out a round blue plastic box, flicking open the clasp to reveal a circle of pills like tiny yellow pebbles.

"Birth control."

"You're doing it?" I asked in disbelief, then brushed my fingers over START HERE, embossed above the clockwise point of the arrow.

"Yeah, everybody is. You haven't done it yet?"

"Lord, no. Mother would kill me." The hair I could deal with, but doing it, already? In three short months, Clara had become another person, broken free of the restrictive and contradictory sexual codes of our Southern upbringing. These codes required skill in the art of interpretation, of wrestling with ambiguities and reading between the lines. The "nice girls" of Pipe Shop, unlike their "fast" counterparts, wore starched white blouses and virgin pins and had all been raised to believe that men did not have sex with the women they planned to marry.

Of course, the codes did not provide for the possibility that some men wanted women not at all, they wanted men but lacked the courage to be bold, out loud, and brazen with it. I had heard many whispered rumors of athletes who lingered in the locker room, long after postgame showers and . . . But in the broad open daylight, they lockstepped with the other teen-aged boys and sipped Coca-Colas from a common glass with girls they groped and fondled in the backseats of compact cars. They boasted of "busting the cherry" or "getting the trim" of buxom cheerleaders and majorettes and putting hickies on their necks.

How could things be otherwise? This was Alabama in the 1960s. Who dared risk ending up like Cooper Abernathy, whose four brothers nearly beat the breath out of him? One by one they pummeled him almost to death when they came home and caught him sucking off another football player in their parents' bed.

That women might front off with men was utterly unheard of. That is, that they might also purchase the shell of normalcy, just like Naomi's mother did, occurred to few, if any, in Pipe Shop. Mr. Mitchell did not beat his wife when he found her with Miss Eloise Richardson, but he ran her off that very day, without allowing her to say good-bye to her six children, the eldest twelve years old. And when Miss Eloise ran away to find her, leaving her own children in the lurch, the folks in Pipe Shop never forgot about it or forgave her. Of course, grown-ups tried to hide the most salacious forms of scandal from children, but soon after this explosive news they temporarily abandoned caution and spoke openly of a scene that had rocked the neighborhood as nothing else in recent memory.

So there we were, knowing nothing of the range and variety of sexual expression, but we were certainly well tutored at the complicated dance of dalliance and flirtation, of loving expressed timidly and in code. Passion and sweaty petting held safely in check just before they overflowed to messiness.

Mother had loaned me her charge card to Parisian, where I found a simple white *peau de soie* dress—empire line with a scooped neck and capped sleeves. Because my dress was so plain, I went to Goldstein's fabric store and found a piece of silver sequined elastic that Mama handstitched to the bodice. Butler's Shoes had one pair of silver pumps left in my size, and I took Clara's dare and plunked down $2.50 for V-shaped rhinestone ornaments and matching silver stockings that sparkled through and through. The shoes still pinched a bit, but pinching was a small price to pay for being fly.

My escort to the Debutante's Ball was Winston Ringstaff. His mother, Carrie, surprised me with a pair of cameo earrings as a present. We all marched into the auditorium in our long white dresses, looking stiff and hugging our arms against the dampness of the auditorium, which doubled as a gym. Brown aluminum folding chairs were lined up in rows on either side of an aisle covered with lengths of white paper. The oak lectern was wrapped in a white sheet and pinned in front with a droopy red velveteen bow. Despite these ornamental touches, there was no mistaking that we were "coming out" in a gym, marching past scratched-up bleachers pushed against concrete salmon walls, the same bleachers that Tawanna Jones had nearly hit her head on when she fainted just months before in the drowsy heat of the Alabama afternoon.

It was May, just after lunch, and we seniors had gathered in the auditorium to rehearse for graduation. Mrs. Parnell had lined us up alphabetically and was walking slowly up and down the line, checking off names from a yellow sheet of paper. I noticed that her dress was hiked up in back. Mama had made other dresses for her, complaining that she always chose the wrong patterns for someone both swaybacked and hump-behinded, a dreadful combination for fitting. You had to keep nipping and tucking and adding inches to the back of the skirt so the hem could hang evenly all around.

Mrs. Parnell had just shouted "Marsha King" for the second time when Tawanna crumpled neatly in a faint just at Mrs. Parnell's swollen patent-leather feet. A flustered Mrs. Parnell flung her list and clipboard down and ordered us to stay in line while she tried to revive Tawanna. She race-walked back on the sides of her feet, trudging through the heavy doors with a wet cloth to sponge Tawanna's face and pellets of ammonia to hold beneath her nostrils.

By that afternoon, the whole school knew what Tawanna's closest friends had safely guarded for several weeks: She was pregnant. And, on the chance that anyone had missed the gossip, Mr. Quincey, the bow-tied, shiny-headed principal of Brighton High, spilled it for all to hear. The static that interrupted the drone of Mrs. Taylor's trigonometry lecture signaled an announcement from the principal's desk. Over the static's growl, Mr. Quincey blared, "There will be only one body per robe in the graduation line. I repeat, only one body per robe in the procession. If anybody is planning to squeeze two bodies in one robe, don't try it. Don't try it. You hear? You will be discovered and ejected from the line. There will be only one body per robe in the procession."

Tawanna looked straight ahead at the blackboard. I had long envied girls like her on those after-Christmas-vacation Monday mornings. They were majorettes and cheerleaders and homecoming queens who splayed their fingers on ink-blotted rustic desks carved with hearts and arrows—monuments to adolescent love—standing on dusty wrought-iron legs bolted to the floor. These popular girls dated muscle-bound athletes, sported their football jerseys, and "did it" for heart-shaped boxes of Whitman's samplers, Elgin watches, and double-yoked shimmering hearts of going-steady rings. The girls who got watches at Christmas often had babies by the start of the next school year, and the babies passed from mothers' wombs to grandmothers' arms, and the boy fathers disappeared. From time to time, they resurfaced with some trinket and a teasing promise that won them quickies in one-night cheap hotels or sometimes even in their mothers' living rooms. Although they complained about girls like me with whom they could only "sofa sit," these boys obeyed community custom and observed the Sunday evening ritual visits nonetheless. They squirmed on plastic couches in tiny living rooms where "whatnots" stared from mantels and cluttered the shelves of rickety étagères. For these were the girls they had to marry—eventually. The ones who would fill their houses with bric-a-brac and sullen little children who would shatter the miniature cups and saucers from the New York World's Fair and demolish the snow globes with the Washington Monument trapped inside.

With Mr. Quincey's innuendos ringing in her ear, Tawanna asked to be excused. I now felt sorry for her. She had ignored the lesson pounded into all our heads: "Don't let the boys trick you into the family way. If they want you, they'll wait." Or "Don't listen to that old line about, 'Prove your love for me.'" Of course, we practiced the sixties version of "safe sex": sweaty conversation on the phone and grinding in the basement. But the grinding had to stay within the precincts of the basement, and even then, we had to listen out for parents, just above our heads, who listened out themselves for any signs of trespass down below. Tawanna must have left the basement, let the rivulets of sweat flow in unprotected places, let the lubrication of excitement spill to overflowing in her pants. For this, she would be denied the pride and satisfactions of ceremony: the procession through the gate onto the football field, the march across the stage to the strains of "Pomp and Circumstance," the firm grip of Mr. Quincey's handshake as family members cheered to the stately sound of their loved ones' names, the announcement of scholarships, the award of medals, and, finally, two-hundred sixteen gray mortarboards, tossed in the open air as Mr. Quincey shouted through the microphone: "I now pronounce you members of the class of 1968."

Elbowing me in the side, Clara whispered, "You're next," and I tottered toward my escort as Mrs. Ravizee called my name again. "Testing. Can you hear me," she asked while tapping the microphone, amplifying the rustling paper on which her notes were scribbled. When we had all been introduced and promenaded down the middle of the hardwood floor to stand side by side, just like the contestants in a beauty pageant, Mrs. Ravizee beamed to the audience. "Aren't they lovely? Aren't our girls just positively lovely?" Turning to compliment us on our achievements and to encourage us to press forward in faith, Mrs. Ravizee stepped away from the podium, and debutantes and escorts began the dance.

The remainder of this evening is now a blur to me, except for Mother's accident. Her Kodak Instamatic had been blinding me all evening. *Click. Click. Click. Click.* Each time the ice blue flash cube made four rhythmic revolutions on its axis, Mother reached into her silk drawstring bag and hurriedly plopped another on its notch. Mysteriously, as she tried to snap a picture of me dancing with my partner, the flash cube ejected, popping her smack-dab in the middle of her forehead. It left a visible burn, still slightly noticeable even after months of cocoa butter applications.

I interpreted the whole incident as a sign from God that Mother had taken her uppercrust pretensions a bit too far, had strained too hard to put her Sumter County origins behind her, enlisting me, against my will, in the process. I was fed up with hearing her say, "You know, you can make something of yourself. You can go far, if you don't let the boys fool you.

And you know, once they spoil you, they don't want you. I'm pinning all my hopes on you now. I'll help you make something of yourself; just don't disappoint me."

Mother drummed this message into my ear every time I saw her, and I knew, beyond a shadow of a doubt, just what she meant: DON'T GET PREGNANT. Now out of easy reach in college, with temptations all around, I received weekly letters from Mother reminding me not to stray. It was mainly from Mother that I received the few letters stacked aslant in the narrow brass mailbox with combination locks. Engraved within the postal cancellation circle was a rotating arc of cities and states, but the return address was always the same: Viola G. Williams/1404 Ninth Avenue/Bessemer, Alabama.

She folded ten-dollar bills and books of stamps inside several sheets of half-size letter paper, white with thin blue lines. Always brief, her notes written in distinctive Palmer loops, opened with the epistolary trademarks of her generation: "Just a few lines to let you hear from me. How are you? Fine, I hope." Then came the pep talk: "I hope you're studying hard, because what you get in your head, nobody can take away from you." There would be a few more lines of news about where she had been and where she was headed next. And then that signature closing line, dropping like a bomb in the middle of the page, right at the end of the letter: "Be good. Remember you can make something of yourself if you don't lose your determination. Just step high and stay on the path."

So far so good. I had not veered. Had made it all the way through high school, then through the first semester of college without getting pregnant. There I stood with "Bessemer's Finest Young Women." The ceremony over and introductions made, the crowd flowed into an adjoining classroom and lined up for the cranberry punch brimming from Mother's cut-glass bowl and the finger sandwiches and pink-iced petit fours. Winston and I had earlier decided to see the late show of *Valley of the Dolls*. Mother pulled me aside and asked if I had money for a taxi, if I should need one. I didn't, so she slipped a ten-dollar bill inside the pocket of my gray chesterfield. Then tugging gently on the strap in back, she whispered, "Remember what I told you."

Mama had said little throughout the evening; in fact, had smoldered silently ever since Mother picked us up at home and pulled the mink tails from a Parisian shopping bag. She handed the collar to Mama, who looked contemptuously at the freeze-dried face of the little animal that had frightened me so much as a child.

"What am I supposed to do with this, Miss Viola?"

"I thought you might like to wear it for the evening; just throw it over your coat."

Mama stood awkwardly in the milling crowd, holding the little mink tails in her hand. "You-all be careful," she said to me. "Don't stay out too late." I left her and Mother standing side by side, observing detente, and climbed into the car with Winston and his mother. We dropped her off at home and sped back up the Bessemer Super Highway to the Midfield Theater. He bought our tickets and ushered me into the darkness of the theater.

Our routine was always the same. Whenever we sat alone together, away from supervising eyes, it always took a while for us to touch, and then, always and only at Winston's initiation. I would sit, waiting impatiently for him to reach for me. That night I kept shifting in my seat and eventually he reached for my hand. We petted until he whispered, "Let's go outside." And we left in the middle of the movie and walked slowly to the car. When he reached for me, I drew back. "We can't do it here," I said.

He gunned the motor and headed back down the Bessemer Super Highway.

"Where are we going?"

"To my house."

"To your house? We can't go to your house."

"Don't worry. My folks are gone to bed."

He looked at the dashboard clock. "Granny and Daddy have been asleep since eight o'clock, and I know my mother went to bed as soon as we dropped her off."

"I don't care; I'm not going to your house."

He sighed loudly and turned on the radio, frantically twiddling the dial until he found some top-twenty selection and began to sing along. Right then I knew I didn't want to do it, but I didn't have the courage to tell him so. Staring across the median into the lights of oncoming cars, I tried to convince myself that this was the thing to do. I was way behind all the other girls. But in his own mother's house?

I had often gone to their house in Cairo Village, but mainly after school to practice typing on his mother's electric Smith-Corona. I was trying to increase my speed to eighty words per minute, hoping for a summer secretarial job. Afterward I often stayed for dinner. The four of us—Winston, Granny, his grandmother, and his mother—gathered around the kitchen table and near the end of dinner, his father arrived, exhausted from towing cars and pumping gas all day. "I'm working to give Winston a start in life," he would say, but as the college acceptances rolled in, it finally dawned on him that Winston had no interest in inheriting Ringstaff's Service and Towing. He was going to Morehouse to study political science.

With help from his wife's teacher's salary from Oak Grove Elementary, Mr. Ringstaff's service station had financed their split-level house in Cairo Village, a new subdivision in Roosevelt, far out the Bessemer Super Highway, almost to Mrs. Carroll's house in Midfield, where I had ironed those damask napkins all day long. The dream come true of A. G. Gaston, the hotel magnate and black entrepreneur, Cairo Village was considered prime residential property for the better class of blacks. Opposite a tiny park, where Winston and I sometimes went for walks, the imposing house dominated the far end of a cul-de-sac. After my first visit there, I came home and said excitedly, "Daddy, buy us a house in Cairo Village."

"One day," he answered, and changed the subject.

Winston broke the silence with lightsome reassurances. "Don't worry. I'll take care of you. I wouldn't let anything happen to you. I have protection." We rounded the curve in front of the school and drove into the lot, now desolate of all the cars that had ferried Bessemer's finest to the debutante's ball. We parked at the far edge, away from the muted amber orb of light. "Let's get in the back," he said, as he pulled me to him. And without a word I climbed into the cramped backseat of the Falcon and lay down. He climbed on top and muttered more reassurances.

"Where's the rubber?"

"It's all right. Don't worry. It's all right," he pleaded. "I'll come out."

I pushed at his chest and he raised up. "Why?"

"I can't let you get me pregnant. Mother will kill me."

'Termination

The campus physician made the rounds to each of the women's dorms (he never went to the men's) at the beginning of every year to lecture us on the importance of birth control. Of course, the lecture, like everything else I'd already heard about sex, was delivered in code. "Now you can get pregnant," Mama had said awkwardly as she handed me a box of Kotex and a brand-new elastic sanitary belt that reminded me of a slingshot. That's all she said when I got my period the spring I turned fifteen. When I paused, searching her face for the information about pregnancy I assumed was sure to follow, she added, "If you miss your period, that's the sign that you're pregnant, so remember to keep your dress down and your pocketbook closed." I swallowed two aspirin while staring out the kitchen window, then withdrew to my bed with a booklet on reproduction that the nurse had handed out in school; actually, it was a thin pamphlet with pastel drawings of a woman's pelvis: pale pink ovaries and lavender fallopian tubes.

The campus doctor sprinkled his dorm lectures not with references to pocketbooks that needed closing, but to barn doors closed too late, his metaphor for coitus interruptus, or as we used to put it, "coming out." "This method of birth control," he said, "is just like closing the barn door after the horse is out." Warming to the snickers he had coaxed from all of us who packed the "receiving room" of Rockefeller Hall, he laughed too, closing with the crowning witticism I was to hear from him over the next three years: "And for all of you who rely on that most favored method of birth control, let me make it absolutely clear: Hope is zero percent fool-proof." I had certainly proved him right on that count. Timidly suggesting that my new college boyfriend, Richard, use a condom, I relented when he complained that it wouldn't feel the same. He would come out in time. And time after time, I hoped he would. He never did, and I did not protest, fearful that he would return to the homecoming queen, who reminded me of all the high school majorettes who got the sweetheart rings.

I had spent the whole first semester of college struggling to make it to 8:30 biology classes, to make new friends, finally finding my niche with a group of four other Southern firstborn women who lived on the second and third floors of Rockefeller Hall. We walked together every day to Tompkins, the dining hall, stopping to tease Tom Joyner, the campus disc jockey, who sat inside a glass booth and spun the latest forty-fives. We jerked and wiggled our bodies as we inched through the serpentine line to reach the steam-clouded stalls and pointed again to turkey fricassee or cutlets of mystery meat. Legend had it that the cutlets were ground pigeons plucked from the huge flock that swarmed around Tompkins Hall. On Friday and Saturday nights, we skipped the dining hall and ordered fried chicken instead, from Thomas Reed's Chicken Coop.

Often of an evening, with orders for the others, Ginny Hitchcock or Joan Floyd and I would walk down Old Montgomery Road to the Coop, jeans pulled over pajamas, and scarves covering the pink sponge rollers in our hair. Back in the dorm, we played dirty Hearts atop Ginny Hitchcock's steamer trunk until the wee, wee hours of the morning. By the end of first semester, we had all gained several pounds from this late-night orgiastic feasting on chicken and french fries and vowed to break the ritual at the very start of the new year.

Resolution still intact, I scouted around for alternatives to fill the former gaps of weekend nights. Winston had stopped writing from Texas, because I had failed to "prove my love for him." That is, I had not gone all the way. Worse, I had led him to believe I would, as a Christmas present to him. His last letter indicated, in no uncertain terms, that "unless and until you are willing to prove your love for me, it's best for us to start seeing other people." With no prospects in sight, I became a basketball junkie, which is how I met Richard Hancock, the near-seven-foot center from Detroit.

He fell in step with Gwen Rigby and me as we headed back to Rockefeller Hall from a game. Tuskegee had won, and Richard was the leading scorer. So engrossed were we in our conversation that we did not hear his footsteps, muffled by pine needles strewn all along the unlit path that wound away from Logan Hall. "How did you enjoy the game?" he asked in that cocky way of his, as he approached us from behind. I jumped and said, "I didn't hear you coming."

There he was, the man who figured almost nightly in my diary, standing in the flesh, the thick white towel ringing his neck, forming a halo in the darkness.

"I been walking behind you-all since Logan Hall, but you so busy yakking and jabbering, it's no wonder you couldn't hear me."

Gwen laughed and called him "Hard-hearted Hancock," the name he got for wearing such a mean and fearless scowl at basketball, a face made still more scary by his beady, bloodshot eyes. I did not say too much that night, not even when Gwen left us to play Ping-Pong in the student union, and Richard walked on with me to my dorm. Underneath the lamp above the door at Rockefeller, he said good night and hoisted the red duffel bag onto his shoulder, the gold-embroidered Tuskegee tiger clawing at the sides. "You played a good game," I said, and rushed inside to join the late-night card game and to boast that Richard Hancock had walked me home. "No shit."

When the team made it to the SIAC finals one month later, I bought a ticket to the tournament and showed up in a pair of green velour hot pants and knee-high boots and watched the team from third-row center, near the court. They lost the championship, and I seized upon the idea of writing a personal letter to every member of the team. On the deckle-edged blue vellum paper that Mother had given me for Christmas, I praised the rebounding skills of this one, the passing skills of that one, and the dribbling of another. For Richard I reserved the most heaping praise for shooting, since he had scored a record thirty-two points. It turned out that he was the only one of the team who answered my letter, hand-delivering it to Rockefeller Hall.

He was glad to see me again and couldn't quite believe I was the kind to write letters to a whole basketball team. I seemed so shy. "That's why I write," I said. That's how it began—with the letter, and quietly, before I realized it had happened. We started meeting on the side of the George Washington Carver Museum. He always waited for me on the top step and, together, we descended to the building set in a hollow several feet below street level. I was still stuck in the groove of heavy petting, then retreat, but, after just a few meetings, Richard echoed Winston's words: There were many girls who'd give him more, who had already. He had no time for teasers. I gave in the very night he ran back up the steps, leaving me with the parting shot of insult, "Call me when you get tired of acting like a goody-goody little churchgoing girl from 'Bama." "Don't go," I said, and there, at the Carver Museum, while steadying myself against a pebbled concrete ledge, I first had sex, hidden behind the wall of hemlock trees whose ominous branches reached out to touch our shoulders. His spasms ended, we walked together in silence until we reached the front of the dormitory. The lights in the foyer were brightly lit and people milled about the office. I lingered on the steps, wanting urgently to wipe away the glob of semen wet between my legs, yet not wanting to answer any questions about my "date."

*　　　*　　　*

"What was the date of your last period?" the doctor asked. Richard had borrowed a teammate's car and driven to Opelika, where, he explained, we would not run the risk of having anybody see us. I took the pocket calendar from my purse and showed the doctor the date. It was circled in red. For almost nine weeks I had counted and recounted the days of the calendar, cramming the tiny blocks with points of red and blue and green. "Fill this up with urine and give it to the nurse. When you finish, have a seat in the waiting room." I joined Richard there, where he sat flipping through *Sports Illustrated.*

"The urine sample was positive. Let's see how far along you are." The white paper rustled as he patted the edge of the examining table and asked me to remove my underwear. The examination finished, he said, without even casting a glance my way, "You can get dressed now," and pulling off the rubber gloves, he opened the door and beckoned for Richard.

His starched white lab-coated back to me, the rotund doctor faced Richard and said, "She's almost four months gone." Not a word did he say to me, but after the space of a gasp, I spoke up:

"I'm not four months pregnant. I can't be."

"Young lady, I've been delivering babies for thirty years. Trust me."

In the car, Richard let me know that I was on my own. I had tried to trick him, he said, but it had blown up in my face. If I thought he was going to marry me to take care of another man's baby, I had another think coming. Only later did I learn that the portly doctor from Opelika had used the ruse of "certain" dates to help many an athlete evade his responsibilities to a pregnant student.

In this era before *Roe* v. *Wade,* girls in dormitories all around the campus kept underground lists of abortionists. After many false starts and missed connections, making up my mind and changing it again, I settled on one, a midwife in Phenix City, Alabama. I could have gone to a woman who lived in the projects right outside the Tuskegee city line, but I was afraid someone might recognize me.

The woman was very tentative on the phone and gave me strict instructions: I had to come alone. I was to take the 12:30 bus from Tuskegee that arrived in Columbus, Georgia, at 1:30. Her son, who would be wearing a green fishing hat and a brown corduroy jacket, would meet me at the station and then drive me to her house on the outskirts of Phenix City, a short jump across the river from Columbus.

It took me a few minutes to pick her son out of the knot of people standing outside the station. His hat was really slate gray, not green, and he looked much older than I had imagined. "Are you Readus?" He nodded yes.

The faded yellow Buick rattled over winding country back roads still tracked from recent rain. Although it was unusually chilly for the last week of March, the sky that day was bright. I was glad I saw no hint of rain, for I had images of this rickety car, with its wire hanger for an antenna, rutted in the mud or, worse, the road itself transformed into one long wading pool.

Readus drove without a word, slowly, deliberately, looking straight ahead. As he steered the car around craters in the road, I fought the rising fear of what lay ahead by concentrating on the streaking countryside—the blackened timber, the roadside stores, the shrunken tar-paper shacks plopped down in the middle of rolling fields, white sheets and feed-sack dresses pinned on clotheslines swaying in the wind.

As soon as Readus stopped the car just on the side of the shotgun house, my misgivings seized me and the morning coffee refluxed in my throat. I choked it down, but it rose up again as soon as I stepped into the house, which smelled of cold cooking grease and camphor. Gesturing to a large velour recliner pushed against the papered wall, Readus offered me a seat, then headed toward the back. I surveyed the room, which was dimly lit and spare of furnishings—a cold stove, a green plaid couch with matching chair, a floor-model television, crumpled balls of tinfoil on the rabbit-eared antennas, a bowl of plastic fruit on a side table. And above the mantel, in a dusty frame, a triptych of John and Robert Kennedy and Martin Luther King Jr.

A few more minutes passed before she limped into the room in lace-up Hush Puppies and said, "Come on back here." I don't know why, but I reached for my umbrella. "Leave your parasol in here." I could not meet her eye to eye; she looked too much like women in my neighborhood back in Pipe Shop. Grandmothers they were, not the ones like Mother, but like Miss Hattie and Grandma Edie, the ones who wore thick brown cotton stockings, sat and rocked on porches, went to midweek prayer meeting, and dipped Garrett snuff from tins nestled in their apron pockets. Whenever I try to conjure up an image of the midwife, I can only see the washed-out housedress that she wore and the two gray braids like drooping tusks on either side of her head.

I followed her back to a tiny box of a room where a brown metal chifforobe was opened to reveal dingy sheets and towels. A dingy floral bedsheet suspended from an overhead bar formed a makeshift screen around the corner cot, propped on one side with a mail-order catalogue. She asked for the three hundred dollars right up front and I counted out into her hands the crisp twenty-dollar bills borrowed from one of my teachers.

"I don't need you to take off all your clothes, just your panties and your underskirt." I did as I was told and stood barefooted, shivering on the cold and gritty linoleum, hugging the garments to my chest. Taking them from my hand, she shoved them underneath the wooden bedside table with a kerosene lamp on top. Then, latching the door, she pulled the plastic window shade, and next the string that lit the naked lightbulb dangling from the ceiling.

From the bed, I watched her remove plastic tubing and other supplies from a bag inside the dresser drawer. First I lay there on the musty sheet, listening to her hum an unfamiliar tune, then terror seized me once again. I raised up on my elbows, prepared to change my mind, I thought, then remembered Mother's "be goods" and lay back down again. In the middle of a bar, the humming ceased and she stood beside the bed to prepare me for what would happen "way over in the evening": labor pains and blood and then the baby. Like Readus, she was taciturn, saving her words for only what seemed absolutely necessary. I wanted her to grip my hand, just like husbands grip the hands of wives in childbirth scenes in movies, but she didn't. She squatted down on a three-legged stool and resumed the dirge-like tune.

"Scoot down," she said, then pushed my skirt around my hips and pried my legs wide open.

"Don't go closing your legs now. You shoulda closed 'em long 'fore now." I had heard this caustic language all my life, spewing from the mouth of every older woman that I knew.

An hour passed, maybe two. I don't remember. I stepped back into my panties, my stockings, my slip, and followed the humming midwife to the front door. She whispered, "Remember, don't go making mention of my name to nobody or I could get in a whole heap of trouble and, if that happen, y'all girls over at that college will be in a sho-nuff fix." I nodded my head and mumbled, "Yes, ma'am."

Calling to Readus, who was napping on the couch, the woman said, "She ready." He pulled on his scuffed-up brogans and lifted his coat and hat from the recliner. The front door banged behind him and I soon heard the motor gunning. "I don't reckon you'll have no trouble, 'cause you ain't but two months gone, but if something go wrong, go on over there to John Andrew Hospital and they'll take care of you." I tiptoed down the steps to the waiting car parked just outside the doorway.

Days later, the infection set in—fever, chills, blood—and I knew I had to go to the hospital. Checking me right in, the doctor gave me the bare facts, fastening on me a candid look that said, "How could you?" but a touch that said, "I understand." He had to do a D&C, but because I was under twenty-one, he needed my parents' permission. Dying would be easier, I thought. He cut a deal with me, explaining that this was a simple procedure, and I could explain it to my parents as such. They could then send a telegram of authorization. But if they called to ask him any questions, he was legally bound to answer them.

I plodded to the phone booth at the end of the hospital corridor, closing the narrow folding door behind me as the light flickered on inside. Dropping the dime into the slot, I placed the collect call and struck up my familiar banter when Mama accepted the charges. I don't know now what I told her, but I do remember hearing fear, motherly concern, and intuition rising in her voice.

"I'm taking the bus down there in the morning," she insisted.

"But, Mama, that's not necessary." I began to sweat inside the telephone booth as she reiterated her plan to come by bus tomorrow. Daddy could pick her up on the weekend if Mother had improved.

"What's wrong with Mother?"

"She had a stroke."

"When?"

"Almost a week ago."

"What? I don't believe it. I just got a letter from her last week. Where was she?"

"She was at home."

"But I thought she was on a job in Mobile."

"Yeah, that's where she was, but she had come back home. Hadn't been back from down there much more than an hour when she had the stroke. Mr. Fred said they were just sitting at the kitchen table talking when she slumped over, right there. She was still in her uniform, hadn't even taken off her shoes and stockings."

"Why didn't anybody call me?"

"We didn't want to worry you before we knew anything. Plus, we knew you would be coming home anyway for Easter."

"But Easter's almost a month away."

I recovered my wits and persuaded her that she should stay at home with Mother. A telegram was all the doctor needed. This was a routine procedure that would probably rid me of the awful cramps that confined me monthly to the bed. That's where we left it. I hung up the phone and stumbled out of the booth.

I couldn't believe it. Just last week—the very week I'd scheduled the abortion—I'd received another of Mother's famous "be good," "stay-on-the-course" letters, along with a clipping from the *Birmingham World* about the Debutante's Ball. It was a newsy letter, longer I think than any she had ever written. She was on her way to Mobile and wrote that the Bessemer Board of Education had finally granted Reggie's petition to be transferred back to Brighton High from W. A. Bell, where he could get a decent education from teachers who were competent and caring. "These people are bound and determined to ruin black children's education," she had written, but, "Thank God, Reggie is a fighter." The letter seemed hurriedly written, and some words were, uncharacteristically, illegible. It took me a few seconds to puzzle out "determination," a word that cropped up in all her letters to me. "Never lose your determination," she had written, but the "de" of "determination" was blurred, and so it looked like "'termination." But even without the prefix, I knew that it could be no other word.

She enclosed a book of stamps, a ten-dollar bill, and the clipping of the Debutante's Ball:

> *I've been meaning to send you this since the first of the year, but it's just been first one thing and then another. You look so nice in the picture. Mrs. Berger says you've grown up to be a lovely young lady. I haven't had a chance to get the pictures developed from the ceremony, but will send you some as soon as I do. I talked to Papa yesterday and he sends his love to you. He says look out for a lemon pound cake in the mail next week. Well, let me bring these few lines to a close. Just stay on the path and keep on making us proud. I'll see you Easter Sunday. With all my Love, Mother.*

The story filled two narrow columns.

18 DEBS MAKE FORMAL BOW TO SOCIETY

They created a perfect picture of winter beauty in floor-length dresses of winter white and the traditional single strand of pearls. Geraldine Lancaster, the queen of this year's group, wore a headpiece of tulle and silk taffeta, ornamented with iridescent sequins. Miss Clara Oliver and Sonya Gamble lighted the eighteen candles, which cast a soft glow on the decorative background of red poinsettias.

Mistress of ceremonies, Mrs. Mable Ravizee, presented the parents of the debs, who were themselves visions of grace and dignity as they took their places in the festive hall.

It was classic reporting for the *Birmingham World.* All the language and the frippery of high society for a ceremony in a gymnasium, the orange basketball hoop high above Miss Ravizee's head.

> *Presiding at the refreshment table were Mesdames Sylvie Haynes and Mahalia Vaughn. The table was covered with white tulle over a red satin underskirt, with a centerpiece of red and white chrysanthemums resting on a blanket of ferns and magnolia leaves. Completing the picture was a large cut-glass punch bowl brimming with cranberry juice. Approximately 150 guests enjoyed the occasion.*

"Mesdames?" I scanned the rest, shaking my head and clucking as I read the last paragraph:

> *Mrs. Mable Ravizee, debutante committee chairman and mistress of ceremonies for the occasion, expressed hope that the presentation of the debs will serve as an inspiration to other young girls to be morally and spiritually above reproach, so that they too may be presented to the Bessemer social world as young women representative of the best our city has to offer.*

After the Stroke

When you coming home?" Papa asked when I made my weekly call to check on Mother's progress. Six weeks had passed and I was still hiding out in Tuskegee, dodging Mama's questions and burning accusations.

"I have finally found you out. Thought you had me fooled, didn't you? Walking around like butter wouldn't melt in your mouth."

The insurance company had refused the claim and the hospital bill was left unpaid; they did not cover "that" procedure, Mama said. She couldn't bring herself to say "abortion." Shocked, I cradled the phone, then staggered back down the corridor, in the dawn of Sunday morning.

After that conversation, hiding seemed my only option, but when Papa, who seldom asked for anything, ended our conversation with, "Come home soon. Mother wants to see you," I knew I had to go. I boarded the first bus out the next morning, calling Papa from the station to say I was on my way. It was the first time I had been to the Greyhound station since that Wednesday in March when I had departed for Columbus, Georgia, in a bid to stay on the course that Mother had set for me.

A taxi dropped me off in front of 1404 Ninth Avenue, and I was shocked at what I saw. A blunt negation of its former self, the house looked so dejected. It had been hastily reconstructed to meet the greedy claims of illness: the strips of wood on the slanted ramp still showed the blue-crayoned markings of Fountain's lumberyard; the threshold had been widened to make the wheelchair's passage through the door a little easier. The huge terra-cotta pots, minus the customary white impatiens, were shoved into a corner of the porch.

I let myself into the empty house and walked through to the kitchen, where I found a note from Papa propped against a large carton of Barber's milk, left open on the kitchen table. They were gone to Mother's therapy session and would be back by three o'clock. A plastic tray was littered with balls of half-chewed food, and a crooknecked straw floated in a glass of milk.

Knowing how independent Mother was, Papa had enrolled her in the Spain Rehabilitation Center soon after her release from the hospital. The doctors gave him little reason to hope; it was doubtful that she would ever walk again. What did they know? The night of the stroke they had only given her a week to live, but Papa had refused their prognosis, reasoning that if Mother could vault herself out of Sumter County, Alabama, in 1922, when she was barely fourteen years old, and then pilot herself through the worst economic crisis in American history, then she could surely learn to walk again.

I opened the refrigerator, pushed aside jars of Gerber's baby food, and poured myself a drink of water. Glass in hand, I roamed every square inch of the house. In the dining room, the crystal punch bowl was still poised atop the credenza. It was overflowing with get-well greetings and cards from florists far and wide, some still pinned to red and yellow ribbons. I relived the many times I had lowered this leaden bowl to the center of the table, bedecked in crisp white damask, and poured ginger ale over blocks of lime sherbet, exhilarated by the clouds of froth the bubbles made. The glass-doored corner china cabinet was still stacked from top to bottom with plates and saucers, cups and bowls, monogrammed glasses, and covered dishes painted with idyllic scenes of corseted white women in hooped dresses, holding parasols by the edge of a pond.

Mother's room was transformed beyond all recognition. The shades were tightly drawn, and a portable john, its plastic seat a dingy eyesore, crowded the corner of the room where the bowfront dresser stood. Out of its drawers had once spilled camisoles, silky lace-edged slips, and long satiny nightgowns with spaghetti straps. Atop the dresser, the clear crystal bottles of sweet perfume that had long reflected in the mirrored tray had surrendered their place to plastic bottles of pills. Lysol could only faintly mask the nauseating smell of sickness.

Unable to bear the scene inside the house, or memory's avalanche, I stepped outside to watch the passing cars and transfer trucks speeding up and down the Bessemer Super Highway, south toward Tuscaloosa and north toward Birmingham. When two hours ticked away and Mother and Papa still had not returned, I thought a walk would calm my restlessness. Facing the rushing traffic, I strolled up the highway, passing Macedonia, now cheek by jowl with junk-food joints, pawnshops, and one used-car lot after another. For a moment, I wished that I had the means to sashay onto a lot and plunk down cash money for one of these white-sidewalled cars waxed as glossy as a new prosthesis. Then, I would drive and drive, toward no particular destination, just a place where no one could ever find me.

At the foot of the Bessemer Super Highway bridge, I halted in my tracks. Ten years had passed since the dead girl's body lay hard by where I was standing, and when the terror that scene induced bubbled right back to the surface, I turned on my heels and headed south again. As I neared the house, I could see the canary yellow Chevrolet that replaced the blue station wagon that had been Mother's car for many years.

Once inside, I followed the sound of Papa's cooing and prattling to the bedroom. Reaching the threshold, I heard him say, "It's all right, Miss Vi; you don't have to go back there if you don't want to."

"Back where?" I asked, leaning down to hug her, feeling her pulse beat, the sharpness of her bones through the thin batiste nightgown. Mother mumbled my name over and over again and "I'm so glad to see you," but all the words were garbled, like a toddler's first efforts at speech.

"To Spain," Papa translated. Mother's gown gaped open at the neck, and I could see her flesh sagging on the cartilage of her throat. Even her chin cupped downward like a pointless pelican's bill. For the next few minutes, I couldn't speak as I adjusted my eyes to the astonishing speed of her deterioration. I had seen her last on New Year's Day, just after the Debutante's Ball, rushing about the house, snapping pictures, even at age sixty-two, still in the trim and vibrant form I'd always known. Mother had always seemed ageless, changeless, immune to the ravages of time, easily mistaken for a woman twenty years her junior. There had been no sprinkling of gray strands around the temples, no crescent-shaped pockets of flesh just below the kneecap, no bladder that opened when pepper forced a sneeze, no bunions to misshape the high, elegant arch of her narrow feet or rheumatism to knot her fingers, no liver spots to mar her lineless face. Time had chosen not to exact its toll on Mother bit by bit, but to snatch it, harshly, all at once, without the courtesy of preamble, demanding payment in just a few short months for what it had deferred for years.

The telephone gave me a few more minutes to collect myself. It was the pastor coming for a visit. Mother wanted a bath, so I volunteered to run the water, something I'd done ever since I was a girl. When again I failed to understand her slurring speech, Papa said, "She says don't forget her bath salts; they're on top of the commode." There, next to the displaced bottles of perfume, in a square, wide-mouthed jar, were the coral-colored bath salts Mother had ordered from Wisconsin for as long as I could remember. The salts were packed in floral boxes, which she saved for me to store the various odds and ends I habitually hoarded as a child. In the old-time way, I poured two scoops into the water and lowered my face closer to the rising steam. "Steam works wonders on a woman's skin," Mother used to say.

I called out, "Water's ready." In his new falsetto, Papa was still baby-talking and sweethearting Mother. It was annoying; I wanted him to stop. She was not a baby. He lifted her gently from the bed, cradling her in his arms just before lowering her shriveling frame into the wheelchair and rolling toward the bathroom. I ran the iron quickly over the clean night-gown and bed jacket I had found in the drawer and carried them to the bathroom. There, in the doorway, I stood still and watched as Papa, who seemed oblivious to my presence, worshipfully handled Mother's body like it was some icon in a sacred rite. He propped her disfigured body on the lid of the toilet seat while he dried her off, gently kneading her neck, her shoulders, then the breasts that held on to a little firmness. Slowly squirting the milky lotion in his palms, he smoothed it first on the left hand, the one the stroke had mutilated and twisted inward toward her side, and one by one, he gently caressed the formerly elegant fingers. Then he kneeled down on the floor and lotioned her spindly arms and legs. Feeling that I was intruding on a very private ritual, I left the room.

Papa had probably seen and touched more of Mother's body these last two months than he had during the entirety of their twenty-five-year marriage. She had always seemed to shun the touch of his thick, blunt fingers, the fingers I see whenever I taste a slice of lemon pound cake.

He greases, then flours, the bundt pan. Then with his naked fingers, he creams the butter and sugar. Now he heats the eggs. The fork tinkles against the speckled bowl. Then he sifts the flour and the baking powder and folds them in. It seems that hours pass before he shouts, "Gina, Miss Priss, you can come lick the bowl."

When the semester ended a few weeks later, I decided to move to 1404 to help Papa with the exhausting job of caring for Mother. Besides, I could not go home. Mama and I hadn't spoken since that early-morning conversation, in which I neither admitted nor denied having had an abortion. I dreaded yet another confrontation, although there were certainly many times that summer, before we patched things up, that I actually began to feel that Mama's wrath might be more bearable than watching Mother's slow decline.

The summer stretched into an endless pack of days of suffering Auntee's histrionics, lifting Mother's dead weight, chopping up her food into bite-sized pieces, and spooning it into her churned-up mouth. All this took on a rhythm ruptured only by the telephone, which, for fleeting moments, animated Mother's listless face. Former clients, who had not heard about the stroke, would call to see when she might have a break in her schedule. Either I or Papa or Auntee would whisper to the party at the other end that Mother would not be working again. I'll never know whether she actually heard us or simply intuited from the lowered pitch of the voice, a twitching gesture, a drooping shoulder, or the tilt of the head, but, as we talked, she would motion desperately for the phone, waving her good arm in the air, howling between struggling to speak her garbled words—"Tell Mrs. Berger I'm coming back next month." Always next month. I vividly remember one morning when I took the call from Mrs. Berger and was too slow in passing the phone to Mother. She seized the silver bell in easy reach of her good side and clanged it for dear life. The cacophony of the bell, the conversation, the television's din of Lucille Ball as the Vita-Mita Vegamin Girl, were at once deeply comic and exquisitely sad.

If Mother couldn't go back to work, then she would not lie still. Long accustomed to gallivanting hither and yon, she insisted on a daily outing in the car, following their morning rituals—bath, breakfast, and reruns of *I Love Lucy*. After buckling her into the front seat, collapsing the wheelchair, and loading it in the trunk, Papa often had to lean against the car to catch his breath. Witnessing this day after day, I feared he too would soon collapse. But never complaining about his own fatigue, Papa cheerfully ferried Mother to a rotating group of friends and relatives before wending their way home again.

Neighbors and church members had told him that all this go-go-going, especially in the heat, was too dangerous, and besides, it prevented Mother from facing the brutal fact that her going days were done. Spurning all such suggestions, Papa kept his visits to the meddlesome few and far between, and rationalized that they were just glad to see Mother so humbled. The morning outings seemed a small price to pay for a small dose of pleasure for Mother.

One afternoon, I changed the linen on her bed as Papa commenced the ritual of dressing Mother—slipping on her stockings and moccasins, powdering her face. And what did she want to wear today? Shalimar, Arpège, or L'Air du Temps? Then he squirted the same behind her ears, and gently stroked her neck. Having just come back inside from watering Mother's roses, withering in record-high heat, I was determined that they should stay home that day.

"Papa, do you know it's ninety-eight degrees outside?"

"What of it?" He resumed his low whistle of some hymn and kept right on dressing Mother.

"Papa, it's entirely too hot for you and Mother to be traipsing around from house to house."

When he did not respond, I stepped up the pressure, letting fly my fear that, if they persisted in this maddening pace, they would both end up in wheelchairs. Papa was a man who measured his words as carefully as he did the flour and sugar that went into his lemon pound cakes. But that day, he hurled words back at me faster and more hurtful and perplexing than any I had ever heard him utter.

"Are you jealous, because you don't have anybody loving you the way I love Miss Vi?" I still can't decide which was worse: the words themselves or the shocking fact that they had come from Papa's mouth. From the man whose love I had never doubted, whose love I never had to strain to get. I could call him anytime there was a crisis at home on Eighteenth Street, and say, "Papa, come and get me, quick," and he would answer, "I'll be there directly." And he would be.

When he noticed my play-at-teaching sessions, when I was still quite young, he had laughed and encouraged me. He helped me set up my first mock class in Mother's backyard, dragging chairs from the kitchen and unfolding the tin-top TV tables. He even made the Kool-Aid that I used to bribe the children in the neighborhood to sit as I paraded around the yard, aping the mannerisms of Miss Foster, who was still my favorite teacher. Mother had given me a subscription to the *Weekly Reader,* and for long stretches of summer days, I would stand there, out in front of my pupils, reading to them from its columns until the Kool-Aid and potato chips ran out. And when I said, "Papa, teach me how to drive," he propped me up on pillows, just as he had done with Gina. After I had inched the car forward to the mouth of the garage, he reached over to steer it gently in reverse, and said, "That's good, Miss Priss." And when Mrs. Harvey entered me in speaking contests all around the state, it was Papa who taxied me and sat in rapt attention on the front pew, puffed up, nodding his head and beaming praises with his eyes. This attack was then doubly wounding, not just because of our special history, but because, at the time, it was true.

They braved the heat that day. His fishing hat askew and his shirt back drenched with sweat, Papa unloaded Mother's now useless body onto the thick towel he had smoothed down to keep the vinyl car seat from scorching through the cotton housedress and the nylon stockings to her thighs. I crouched on the steps as the car shimmied over the gravel drive at hearse-like speed. In less than an hour, they had circled back home. I looked up from writing thank-you notes when he wheeled her past the table, slumped sideways in the creaking chair. She waved at me from the dusky hallway, and it was plain to see in her dispirited eyes a highway that stretched from Bangor to Miami.

When he had settled Mother in the bed, Papa stopped at the threshold of the dining room and scratched his back against the doorjamb. Apologizing without apologizing, he muttered, "I see you used the cards." He had given me Mother's monogrammed notecards early that morning, to write thank yous, along with stamps of wildflowers. It seemed oddly inappropriate to use them, since Mother could not write them for herself. But I was still upset with Papa. All day long his words had returned to me like ants to crumbs of Sunday morning coffee cake. I needed to escape the house. Miss Berger's note, written in a spidery hand, gave me the opportunity:

Dear Fred,
Fritz and I are thinking of you and Viola at this shocking time. To see her, always so vibrant and elegant, reduced to her present state, is such a shock and nigh unbearable. We miss her so much and can't quite believe she isn't here. Nebo, who had grown so attached to Vi, keeps hovering around the door of her room, wagging his little tail. Laney is still away at school and asks about Viola constantly. She is planning a visit to see her as soon as she gets home next week. I pray that you and your family are bearing up under this cruel strain and that Viola will be blessed with full recovery. From my own mother's case, though, I know that such a prospect is quite remote. If there is anything Fritz or I can do, don't hesitate to call us.
                                                Sincerely,
                                                Julia (Mrs. Aaron) Berger
P. S.
Would you like for me to bring Viola's belongings to you? I can bring them when Laney comes. There are odds and ends in her closet and dresser drawers. As we are in the process of hiring another live-in, who will take Viola's room, I wouldn't want any of her things to get misplaced. Of course, I hope you know that we'd take Viola back tomorrow if we could, but right now, Mother requires round-the-clock nursing care. She too has been quite cantankerous since Viola's been gone, and is convinced that no one can care for her the way Viola did.

That morning, as soon as I had finished reading the note, also on crisp, white monogrammed paper, I spontaneously dialed Alpine 91523, and someone had answered, "Bergers' residence" just as Mrs. Berger picked up another extension and chirped, "I have it, Millie." I could come right away, if I wanted. She'd be home all afternoon; would be glad to see me.

"Papa, I want to go to Mountain Brook to pick up Mother's things.

Mother's Effects

I had last seen Mrs. Berger's house when I was still at Brighton High. Gina and I had gone with Papa to visit Mother on a Sunday afternoon, soon after Gina had passed her driver's test. Papa repeatedly cautioned her to slow down around the hairpin turns. I remember this day so well because the long-awaited magazine had come. Mother had told us all about the photographers and the women with the flipped-up bouffant hairdos who stayed all day at Mrs. Berger's house just to write a story. The house was the focus of a six-page spread with shots of sweeping vistas everywhere: the windows that ran from floor to ceiling in almost every room, the double French doors that opened onto a patio, the lush garden in riotous bloom, expanding in the distance as far as the eye could see.

Gina and I had pored over the glossy pages of this *House and Garden*–type magazine—oohing and aahing until Mother said impatiently that we could take a copy home. We did. And for the longest time, the magazine—I think that it was called *Gracious Living*—was stacked atop the issues of *Ebony* and *Jet* on the coffee table in Mother's living room. We lost no opportunity to casually mention, when someone outside the family was around, that Mother worked inside this sweeping mansion atop Red Mountain.

When Mary Alice Fallin came early one Friday night to pick us up for a football game, she browsed as Gina squeezed into her majorette suit. I sat with her in the living room, where she thumbed through the magazines on the coffee table. When she picked up the now-battered copy of *Gracious Living,* I chirped up. "You see this house," I said and pointed. "My grandmother works here."

"Oh yeah?" Mary Alice answered in that waspish way of hers. "So what? It's not your house."

"I know it's not my house, but I've been in it."

"Why you so proud to say you've been in a house that don't belong to you, where your grandmother cleans up other people's shit?"

"She does no such thing; she's a nurse."

"Where is she?"

"Over there in Mountain Brook."

"I mean where is she in the pictures?" The question stopped me in my tracks. For the first time, it hit me that Mother wasn't in any of the pictures, and that it did seem strange. It was just Chipper and the Bergers standing in front of waist-high reddish-pink azaleas, clumps and clumps and clumps.

As I climbed the steep gradients of the sinuous mountain road, shaded by skimming pines, I was reminded that most of the sprawling estates were invisible from the road. The only signs that houses might be some-where near these ivied embankments were the redbrick pillars topped with wrought-iron lanterns that marked the entrance to these grand and gated mansions.

Before I knew it, I was at the turnoff that would head me up the moun-tain to Mrs. Berger's house. I wept as I remembered all the days of my child-hood when I would gleefully read WENONAH/WEST OXMOOR ROAD/SHANNON, which was the sign that we would soon arrive in Mountain Brook.

Over the river and through the woods to Grandmother's house we go.

"Are we lost Papa? Are we lost?"

"No, Miss Priss. We not lost."

I had a child's sense of timing, the sense that good things take much too long to get to, and Mother was my good thing then, that day in mid-March, just before my tenth birthday. She had a surprise for me.

It was a seemingly endless trip round and round the winding roads, deeper and deeper into the woods, higher and higher up the mountain, the car straining to make the climb until we finally reach the house where the automatic six-foot wrought-iron gate opens to admit the station wagon. It clicks shut as suddenly as it opens and we hustle out of the car, up to the sprawling house with the huge glass windows on all sides, and the spread-ing branches of trees that look like they have long extended arms with fringe. Wearing her nurse's uniform, Mother meets us at the side door that leads us to the kitchen, where she is frosting the German chocolate cake, my birthday cake.

Papa sits at the table, and Gina and I, on thick-padded stools at the counter, care-ful, in Mother's presence, not to rest our elbows on the table. We are about to eat. I see the blue-striped boxes with the yellow ribbons. Mother lights the yellow candles on the cake. I make a wish and blow out the candles and we sing "Happy Birthday." We eat the cake. The icing has a lot of pecans. Mother knows I like pecans. I open my pres-ents. I am so happy. It's my first watch. A Timex, just like Gina has, except her band is dark, dark brown and mine is navy blue. The band is too large. Tomorrow, Papa

*will take it to the shoe shop and get more holes punched in. I want to wear it any-
way, right now. I won't lose it. I have two more presents. I don't like the ruffly blouse;
I don't like ruffly things, but I don't tell Mother. Mother says you should always be
glad when people give you things and just say thank you. I like the teeny-weeny bottle of perfume with a pink heart on top. Gina opens her present too, but it is not her
birthday. She likes the wide-tailed skirt with squiggly things all over it.*

*I want to see the house. Gina has already seen it. That time she stayed all night
at Miss Berger's so they could all go to Florida early in the morning. I could not go
to Florida. I was too little. Gina and Papa stay and play dominoes in the kitchen.
Mother pulls back the funny wooden doors that peek out from a narrow strip in the
wall. I like them. How come they do that? Mother tells me they are pocket doors. I
want to pull the whatchamacallit to see the door go back inside the wall. Mother
says it's not a plaything. I lean my face real close and try to see inside, but the door
is in the way. In the hall, there's a great big mirror at the top of the stairs. It's way,
way taller than Daddy. I want to go up there. I've never been inside a house with
stairs. Mother says we can't go up there. We can only see the dining room and the
library and the place where she sleeps. I cannot touch the books. There is a ladder.
Mother says it's so Miss Berger can reach the books way up high. The dining room
is big. I rub my hands over the tall blue chairs. They are the same color as the plates
that have some white in them.*

"How come they keep the plates on the wall, Mother? Do they take them down
when they eat?"

Mother laughs, "No, honey, these plates are just for decoration."

"Oh."

*Below the plates there is a high-backed chair. It's not like the other chairs. It is
a dark color, maybe brown. A piece of velvet ribbon is stretched across the arms.*

"How come they have ribbon on the chair, Mother? You can't sit down in it with
the ribbon."

"They don't want you to sit in it; it's very, very old."

"So is it for decoration too?"

"I guess you can say that."

*I see the chandelier on the great big table. It's in the middle of the room. I can see
my face too. The table is so shiny. Over the mantelpiece there is a picture of a lady.
She has on a long white evening dress. It drags on the floor and I cannot see her shoes.
She has on a green necklace that looks like the bottle ginger ale comes in. You can even
see her titties. Her hair is dark brown and it is piled way on top of her head, and
then she has two curls, kind of like Shirley Temple curls, hanging down on her ears.*

"Who is that lady, Mother?"

"It's Mrs. Berger's mother."

"Who is this in the teen-inchy picture?"

"That's Mrs. Berger."

"It don't look like her."

"Doesn't. Doesn't look like her. She was much younger then—in college. She painted it herself."

I stare long and hard at the lady's face in the fancy gold frame. "How come? How could she see to paint her own face?"

Mother laughs and teases me about this all the time.

It is almost dark when Papa drops me off at home. He thinks I can't tote the cake and the bag with the presents, but I know I can. But he still makes me take them one by one. Everybody says I'm clumsy. I hold the cake tight in both my hands and I walk real slow up the steps. I'm trying to keep from tripping over my feet. I give Reggie his Etch-A-Sketch, his Harold and the Purple Crayon, *and the little bag full of Hershey's Kisses. Bumbiddle screams for the kisses. He likes to pull the little tissue-paper string. He has a present too. ABC blocks with different colors—red and blue and green and yellow—but he just wants the Kisses in the silver paper. I can't wait to show Mama my watch and tell her all about Miss Berger's house. I start to tell her all about the funny doors inside the wall and the great big mirror, but she does not want to listen. She says, 'I know all about that house on Saugahatchee Road.' Then she pours herself some whiskey in a jelly glass and sits down in the big blue chair with the elephant feet.*

I overshot the driveway two or three times, driving up and down a winding stretch of Saugahatchee Road before I saw the tall pillars with the swinging lanterns and the discreetly lettered sign: PRIVATE PROPERTY—NO TRESPASSING, and chugged up the steep incline to the gate, watching it creep open, still fascinated by its hidden mechanism, still in awe of this sprawling estate.

Millie, the housekeeper, met me at the door. "My, my, ain't you just the spitting image of Viola. Lord have mercy. How is she? Bless her bones." Inside, the house was much as I remembered it all the times before. Still full of mystery. Now standing there again at the foot of the sweeping staircase with its varnished balustrades, I looked up at the colossal mirror in the gilded frame, still amused at my image blurred and diminished by the distance. Out of the corner of my eye, I could see the edge of the dining table and the blue velvet draperies tied back with thick gold cord.

Millie ushered me into the library with the red damask walls, where Mrs. Berger sat doing needlepoint. She stood up, brushing her wispy, silvery hair away from her swarthy brow. Pleasantries exchanged, she offered me iced tea and asked me questions about Tuskegee. A nervousness came over me, although I don't know why, and I politely refused, offering the excuse that I had to return the car to Papa by three o'clock. She begged me to delay long enough so she could cut some flowers for Mother, and I followed her down the soapstone path, her clogs *clip-clopping* on the stones, and into the well-tended garden, where she chattered as she moved among the flowers, identifying them for me with each new snip of the scissors.

I headed down the winding mountain road dwarfed on either side by towering pine trees rising like church steeples and skimming the sky. I passed the golf course, the ivy-covered lawns, and the man-made lake shaped like a giant bolo bat. As I sniffed the honeysuckle wafting on the breeze, I looked in the rearview mirror at Mountain Brook receding in the distance. I would not see this place again.

I did not go straight home that day. I stopped at Highland Bakery for an ice cream cone. I decided to linger inside the bakery's air-conditioned comfort just for a little while before returning to Mother's house and the liniment scent of sickness. There, in the coolness of the bakery, I was stricken with an uncontrollable curiosity about Mother's effects, stowed in two shopping bags resting underneath the dashboard. The woman wiping off adjoining tables gave me the strangest look as I lugged one of the bags into the bakery, dripping pistachio ice cream on the newly mopped floor.

I looked all around the room, which was empty except for the woman, who glared at me as she brought back a mop to wipe the floor again. My heart was pounding so hard, it seemed that it would burst right through my chest as I began to stack items on the table. Mother was always a very private person, never leaving *anything* lying around that needed hiding. Here I was doing something that Mother, Mama, and Grandma Edie had always forbidden me to do: ramble in other folks' belongings.

There was a small, sepia-tinted photograph of Aunt Dallas, matted on faded, tattered silk moire and encased in a silver frame; an unopened package of white shoestrings; a thimble, a pewter letter opener, a near empty jar of cold cream, multicolored spools of thread, a box of notecards, a fountain pen, and a bottle of ink. And there, wrapped in Mother's navy blue sweater, was the jewelry box I'd made for her at Vacation Bible School so many years ago. Some macaroni shells were lost and particles of glitter had flaked away, but there it was, used not for jewelry but to store Mother's usual newspaper clippings and letters and two of Reggie's childhood drawings.

Reverend Lockhart was the focus of several clippings announcing various speaking engagements around the city.

"Voter Registration Workers to Hear Rev. Timothy Lockhart, Thursday, June 10, 1962. Subject: 'The Negro's Destiny in a New America.'"

There were even clippings about his assassination:

"Death Angel Takes Rev. Lockhart," "Rev. Timothy Lockhart, A Fallen Martyr in the Cause of Racial Justice," "Rev. Timothy Lockhart, Funeralized Saturday."

I folded the clippings and placed them back in the jewelry box.

I had not planned to read the letters. Mother had always said, "Never open anyone's mail; it invades their privacy," but what harm was there in reading my own letters to Mother? I asked myself. I had written them after all, the first, soon after I had arrived at Tuskegee:

September 10, 1968

Dear Mother,

Just a few lines to let you hear from me. I am doing fine and adjusting pretty well to college life. I am taking basic economics, English composition, biology I, sociology, world literature, and swimming. I hate the economics class, but it is required for my major. I hate swimming too, but everybody has to take a physical education class. I still can't bear to put my head under the water. I like my English class a lot. This week we had to write a personal composition, and I wrote about Bumbiddle and how I gave him his name. The teacher liked it a lot and read it out loud to the class. I was very proud. I also like my sociology class. When you all come for Parents' Weekend, I want you to meet my teacher, Mr. Gomillion. I think you'd like him. He has told us all about gerrymandering in Tuskegee. I couldn't believe that he had sued the mayor of Tuskegee and it went all the way to the Supreme Court. I bet he knows Reverend Lockhart.

My roommate is growing on me. You were right; I just needed to give her a chance. Thanks for the money you sent me and the clipping about Reggie's petition to the Bessemer Board of Education. If they have sent all the worst teachers to W. A. Bell, then he should be allowed to go back to Brighton. There are so many good teachers there—Miss Edwina Reed, Mr. Pouncy, Mrs. Mittie Robinson, Mrs. Bonner, Mrs. Boswell, and Mr. Yarborough, and Dr. Dulce Tabares.

Well, I should bring this letter to a close so that I can study for my economics quiz. Don't worry, Mother, I don't intend to throw this opportunity away. I know you are right. "What you get inside your head no one can take away from you," so I am following your advice to study hard and do well, because, as you always say, "Education is the key to progress."

Love,

Your granddaughter,

P. S. I love you oceans and oceans.

There was a letter from Mother's niece, Lillie Mae in Sumter County. I rationalized that reading it was all right too. It was just family.

Dear Aunt Curly,

   How you doing? Fine I hope? Just a few lines to let you know that we recieved the money and the cloths you sent the children. It was a great big help. We all doing all right. The Lord blessin us with a reasnable potion of health and strenth. The Dr. can't make out why Peter having so much trouble to catch his breath, but I have faith the Lord will make a way. We planning to kill a hog long about the end of the month, so you and Uncle Fred should come down home and get some meat to put in your deep freze for the winter. Peter keeping count of what we owe you and we will pay you back soon as we can.

   May the good Lord keep rainin his blessings on you and Uncle Fred. Give Stella and Gina and everybody our love and keep us in your prayers. We will do same.

Your neice,
Lillie Mae Mack

Folded in with Lillie Mae's letter was a clipping from the *World*. Dated May 15, 1959, it was a letter to and response from L. S. Craig, Marriage Counselor:

Dear Counselor:

   I am writing you because I have no other person that I can talk with, concerning my problem. A few months ago, I saw my mother sitting in a parked car, making love to another man. I do not know just what to do. I want to tell Daddy, and I want to tell Mother how bitter I am toward her and how she hurt me. What should I do?

Dear Counselee:

   I understand how a boy idolizes his mother and esteems her. Your disappointment, bereavement, and resentment of the other man are thoroughly understandable and natural. It is most unfortunate that your mother engaged in infidelity. Now, that has happened, and nothing can change what has happened. The important thing is to see that your whole life is not colored by this unfortunate experience. You should find some way of telling your mother that you saw her. It is going to be difficult, and will be most embarrassing, to you and your mother, but it will probably serve to shock her to a sense of decency. You should not mention this to your father

or any other person. Try to face reality: Your mother is human and is as
subject to making mistakes as any other woman.

I lost track of time there in Highland Bakery, and when I looked up and glanced out the window, the sun was going down.

Except for the whir of window fans, all was quiet when I stole into the house. I tiptoed down the hall to Mother's room and stood in the doorway. The sputtering window fan was whipping the layers of white voile curtains into cumulus clouds. There they lay in the four-postered mahogany bed, peacefully sleeping amid white tousled sheets, Papa cradling Mother in his arms.

PART
FIVE

Going to Indiana

For the remainder of my college years, I camped out at Mother's house during holidays and summers. The tension at 1805 was as thick and dense as fatback and just as difficult to digest.

The summer following graduation from Tuskegee was by far the hardest: I would soon be leaving Alabama. Before I left for Indiana in mid-August of 1972, I had never lived outside the state, and my travel had been restricted to school trips to Mammoth Cave in Kentucky and Look Out Mountain in Tennessee. When Daddy drove us to Buffalo, New York, in 1967 to bury Martha Faye, that was my first trip beyond the states that bordered Alabama. Now I would be going to a place I'd never been and where I didn't know a soul, besides.

This had long been my fantasy: to live anonymously among people who would not be captive to conventions of the South, people who would not hang the albatross of great expectations round my neck. But, true to the nature of desire, the closer I came to fantasy's fulfillment, the more it withered in appeal.

Circumstances at home didn't help the matter. Mama was ill with stomach trouble, which drinking did not help; Daddy was out of work again; Reggie had just finished high school and was working on an assembly line at a chicken factory way out in Birmingham; and Bumbiddle, sullen and withdrawn, was losing all interest in school. Always a quick student, with an aptitude for science, Bumbiddle was an early casualty of the "integrated" public schools in Bessemer, most now disintegrating and packed with students who could not flee to private academies.

I was awash with guilt about the whole situation, but felt powerless to change it. I decided that the least I could do was spend my last two weeks in Alabama back at home in Pipe Shop. At some perhaps unconscious level, I hoped it might be possible to re-create the exultation that had marked my departure to Tuskegee almost four years before.

So much had changed in those scant years since I had left for college and much too fast for reckoning, but in the final days before I left for Indiana, everybody gathered on the porch on Eighteenth Street again—Papa and Mother, Daddy and Mama, Grandma Edie, Reggie and Bumbiddle. For the life of me, I can't remember why Auntee and Gina weren't there, and when I've asked them, neither one recalls the day of the small cookout we had in honor of my leaving. The rest of us sat there, though, enjoying the fragile peace that had settled over the porch.

That was the day that Reggie, always more limber than anybody in the family, squatted barefoot on the porch to paint my name and new address in mustard-colored letters on my dark green trunk:

1009 GRADUATE HOUSE EAST
PURDUE UNIVERSITY
WEST LAFAYETTE, INDIANA 47906

My three Samsonite suitcases were already stuffed to bursting, and piles and piles of fabric and other clothing were mounded on the bed. When Reggie teased me for being a pack rat and volunteered that, as far as he could see, this trunk would not hold all the junk still piled back on that bed, I broke right down. I had been called a pack rat all my life; there was no reason for me to cry, but I had been so high-strung and edgy all that summer that a simple, innocent statement, not meant to harm at all, had unstopped the reservoir of sadness that I had dammed up inside for months.

"I didn't mean anything by it," Reggie joked. "I can't believe it, you have graduated from college and you're still a crybaby."

"I'm not crying about what you said."

"Well, why you crying, then?"

"I'm crying because I'm leaving." And he said, "You don't have to go." Mama started singing out of tune, "Going to Indiana, sorry but I can't take you," and we all laughed. Daddy said, "Indiana's got too many syllables; it's got to be Chicago or it won't sound right."

After that, it was a lovely afternoon, with no talk of disease and layoffs and accumulating debts, just stories and nervous laughter, most at Daddy's expense. Mama began the teasing about Daddy's white vinyl platformed zippered boots, so out of character for him. "You used to have such good taste," Mama started in. "What possessed you to buy these go-go boots?" Daddy claimed that Buttercup had given him the boots because they were too small for him. He wore them simply to spare Buttercup's feelings, or so he said. We snickered and Daddy took it all in stride.

Although he was only forty-nine, that day he looked so much older, no longer the handsome, clean-shaven, charming man, but one who had balded and whose jaws had caved in from tooth extractions and neglected meals. He cut a ridiculous figure that afternoon, there in the white boots and the black beret he wore to cover up his bald spot.

That night, Mama took a turn for the worse, and Daddy, Reggie, and I rushed her to the emergency room. Bumbiddle stayed at home. The wait seemed endless, but finally Daddy and Mama approached us, Daddy clutching a prescription in his hand.

"What was the matter?"

"Some kind of infection. We have a prescription."

I wanted to know more, but then again I didn't. I held my tongue and fixed my mind on Grandma Edie's remedies and her opinion of doctors, most of whom would be entirely unnecessary, she insisted, if people just took black draught and cod liver oil every spring and when their bowels were "caustive." Plagued with sore throats all my life and tired of antibiotics, I once resurrected her remedy: a mixture of salt and black pepper moistened with turpentine. I can't say that it worked, but maybe that was because her hands were missing, gently massaging my swollen glands.

The next morning, Mama felt well enough to eat. She managed to keep the oatmeal down, then settled back in bed. In three more days, I was to leave, and this filled me with such guilt and foreboding, I had to leave the house just so I could think. Not surprisingly, I found my way to Mother's. All my life, I'd looked to Mother when confronted with dilemmas, but since the stroke, I had not thought her capable of sound advice. That day, however, when I brought her lunch tray to the bedroom, she proved me wrong. For the past several weeks, Mother had apparently observed my moods and movements far more closely than I knew. I propped her up in bed and fluffed her pillows, then smiled as she began to feed herself with her right hand. It was a small victory, which had taken her years to achieve, and not because she lacked the physical capability, but because she lacked the will.

I had not talked much to her and Papa about going to graduate school, especially after he shocked and offended me with his prediction that I was educating myself right out of the marriage market. A thimbleful of feminism in my belly, I hurled at him with all the venom I could muster, "I'm not up for sale."

That afternoon Mother's eyes trailed me all around the room as I distracted myself by dusting the dresser, shoving the pill bottles neatly in a pile, then folding newly laundered sheets and towels, stacking them in the armoire. When she finished her soup, she pushed the bowl away and said, quite plainly, "Go get the suitcase."

Her speech had improved the last three years, but at that moment, it seemed clearer than anything she'd uttered since the stroke. And yet, not quite believing what I'd heard, I asked her quizzically, "What did you say, Mother?"

"Get the big gray suitcase."

"For what?"

"To take to Indiana."

As the years have passed, I've often thought about that day. I had only talked in passing in cryptic ways about what lay ahead, but it seems that all my years of following in Mother's tracks had made words unnecessary. Gesture was enough. She divined exactly what I was feeling: I was afraid to go, but I knew that if I didn't leave that summer, I might not leave at all.

Mother's diction seemed to sharpen even more as she issued her directions that afternoon: "Sometimes if you try to save people, they will drown you too, and then there'll be two bodies facedown in the water."

She persuaded me that I could do everybody far more good by leaving than by staying put, and I trusted her assessment, just as I had always done. Leaving was Mother's angle on ascent. With difficulty, I heeded the simplicity of her two final words to me that day: "Go. Go."

Miraculously, Daddy often got recalled to work at moments of great crisis, and then the tables seemed to turn, just as they had before I went off to college, just as they were turning now. Mama even felt so much better that she was able to see me off. Daddy was working and so he didn't come, but I was heartened that as he left for work that morning, he wished me all the best.

Mother spoke up at the baggage counter.

"Do you charge for extra bags?"

She reached into her pocketbook, but Mama said that she would pay, fishing in her purse for the crisp new bills, then smiling in my direction. The man hefted Mother's steel-gray suitcase onto the platform, her initials, V. G. W., glowing just above the metal clasp.

Christmas 1972

Reggie met me at the airport and filled me in on his new job—this one at a plant in Birmingham, where he worked nights processing galvanized steel for chain-link fences. By day he took classes at Miles College, but fell asleep from exhaustion in the middle of the lectures. I laughed and said sometimes I fell asleep myself, in one class in particular.

Taught by a professor who would be retiring the following year, the class consisted of his reading passages from books and asking the same question about each one: "What do you see here?" One day he varied things a bit and shuffled into the class, paused just at the edge of the desk, and asked, "How large was the raft that Huck and Jim floated on down the Mississippi?" The class erupted into paroxysms of laughter, until the teacher's expression made it plainly clear that he had not meant the question as a joke.

I was barely weathering the awkward uncertainties of racial intermingling, of furtive glance and fond embrace, and already squirming in my role as unsought resident expert on Southern affairs. I brought it on myself by enrolling in a course in Southern literature. The atmosphere was supercharged with tension, and I felt constantly on the spot to pose as an authority on all questions regarding Southern race relations that arose. Many was the time when I wanted to shout out loud to the ghoulishly curious that, yes, awful things did happen in this place we called "the South." Yes, firehoses and police dogs were turned on demonstrators; the television cameras didn't lie. But no, I had not heard blond housewives shout "Go back to Africa" to innocent black schoolchildren, although I did not doubt that they had. There had been no move to integrate the schools I attended and, when Reggie and Bumbiddle began to test what passed for desegregation in Alabama, it was almost fifteen years past *Brown.*

At home, Grandma Edie said the grace at dinner and gave thanks to God for my safe landing, interjecting in the blessing a plea for understanding why anyone in their right mind would want to sit up in an airplane.

"What kind of grace is that, Grandma?" I teased.

"Ain't you scared of that plane?"

"No, ma'am, I'm not."

I have precious little memory of this Christmas as Christmas, perhaps because it will be forever identified in my mind with one more awful event: Grandma Edie's passing. She had seemed so well, so high in spirits, but barely had I landed back in Indiana two days after New Year's when I had to turn around again. Grandma Edie had died in her sleep in the very bed where Daddy Les had died eight years before. In her eighty-eighth year, she had died clothed in her right mind, as had been her constant prayer.

From that point on, the seven years of graduate school blurred into a series of deaths and one thick book of funerals. I sometimes thought it seemed that no one could survive Grandma Edie's passing. Or maybe they were simply hoping, at some unconscious level, for the final peace that shone on her face the night she died. Mama would describe it repeatedly as the most restful expression she had ever seen her wear.

Grandma Edie's passing affected Daddy most of all, because she had raised him and doted on him ever since he was a little boy. No matter how much she chastised and scolded Daddy, Grandma Edie's heart was eternally tender where he was concerned. She had shared her worries with Mama about the dismal situation at U.S. Pipe, that each year grew more desperate for workers. She hid her worries from Daddy, though, offering instead calm and faithful reassurances that "things would work out all right." That Daddy failed to muster the faith she never lost, made him and all the rest of us stand back in awe, just as we did when we stood in front of the portrait of her, Crockett, and Daddy Frank. In the portrait, as in the house, she was right there at the apex.

I often see Grandma Edie in a recurrent dream. I have received word that she is dying and have been summoned home from some far distance to say my final good-byes. I'm in a plane in bad weather. It circles and circles the city for a long time before it is cleared to land. In the dream, no one meets me at the airport and I must plod with luggage in each hand down the Bessemer Super Highway. It seems that the ground beneath my feet is mushy, and with each step I sink ankle-deep into the mush. Cars pass to and fro, shining their blinding headlights in my eyes, but no one offers me a ride. When I finally make it home and to the room where Grandma lies in the metal bed with chipped white paint and flowers, she is already dead, her gray braids lying limply on the pillow. I stand by her side and fix my eyes on her deep brown face, so much like the rich, waxy soil of the Black Belt of her birth. She lies atop the covers in a luminous white shroud that comes just above her ankles. The brooch she wears in the portrait with Crockett and Daddy Frank is pinned securely near her neck. I rest my hand on her forehead and utter the benediction, "God rest your soul, Grandma." She raises straight up from her bed, her two gray braids drooping to her shoulders, her arms stretched high above her head like scepters. Suddenly she is radically transfigured. The shroud falls from her shoulders and she is naked. Her skin is as smooth as a newborn baby's, and her face turns into mine.

Voilà

Mama didn't work on Friday. It was the day Mr. Shannon brought the mending after the steam presses shut down at one o'clock. Mr. Raymond Shannon, a muscular, pock-faced man with a crew cut, owned Dixie Cleaners with his wife, Dot, who was as frail as he was muscular. She reminded me a bit of Lucille Ball—not just the red hair (which Mama said she dyed), but the eyes, the bug eyes that locked at times in dumb expression, making her look a little drunk. Insanely jealous of the black female workers that Mr. Shannon seemed to prefer, she never left the premises when he was there.

An enterprising pair, the Shannons had owned the business for as long as anyone could remember, building it up from nothing, as Mr. Shannon used to boast. Each year Dot softened her brushes and added another hand-lettered line to Dixie's expanding list of services.

SILKS HAND-FINISHED

WEDDING GOWNS CLEANED AND PRESERVED

PROFESSIONAL LUGGAGE REPAIR

DRAPERIES AND BEDSPREADS, BLANKETS

It was when they added

COMPLETE MENDING AND ALTERATIONS ON PREMISES

that Mama presented herself at the cleaners, during one long stretch of summer when the Pipe Shop had laid almost everybody off. The first seamstress had quit the job a mere two days after starting because she could not tolerate working for a bad-tempered woman who stalked her every move, but more, because the seamstress ignored Dot's order forbidding her to wear those skintight clothes. She would rather quit than don the shapeless dusters that all the other women wore. Mama's cousin Tootsie, who had worked at Dixie Cleaners for several years, mentioned that she knew someone who might like the job. Mama was hired immediately and worked there for almost twenty years. It wasn't long before she was running the presses, too, if mending and alterations were caught up. On Friday afternoon, Mr. Shannon delivered whatever mending jobs customers had dropped off that morning, along with Mama's pay, having calculated her wages due directly on a tiny manila envelope, the size used in church for tithing. She earned minimum wage for pressing, and a sliding scale for mending by the piece.

Departing from a years-long pattern, Mama went to Dixie Cleaners on the Friday before Mother's funeral to clean and press her burial clothes. Jollie, one of the women Mama worked with, had offered to prepare the suit as a kindness to the family, but Mama quietly insisted on discharging this task herself. It was customary to bury women in negligees of powder blue or pastel pink, but everybody in the family, including Papa, agreed that negligees were not befitting Mother. We decided that only one of her signature outfits would be appropriate: a navy blue suit. These suits, that changed as fashions changed, identified Mother as certainly as Grandma Edie's whiskered mole did her. Mother insisted that every well-dressed woman needed a discreet navy blue suit, preferably one that could be worn in every season. It was versatile, she said, and complemented practically any other color—not just the conventional ecru blouse, but chiffon scarves of chartreuse, fuchsia, and vermilion that often trailed from Mother's neck.

I had started out from Indiana the morning after Auntee called me with the news, and as soon as I arrived, was swept up, as I had been for many years, in preparing for another funeral. The day I went to Mother's house to fetch the suit, I rummaged through her closet as I had done ever since I was a girl, breathing in the faint scent of her perfumes. When I came upon the suit, crushed between a crowded rod of other garments on padded satin hangers, I could not help but whimper.

I had dropped the suit off at Dixie Cleaners, walking the few blocks to the low-slung building opposite U.S. Pipe and Foundry. I'm sure it is only my imagination, but the hiss of the steam seemed muted that day as Mama raised and lowered the pressing lid down on the pencil-straight skirt. Pushing the pressing stool she sometimes used in my direction, she said, "Sit down, I'm almost done. I just have the blouse to go. You know I have to do this right. I can't have Miss Viola standing over my shoulder inspecting the job." I sat down and bantered with the other women who had kept me in hysterics all my life. Jollie, who cleaned the wedding gowns, teased me about not being married. As she stuffed blue tissue paper inside a lacy sleeve, I remembered all the many days I'd seen these dresses dangling limply on wide-winged hangers, awaiting the necks and arms and pointy breasts of beaming brides, the brides who would teeter down the aisle on white satin spool-heeled shoes, braced on the arms of their fathers. I had even imagined myself in one of these dresses with Alençon lace, but the fantasy had faded long ago.

Mama gently guided the suit through the plastic sheathing and we left together, stopping along the way at Blankenship's for a carton of eggs. Mr. Stansell's funeral car pulled up soon after we arrived back home. He'd come to get the suit. He was in the neighborhood and thought he'd save us a trip up the Bessemer Super Highway. I was about to pass it to him when, matter-of-factly and with a level tone, Mama dropped a bomb: "Wait, I want to do it. I want to dress her. Would it be all right?" I was flabbergasted. While relatives did not normally dress their loved ones—most were too bereaved for that, Mr. Stansell said—it was by no means unheard of. He knew people who had done it in the past. Totally shocked and unprepared for this turn of events, I stood stock-still on the porch as Mama and Mr. Stansell drove away.

What would make her want to prepare her mother-in-law for burial, the very person who had barnstormed her way through Mama's life and fought to manage every aspect of it, right down to when and where she married?

The account of how my parents came to wed was a favorite of mine. Mama often told this story after some disagreement with Mother, prefacing it with, "Oh, yeah, Miss Viola and I have our differences, and don't always see things eye to eye, but I don't have anything against her and I know she can't possibly have anything against me. Couldn't have. She put me with your daddy, and he was the only man I ever loved.

"It was funny the way it happened. We had been courting for going on three years, ever since we both worked uptown. We mainly got together on Saturday nights and Sundays. We might stroll up to the Lincoln on First Avenue and see whatever picture was playing. Sometimes we might visit with other couples. Or we might just walk, nowhere in particular. We just liked being together, so it didn't much matter where we went. On Sundays, Wiley went to Miss Viola's for dinner, and after a while, I started going too. She told him to invite me. Practically every Sunday, soon after I got home from church (I was going to New Bethlehem then), he would show up at our house. My daddy liked him. Thought he had a good head on his shoulders, so after they passed a few words, and took a nip of Old Grand-Dad, we would stroll on down the Bessemer Super Highway to Miss Viola's.

"She was always nice to me, always took an interest in what I was doing.

I think she liked me because I was on the quiet side, around her anyway. Since she and Stella were always squabbling, I guess she was just glad I didn't talk back to her. She would try to shame Estella by saying stuff like, 'Why don't you act like a lady? Look at the way Jim carries herself and the company she keeps. You don't see her alleycatting around with every piece of trash in Bessemer.' It would make Stella so mad; make me mad too, because, for the longest while, Stella took it out on me, wouldn't give me much more than the time of day. But when I got engaged to marry your daddy, things got a little better between us.

"I never will forget it. I remember it just like it was yesterday. It was the first Sunday in May, one of those Sundays when Miss Viola pulled out all her fancy things—her special dishes, her silver, the damask tablecloths and napkins. Napkins so big you could just about wrap yourself up in 'em, the little crystal salt dishes with the tiny little spoons, the water goblets with her initials—all of it. Plus, she had done all the cooking, except Mr. Fred had made the pound cake, as usual. I don't know where Stella was that day. Anyway, Miss Viola went all out. She made smothered chicken *and* roast pork, dressing, her famous icebox rolls, creamed corn and fresh green peas, seems like the sweetest, greenest peas I ever tasted. That day I helped her set the table. Everything was so fancy that I thought Reverend Powell must be coming. He was the pastor of Macedonia then. But she said no, it was just family—her and Mr. Fred, Fred Jr. (he was just a little bitty boy then, barely walking), your daddy, and me.

"Well, sir, that Sunday, after we had finished eating, we were still just sitting around the table, when Miss Viola clinked on her glass and turned to Wiley. He was sitting to her left. She said, 'Wiley, do you love Jim?' and he said, with a puzzled look on his face, 'Yes, Mother, I do.' And then she looked down in my direction. I was at the other end of the table next to Mr. Fred. Fred Jr. was sitting on my lap. She said the same thing to me. 'Jim, do you love Wiley?' And I said, 'Yes, ma'am, Miss Viola.' And then she said, 'Well, why don't you-all go on and get married. No need in wasting time.'

"And that's the way it was. Now, I want you know that I was no more thinking about marrying than a hog is thinking about a bath. I liked working for Dr. Davis and running my little sewing business on the side, but after Miss Viola brought it up, I started turning it around in my mind, and we got married in September, on my birthday, September the fifteenth, 1943, right in Miss Viola's living room. I was twenty years old. I made myself a blue crepe suit tailored right down to the bound buttonholes. I found the most beautiful roll of bronze-colored soutache and tacked it around the collar and on the pocket flaps. It was sharp, now. I found a hat at Loveman's that had a little netting on it, so that was my veil. It was a nice wedding. Small but nice. Back then, not too many people had these great big old weddings like they do now. It so happened that Jimmie Lunceford was playing in town that weekend, so we went to hear him and took Stella with us.

"When your daddy went into the army and they shipped him overseas, I moved into Miss Viola's house, and that's when Estella and I got to be close, a little like sisters, but not quite. You just might as well say Miss Viola proposed to me for your daddy. I know he wanted to go along with it, but she was the one who proposed. Since Miss Viola was so particular, I took it as a compliment that she wanted me to marry your daddy. People used to say that she didn't think anybody was good enough for him. Estella told me that he might have married Ernestine when he got her pregnant with Martha Faye. Back then, folks thought you oughta marry no matter what, but Miss Viola wouldn't hear of it, and he would never cross his mother.

"Miss Viola came home as soon as she heard I was in labor, and she and Estella paced up and down the halls with me at Bessemer General Hospital almost that whole day. You didn't want to come here; took me twenty-one hours to get you out of my womb. When they discharged me from the hospital, Miss Viola brought me to her house, and that's where we stayed until I got my strength back. She bleached your belly bands and showed me how to nurse and burp you. And I want you to know, she didn't go back up to Mountain Brook until you had your first checkup.

"Then your daddy and I moved back down the street to our little place in that row of apartments behind Town's Grocery Store. Your daddy always said they reminded him of army barracks. We had a Hide-A-Bed in the living room, where we kept your crib. Scattered pots and pans, kitchen stuff. Miss Viola got us a coffee table and a lamp. And she was the one who helped us find a place when I got pregnant with Reggie. She was right. Two rooms and a kitchen didn't cut it for a growing family. When your daddy came out the mines and went into the Pipe Shop, we moved in here. It was just supposed to be for a little while, but before we knew it, we were here to stay.

"Miss Viola was always willing to help. Now she dosed out advice the way Miss Edie did castor oil, and sometimes you couldn't help but gag on it after a while, but it was all for the best. Every last bit of it. Sometimes, now, I wish I had listened to her. She was absolutely right about all of us crowded together down here, but I don't think she really understood all the reasons why we stayed."

As she snuffed out half-smoked cigarettes, one behind the other, Mama kept eulogizing Mother. "Miss Viola wanted the best for everybody. I know it didn't always seem that way, but she did. She knew what was right, and she didn't bite her tongue about saying it. Some folks didn't like her for it, but it didn't shut her up. She had a sense of herself that nobody could touch—she was fair too. Like when your daddy got out of the army and commenced to running around, staying out late, and whatnot, Miss Viola blessed him out to a fare-thee-well and told me that I needed to put my foot down. 'You don't have to stomach Wiley's mess,' she said. 'If you don't put your foot down, he'll walk all over you. It's in his blood.' I don't know what happened to your daddy then, but when he came back from that army, he was never quite the same. I asked him if something had happened over there, but he would never say. You know he could shut down and close you off one minute and scream at you the next. After he got back from overseas, look like the least little thing could set him off. First, old man Elmore died and his wife sold the tailoring shop, so that upset Wiley. More than anything else, your daddy wanted to be a tailor. He ended up carrying burial insurance for North Carolina Mutual for a while, but the pay wasn't too good, so, quite naturally, that shortened his fuse. Then, everybody in our card group was getting pregnant but me—Louise, Ovetta, Helen—and that upset him. Didn't matter what it was. Things started to look up when Mr. Fred got him on down at Pyne Mine. After a while, we just gave up on having children, and lo and behold, here you come, a whole eight years after we got married.

"Later on, when your daddy started running around again, and it looked like we might not stay together, Miss Viola tried to interest me in learning some other trade at the junior college. She said every woman needed to know how to make a living for herself. She even offered to teach me to drive so I would have a way to get over there (it was in Wenonah) without having to transfer so many times on the bus. I don't know why, but I didn't want to learn to drive. The way these cars zoom up and down that Bessemer Super Highway, sometimes I'm scared just riding in a car, so I couldn't no way never picture myself driving one. I was too old for all of that by then. You have to do these kinds of things when you young.

"Miss Viola never gave up on me, though. I'll always remember what she did when my face started to break out all over. She brought more soaps and ointments in this house than a little bit, trying to help me clear my face up. When none of it worked, she took me to a dermatologist. After the stuff he gave me still didn't clear it up, he said it must just be stress. I should just take it easy. I almost laughed in that white man's face. How could I take it easy? I was working at the cleaners from seven to one, then coming home, starting dinner, then sitting down to sew and do the mending. And I'll have you know, sometimes, after I had finished a job, folks would come up in here asking if they could pay half today and half later on. That's why, after a time, I decided to just go on full-time out at Dixie. I didn't want to keep sewing for half-pay, and I sure didn't want to keep it up for surplus cheese and Mason jars of bootleg liquor.

"You know when I really found out what a good-hearted person Miss Viola was? When she helped put Norman Whitfield through college. You remember Norman? He was Fred Jr.'s best friend. They went all the way through Dunbar High School together. Couldn't separate them. They graduated in the same class. Well, you know, when Fred Jr. went off to Washington, Norman stayed back here. His mother couldn't afford to send him to college. He hung around Ninth Avenue, moping around, moping around, missing Fred Jr. until Miss Viola and Mr. Fred said they would help him go to school somewhere in the Birmingham area. Well, naturally, that could only be someplace like Miles or Daniel Payne Business College, because blacks weren't going to places like Birmingham Southern or Sanford, and definitely not to the University of Alabama down in Tuscaloosa, not back then. He went on out to Miles, I think, then transferred down to one of the Atlanta schools—Clark, I believe it was. And do you know that all that time, they never mentioned that they were putting Norman through school? You know how we found out about it? Soon after Miss Viola had that stroke. Norman's mother told it, when she came up from Mississippi to see Miss Viola. She had moved down there where one of her sisters was. We were surprised to hear that she was coming, but she rode up here on the bus and was sitting right in Miss Viola's bedroom when she told Mr. Fred that coming up here was the least she could do, since Miss Viola had put her son through school.

"If you wanted to make something of yourself, Mother would do anything in her power to help you. And she wouldn't do what some folks do when they help you out. She didn't throw it up in your face or talk it round to everybody in creation to make herself look good. She wasn't just a beautiful person outside. She was beautiful on the inside too. I'm just glad to see that you took some of her medicine."

Norman Whitfield couldn't get to Mother's funeral, which was the following day. He was out of the country on an assignment for his job as a chemical engineer. His mother wired him that Mother had died and he sent a telegram and a spray of yellow roses. I read from one of Mother's favorite scriptures from Ecclesiastes: "Truly the light is sweet, and a pleasant thing it is for the eyes to behold the sun." Miss German had labored lovingly on the program, though she scolded herself over and over again for the one typo on the very front page of the program. She had misspelled Mother's name: "V-O-I-L-A." I tried to reassure her that it was actually rather fitting: "Voilà."

Mama's Pocketbook

"Here your mama's pocketbook. Her dress and underthings in that hospital bag on the washing machine."

The purse felt light. Auntee stood still when she saw my eyes well up, then patted me on the shoulder. "You want squash or creamed corn for supper?"

How could she ask me such a question? Mama had been dead less than twenty-four hours. Food was the last thing on my mind. I had talked to her on Sunday, Mother's Day. Here it was only the following Friday; she was dead. I would later learn that Mama might have lived had the attending physician, actually a dentist who was moonlighting at the hospital, given her an antibiotic instead of Demerol.

I slumped down on the couch and settled into the darkness that envelops Auntee's den in every season, every source of light blocked out. She insists that covered windows trap the heat in winter and the cool in summer, and so some thick panel or heavy drapery covers any opening: the three rectangle windows cut into the front door, the windows that flanked the door, the window in the dining room to the right of the den that anchored the air conditioner. Its deep, insistent rumble set the whole house throbbing. No light, just sound on every side.

The bag was much smaller than the break-your-shoulder bags I now carry around most of the time, but still quite roomy enough for the average woman's necessities, as well as the inessential junk from which she can't be parted. I remember the day Mama recovered it from the kitchen garbage can. I was standing at the sink counter making salmon croquettes. She had lifted the lid and was just about to dump the ashtray when she spied the bag underneath a layer of eggshells and onion peels.

"You throwing this pocketbook away?" I nodded yes.

She shook off the onion skins still clinging to the sides and held it by the straps.

"Why you throwing it away? It looks perfectly good to me."

"No it's not, Mama. It's old and the straps are cracking and the piping is coming away from one of the side seams. Plus, look at these ugly ink spots. My pen spilled all over it on the plane." I put the fork down to show her the black splotches, like Rorschach inkblots, that had formed an unsightly cluster on the lower backside of the whiskey-colored bag.

"Oh, that ain't nothing. I can turn that around to the back and nobody will ever see these little spots. And I can sew the piping back into the seam. We do that kind of thing at the cleaners all the time."

"Mama, I can't believe you intend to go around town carrying this old spotted bag." I suggested that we sweet-talk Auntee into taking us to Parisian after dinner, so we could both buy new bags. She sucked her teeth. "I'm not wasting my good money. This pocketbook is perfectly all right for everyday and it has more room than the one I been carrying."

She reached around me for a dishcloth, dampened it, and squirted Ivory soap on one corner. As I dropped salmon patties into the cast-iron skillet, I watched her go to work on the bag, scrubbing it all around, leaving it clear of the egg whites' drying film, the airborne grit and grime that had settled in the purse's gusset. Just the inkblots remained. When she finished, she held it up again for me to see.

"Look here. I'll get at least another two years' worth of good out of this pocketbook. It's certainly good enough to take back and forth to Dixie Cleaners. Won't a soul out there or at Bruno's Food Store be paying any mind to what's on my pocketbook. Now Bruno will want to know what's *in* it, but that's all, and if he keeps raising his prices, soon won't be anything in it."

Still in shock, I needed the temporary forgetfulness of sleep, but it eluded me. I lay there in bed staring at the handbag on the dresser across the room, and now the splotches seemed like so many misshapen eyes staring at me. I crawled to the edge of the bed and stretched my arm across to reach the purse, then scooted back to rest against the headboard. I pulled out the Mother's Day card again, postmarked just the week before from West Lafayette, Indiana.

I ran my fingers across the black embossed letters and numbers of the gray-striped plastic square still tucked inside the Hallmark card. Everything just as I had mailed it, undisturbed.

WELCOME TO PARISIAN
THE POWER OF MONEY

And then below, in smaller letters: Your Credit Limit is $300. The credit card had been my Mother's Day present to her. Since I was merely a graduate student with a meager assistantship and a part-time job as a receptionist paying only minimum wage, I was amazed at just how easy it was to get. The card was a kind of joke that I had decided on months before, during one of the every-Sunday-morning conversations I had with Mama. Either I would call or she would call, and when I asked my ritual question, "How you doing, girl?" Mama always answered, with laughter in her voice, "Kicking, but not high."

I had initiated this Sunday morning ritual after Daddy died and I returned to Indiana to crank out all the final papers his death had interrupted. These ten o'clock calls highlighted my Sunday mornings and reassured me for one more week that Mama was all right. She took an interest in my papers and the books I was reading, especially Alex Haley's *Roots*. I sent her a copy of the book for her birthday, which ended up making the rounds of her clubwomen, in The Ladies of Pipe Shop, ending with Miss Virgie Lawson. She brought it to me the day after Mama's funeral, thinking rightly that I'd want to have it, to be reminded of the overly sentimental inscription:

To Mama,
    Whose roots run deep within me, sending sprouts of wondrous wisdom and abundant love.

        With all my love, your daughter,
        HAPPY BIRTHDAY

On one of these Sunday mornings, our talk turned to sewing. I was making a dress for an awards ceremony and the needle kept pulling in the fabric. Mama diagnosed the problem almost immediately. "First of all, why you sewing on polyester?"

"It was on sale."

"Well, change to a number fourteen ballpoint needle and next time stay away from the sisters."

"What sisters?"

"Polly and Esther."

I recovered from a laughing spell and asked what she was sewing.

"Between mending pissy pants at Dixie Cleaners and making the dresses for Dot's daughter's wedding, I ain't even had time to sew on a button for myself. I need a dress for the wedding, but I guess I'll have to break down and go into one of these white folks' stores, and you know how I hate that." That's when I decided. I would open a charge account for Mama at Parisian.

Mama had this thing about ready-made clothes, insisting that the seams were too stingy or the workmanship too shoddy or the buttons too cheap. After a time, her resistance seemed irrational to me, and although she never said, I suspected that behind it all was the fact that when stores like Parisian opened up their fitting rooms and sales forces to black women, all her hopes for a sewing business were shot.

Until they were seduced by the illusion of desegregation, women flocked to 1805 Eighteenth Street to get their garments made, especially when the boycotts brought the wheels of commerce in Birmingham grinding to a halt. But when local department stores caved in to the boycott's aggressive demands, Mama's business suffered. Black women, some of whom were now hired as saleswomen, grew to relish their newly won right to try on their hats and dresses in carpeted rooms with padded benches and shaded sconces on the wall. With shopping bags and brightly corded hatboxes from Burgher-Phillips, Pizitz, and Odom Bowers and White, they could stroll to some nearby lunch counter and sit and sip a Coca-Cola and nibble on a Ball Park frank.

The whiff of desegregation had done much to nurture in Mama contempt for fancy department stores, but it was the coat incident that pushed the prospect of patronizing the likes of Parisian beyond the bounds of possibility. Mama had long made most of my coats—the red flannel with pleats in the back, the green wide-wale corduroy car coat with a gold quilted lining, my Sunday coat, a navy blue princess style lined with satin-backed crepe. And then the camel houndstooth check with dark brown velvet collar that I was wearing that Sunday when we were leaving Mother's house. I had just proudly announced that I would soon be going to Mobile to the Library Association meeting. Mrs. Slaughter, the librarian, had offered me a job as her assistant and had decided that I should mingle with other librarians if I was serious about becoming one myself.

Mother looked me up and down and decided that I needed a new coat for the trip. I had plainly outgrown the houndstooth check. My arms dangled from the sleeves and my skirt hung several inches below the hem. At fifteen, I was five feet, nine and a half inches tall and still growing.

"Wait a minute."

She rushed back toward the doorway, digging in a cavernous red leather bag for her wallet. "Here, go buy yourself another coat." She handed Mama the Parisian credit card that bore the name MRS. FRED A. WILLIAMS, SR.

*   *   *

It threatened rain the morning we had planned the shopping trip. Mama, who hated shopping anyway, thought we should wait until the next Saturday. I couldn't bear to wait another week, and so we boarded the bus to Birmingham, pulling the cord at Newberry's, where we stopped first for tuna fish sandwiches on toast and Coca-Cola in the tall trademark bulging glasses with frosted flourish. I was eager to get to Parisian, which was central to my teenage daydreams for a long, long time. I imagined that it was a store only by day. By night it was washed in mysterious light, its sweeping floors turned into one expansive ballroom where men in tails and satin cummerbunds twirled women in billowy clouds of blue chiffon or draping mousseline. I had been there often with Mother to shop for Papa's Sunday clothes. Knowing that he would never buy anything for himself and would wear every piece he owned until it shredded off his portly frame, Mother caught Parisian's end-of-summer sales. Bald-headed men wearing seersucker suits and polka-dotted bow ties leered at Mother as she picked her way through racks of hanging jackets, stacks of unhemmed trousers in lightweight wool, and the limited pile of short-sleeved shirts with 17 ¾-inch collars. At other times, we shopped for her French-milled pastel-colored soaps that felt leaden in the hand. And her perfumes—which sat atop her dresser in a beveled mirrored tray.

The store stretched from one block to the other, and the brass that trimmed its gleaming glass front resembled the entrance of a grand hotel. So imposing was it that any minute you might expect to see stately men in livery and tricorn hats, their white-gloved hands opening doors for patrons whose high-sheened faces gave them an expensive look, just like the reedy, wraithlike saleswomen who stood, erect, behind cosmetics counters or strolled up and down the aisles, threading their way around the marble columns that divided the expansive room. Their hair—honey blond, jet black, silver—was always perfectly coiffed and their lips smeared thickly with cherry red or coral. Although I know they wore no uniforms, they have merged together in my memory, where they stand in black suede or patent-leather high-heeled pumps. They wear black dresses or black pencil kick-pleated skirts and starched white blouses with the collars turned up in back. Ropes and ropes of cultured pearls dangle from their bony throats.

I strode just ahead of Mama, pulling the heavy door open to let her enter first. We walked straight back toward the elevator, where the operator stood just outside the door—a diminutive copper-colored woman who wore a cardigan buttoned from neck to waist. She muttered a pleasant "Good morning," then sat on a low, three-legged stool.

"What floor you going to?"

"We want the coat department," I chirped.

"Say please," Mama said, and the woman smiled and pulled the black-handled lever that snapped the brass lattice shut.

A saleswoman first stalked us with her eyes, her head pivoting nervously on her neck, her snowy hair piled in a bun atop her head. Then she began to haunt our every move. As she tracked us round the room, her skirt swished against her nylons. Standing at our elbows, literally almost breathing down our necks, she provoked Mama to hiss under her breath, "We do not plan to steal." I wanted her to spit the statement in the woman's face, but Mama was usually reluctant to speak up, especially in the presence of whites, so instead, she pulled on the belt of her dress and said, "We're looking for a coat."

"For yourself or for her?"

"For my daughter. Size ten missy. She's tall for her age."

"You don't see anything here?" she asked, pointing to the rack.

"Not yet," I answered. "I don't like any of these."

Trying to be cordial, Mama said, "She's a little hard to please."

The woman seemed personally affronted, but she returned from the stockroom with a blue plaid coat.

"These just arrived today. We haven't even checked them in. All the girls are wearing them in *Seventeen*."

"Do you like it?" Mama asked. I knew how much she hated shopping, and on the rare occasions when I had persuaded her to go with me, I felt the pressure to make a choice long before I was ready. Rushing resulted in many an article of clothing that I actually hated and seldom wore.

"It's all right. I'll try it on." But before I did, Mama began her routine inspection. She always picked store-bought clothes apart. She could abide a messy house, littered with scraps of fabric, cigarette butts stubbed out on lids of empty beer cans, but she insisted on precision in her sewing, ripping out crooked seams, more than once if need be, and pressing and clipping the curves of others until all their puckers disappeared.

First she noticed that there was no ease in the lining; then, that the plaids didn't match. She pointed to the sides, the center back seam, and where the sleeves joined the upper front. And the buttons were sewn on so loosely that they were likely to fall off if the wind blew hard. When the haughty clerk said in a snooty voice, "The manufacturers aren't doing that anymore," meaning matching plaids, Mama quickly answered, "Well, I can see that all right enough, but I'm not buying a garment that is so poorly made."

"Suit yourself," the woman shot back and walked away, leaving her French perfume lingering in the air. We went round and round the rack again and found a double-breasted melton chesterfield that was feather gray. For once, the sleeves fell just below my wristbone and the hem below my knees. Although Mama thought it would be in the cleaners every other week, it passed inspection. Just to be sure, shouldn't we take a look at Loveman's, where garments were even more expensive and generally better made? We found the clerk and asked her to hold the gray coat for an hour. We would be back.

Outside, I reminded Mama that we only had a Parisian credit card.

"I know that. But we can put a coat on layaway and have it out by the time you go to Mobile." When we found nothing to my liking, we returned to Parisian. This time, the woman sat inside the elevator squinting at the fine red-and-black print of a pocket-sized New Testament, just like the ones they handed out in Sunday School. Mama said, "You shouldn't be reading in this dim light. You'll ruin your eyes that way." The woman looked up, smiled, and pulled the lever. When we rested our backs against the oak-paneled wall and the elevator began its slow ascent, I noticed that the woman had removed her sweater and that PARISIAN was emblazoned across the yoke of her khaki-colored dress.

Back upstairs, Mama presented the credit card. The woman looked from hold tag to plastic square and, turning to Mama, asked, "Is this your credit card?"

Mama shook her head no, but before she could elaborate, the woman asked, an unmistakable note of suspicion in her voice, "Then are you authorized to use it?"

"Yes, we are."

"Well, we'll still have to go up to the office. It's for the customer's protection, you understand."

We followed her into the elevator, where she barked, "Fourth floor." I watched the numbers lighting as we climbed. Upstairs at the credit desk, we three stood in front of the counter as the saleswoman explained the situation to the clerk who sat behind the metal cage. Wearing black-framed cat-eyed glasses, rhinestones studding the rims, she glanced from Mama to me as she shuffled through her ledger:

"WARE; WELLS; WHEATON; WILLIAMS, ALVA; WILLIAMS, BENNETT. Here it is, FRED A. WILLIAMS. But it doesn't say here that you are authorized to use this card. A Fred Williams Jr. is the only one, other than Mr. and Mrs. Williams, authorized to use this card."

Mama drew a breath and said, "But we are. Do you think we would be crazy enough to show up in this store and try to charge something on somebody else's card?"

"But that's exactly what you're trying to do." She continued, now a

tinge apologetically. "Your name's not here, and there is no note to indi-
cate that either Mr. or Mrs. Williams has called to make a temporary
exception. I'm sorry, that's how it's done."

"We can call Mother in Mountain Brook," I said. "I know the number."
Mama turned to the woman behind the cage, while the clerk paced the
marble floor. When she stood still for a moment and leaned against the
counter facing me, I could see tiny red blood vessels on her nose and smell
whiskey on her breath. Then I heard Mother yelling through the phone:
"She's my daughter-in-law and the young lady is her daughter, my granddaughter. Let them charge that coat to my account."

"I guess you heard her. Let them have the coat."

"I see you found something," said the woman in the elevator, now wearing
her sweater again. Then Mama exploded. "We found something all right,
but not without a whole lot of rigamarole and Hoosier mess. Just because
they say your money spends the same as theirs, don't you believe it's true,
not for a minute. They don't want you up in these stores no more than they
want to serve you a Coca-Cola. The law's the law, but don't you know that,
as sure as you born, if they could get your money without having to look
you in your face, they'd do it. Every last one of them would do it."

The elevator jerked to a stop on the first floor and the woman simply nodded. As we left the store, the rain fell in whispers. The coat, sheathed in a
white plastic bag with gold PARISIAN lettering, was draped across my arm.
As we stood underneath the green-striped awning in front of Newberry's
to wait for the No.10, I remembered the bag of salted peanuts that we had
promised to bring back for Reggie and the silver kisses for Bumbiddle.

We boarded the crowded bus and sat just behind the driver. Staring out
the window, Mama replayed the incident out loud. Mimicking the saleswoman's high-toned nasal voice, she said, "The manufacturers don't do
that anymore." "Are you authorized to use this card?" And then she sucked
her teeth and said, "Don't get me wrong, now. You have a nice coat. It's
just fine, but I could make a better coat even with my eyes closed."

After Mama's funeral, I wanted nothing more than to sink into a stupor, to
pull the covers over my head, to ceaselessly bewail my loss, not just of
Mama, but of all my loved ones. Papa tried his best to comfort me, offering his timeworn expression: "Don't think of what you done lost; think of
what you got left. You got me, you got your Auntee, and Gina, and your
brothers. Your brothers need you to be strong for them. You the oldest."

"They need me? I need somebody to lean on myself."

"Lean on the Lord; He'll prop you up on every leaning side." When he began to read me the Twenty-third Psalm, I found it more mocking than comforting and tried to tune it out. For six years running I had walked in the valley of the shadow of death and felt no one was with me. And when Papa died himself, just two years later—again, around Memorial Day— things began to seem surreal. From time to time, Grandma Edie had spoken of families being cursed, and despite my rational leanings, I was coming to believe that my family was cursed with death.

I languished there in Pipe Shop until near the end of June, avoiding the big decisions that were staring me in the face. Should I get a job in Birmingham in order to help Bumbiddle through his last two years of college, or should I return to Indiana to complete my dissertation? At that point I had three chapters written, two remaining, and revisions to make on them all. The prospect seemed almost too daunting to contemplate. As I tried to decide about my future, Reggie resumed his studies at the San Francisco Art Institute, and Bumbiddle joined the navy, without discussing it with anyone. Just came home to say that he had enlisted. He had not been able to concentrate on college courses, and there were few jobs in Bessemer at which he could make a decent living. Back in Indiana, I plunged into my work. For the past six years death had interrupted study and study interrupted grief, and so I accommodated myself to this familiar cycle once again.

The day of my dissertation defense, some friends prepared a party for me. I was in a bittersweet mood, as a fellow graduate student, still laboring away at her dissertation and fearing that the end would never near, put a simple question to me: "How do you feel since you've come out the wilderness?"

"Numb, relieved," I answered. "It's a major hurdle over."

"Are you gonna come back to get your hood?"

"No, I'm beyond all that," I told her, although now, looking back, I know it wasn't so.

And with now-remembered smugness, I then allowed as how only the sentimental and those puffed up with pride needed pictures of themselves in caps and cowls and tasseled mortarboards. In time I came to see that I had simply imposed one hardship on myself while trying to avoid another. I had not let myself be sad about that morning when, following my defense, I trod the half-mile to my apartment to sit in the living room with no one, at least not at the moment, to share with me my triumph. Instead, I stared blankly through the picture window at rows and rows of compact cars, imported from Japan, with Purdue Boilermaker stickers inside their windshields.

Museums

I was reading the Sunday papers one morning when I came across a review of an exhibition titled "Passionate Visions of the American South: Self-Taught Artists from 1940 to the Present," on view at the Corcoran Museum in Washington, D.C. I folded up the papers and taxied there that very afternoon in April 1995. Inside the museum, I found myself inexplicably frozen before two paintings, just inside the threshold of a room. The first, *Life Go On,* was a vibrant picture of a chocolate brown heavily rouged woman who seems to have emerged from a darkened, womblike space. One blue bird rests on her head; another, larger bright blue bird with yellow streaks rests serenely in her clawlike hands. The bird in her hand and the bird on her head face in opposite directions.

The second painting was even more prepossessing. Titled *Rolling Mill: Steel Is the Master, Lady Is the Power,* the abstract work, wrought from metal, enamel, garden hose, rope, and industrial sealing compound, was almost frightening in its frenzied strokes. "Thornton Dial Sr., Bessemer," the caption read. Thornton Dial, Thornton Dial, I thought to myself. I know that name.

Down at the museum shop, on a center table, I found a stack of exhibition catalogues. Leafing hurriedly through the biography section, I immediately recognized Thornton Dial Sr. as a neighbor who had lived three blocks over from us all the time I was in Pipe Shop. There he stood, arms akimbo, another painting of massive scale looming in the backdrop. Of my father's generation, Dial had worked at Pullman Standard, the boxcar factory, for thirty years, taking side jobs in construction and maintenance, commercial fishing, and farming. After retirement, he began to devote himself full-time to his art, salvaging materials from the Bessemer countryside for the paintings that now hang in major art galleries and museums and in the homes of numerous private collectors. Thornton Dial had outlasted the decline of iron and steel, but industry still had a powerful hold on his imagination. Seeing Dial's work reminded me of all the afternoons in Pipe Shop when Daddy sat sketching just to the side of the porch, but the sketching ended when he was abruptly reassigned, first the three to eleven, then the eleven to seven, the graveyard shift.

The show at the Corcoran brought another exhibition to mind, on view at the National Building Museum. Called "Making It in the Birmingham District," the show had opened the previous December, close to the twentieth anniversary of Daddy's death. I had planned to go, but it slipped my mind until I saw Dial's paintings, which wrenched me out of late-night reveries of Pipe Shop the neighborhood and forced a confrontation with Pipe Shop the foundry.

I arrived at the building with the rose red bricks that stretched the length of one long city block, in time to join a museum tour guided by a chipper, blond college-age man in shorts exposing the muscular legs of a soccer player. I listened as he extolled the genius of Montgomery C. Meigs, the architect and engineer of the former pensions building, modeled on the Farnese Gallery in Rome. Meigs had taken unusual insurances to preserve the historical record, not just of the building, but of the age. Inside the more than twenty colossal Corinthian columns that he had taken from a church in Rome, Meigs dispersed maps, newspapers, minutes from town meetings, and, of all things, a copper facsimile of the Declaration of Independence. These he stored for historians and antiquarians of a future generation, in case the building ever came to ruin.

Right at the entrance of the exhibition, on the first of four large panels, was an aerial view of Vulcan, standing atop his observatory tower. I stood transfixed, remembering all the times I saw Vulcan when Gina and I rode to Mountain Brook with Papa to visit Mother. We'd always look to see if Vulcan's torch burned red or green, breathing a sigh of relief if it was green. That was the sign that, at least within the last twenty-four hours, no one had died in a traffic accident within the Birmingham city limits.

As school children, we'd gone on field trips to see the world's largest iron man, perched high above Red Mountain, standing guard over the city of Birmingham, six hundred feet below. We climbed the 159 steps of the statue to hear the spiel: Next to the Statue of Liberty, Vulcan was the tallest figure in America—55 feet—and the largest cast-iron statue in the world—120,000 pounds. Vulcan had represented the Birmingham district at the Louisiana Purchase Exhibition in St. Louis in 1904.

"All below you is Jones Valley, named for the first white man who settled here."

A patron bumped against me and broke me from my reverie. Before giving up my space to him, I paused a minute longer to read the Vulcan caption:

WE ALL HALT HERE, AND WELL WE MAY . . . THE LIBERAL MOTHER OF A THOUSAND FURNACES AND FORGES . . . WE STAND IN THE PRESENCE OF ONE OF THE GREAT WONDERS OF THE WORLD, RED MOUNTAIN.

On the backside of the Vulcan image was a blown-up poster of the labor organizer Hosea Hudson and his bride, above the caption:

AFRICAN AMERICANS PARTICIPATED IN THE DISTRICT'S GROWTH DESPITE THE SHAMEFUL POLITICAL AND SOCIAL CONSTRAINTS THEY FACED.

The mood at the exhibition grew more somber and grim and heavy by the minute. All shot in winter's ash gray light, the black-and-white photographs of hoists and gyrators and coke ovens, and the occasional tree, denuded of all foliage, created a sense of overwhelming desolation. The exhibition admitted no perspective, which only heightened the claustrophobic atmosphere of the room. The dimness of the brooding light, combined with the closeness of the room and the tiny print of the captions, pushed the viewer into almost immediate contact with the photographs. Straining for perspective, I backed away and crashed against a folding screen. So there I was, distance all contracted, pulled into an ambivalent embrace with photographs of ruin. One piece of industrial equipment, standing on a crumbling base, looked just like a monster's head, its eyes gouged out like Lear's. I inched my way along the wall, peering to read the captions:

ABANDONED STACKS AND MIXER, TCI
ABANDONED COKE OVENS, BILL GOULD COAL MINE
ABANDONED CRUSHER RUINS
ENTRANCE PORTAL TO ABANDONED IRON MINE
ABANDONED MCCULLY NO. 8 GYRATOR CRUSHER, RUFFNER RED ORE MINE
ABANDONED FURNACE, BRIERFIELD IRONWORKS
MAIN STREET OF ABANDONED TOWN, OLD DORA
ABANDONED HOISTS, CONVEYORS, WOODWARD IRON COMPANY

That's where Papa worked—Woodward Iron Company, or, as it was also called, Pyne Mine.

"My papa works at Pyne Mine. He lives at 1404 Ninth Avenue. His number is Hamilton 58255."

Here were photographs of a paint-chipped, striped metal awning where miners collected their wages. One window marked WHITE, the other, COL-ORED. And there, the company's slogan: KEEP THE WHITE LIGHTS BURN-ING—PYNE MINE.

I had almost made my way around the room when I finally came upon two color photographs shot at U.S. Pipe and Foundry. The only spots of color in the entire exhibition, the first was of an iron pour. Because nothing of the process could be seen save for bursts of light—sulphur, saffron, sapphire blue—the picture seemed quite abstract, dependent on the caption for identification. I couldn't have predicted how the next picture would affect me.

I read the caption first:

EXTRACTING A 24-INCH PIPE, U.S. PIPE AND FOUNDRY, BESSEMER

A lone black man in a white helmet was bent over a row of pressurized valves as the pipe emerged from a giant mold. At first glance, the pipe looked just like a cannon pointing at my chest, and the mold like a long, deep birth canal, both pipe and mold dwarfing the image of the man. I could swear he looked a bit like Daddy, although this must have been my imagination running away with me. I had no warning, did not feel it coming on, but I stood there staring at the man until I began to sob, wracking sobs that brought another patron to my side.

"Are you all right?" she asked. I nodded yes, but when I did not collect myself, a guard came over and ushered me gently outside and to a bench between two of the marble columns. I sank down there, heaving, and when the patron left the gallery, she approached me once again. "Are you sure you're all right? Would you like for me to call a doctor?"

I faintly recall a barrage of other questions of concern, before I caught enough breath to murmur, "I'm all right. I'll be all right. I just need to sit here for a while."

I don't remember how long I sat there leaning against the pillar. It could have been ten minutes, or an hour. When I came to myself, I was clenching my skirt in my hand. I rose, and for a moment felt an acute sensation of vertigo. Fearing that my legs would buckle right under me, I leaned against the column for support. Braced, I hobbled out of the building and across the short expanse down into the subway, passing a line of giggling schoolgirls as they fed coins into the fare machine. Hearing them approaching at my back and not wanting them to see my tears, I walked farther down the platform. My whole body felt naked, stripped clean like the bark of a tree that has been struck by lightning.

*   *   *

I missed my stop at Dupont Circle. Without realizing it, I had ridden all the way to Silver Spring. The static of the train announcement brought me back to myself again. The train had come to the end of the line and all passengers must disembark. I staggered off and sat on the slatted bench waiting for the train in the opposite direction.

As the train howled and lurched through the darkness of the tunnel, the image of the helmeted man and the valves and the pipe emerging from the giant mold was still vivid in my mind. I could not help but think of Daddy. For more than twenty years I had tried to banish him from memory, but here was the repressed returned. Every which way I moved, I bumped into another reminder, not just of Daddy, but of U.S. Pipe and Foundry. Many a time, especially during my college years, I would listen as family members—one by one—laid Daddy's woes and squandered hopes at the feet of U.S. Pipe. I mustered not a mite of sympathy for the view they took of him. I was always ready with a sharply rational rejoinder, quick to interject that work was not the measure of the man and thus it could not explain everything. There was more to a man than his work. But now it slowly dawned on me that, while all this might be true, there was also more to Daddy's work than I had ever known or cared to know. I was now compelled to seek that knowledge, which I could only glean by going back to Pipe Shop once again.

P A R T

S I X

Who's turned us round like this, so that we always,
do what we may, retain the attitude
of someone who's departing? Just as he,
on the last hill, that shows him all his valley
for the last time, will turn and stop and linger,
we live our lives, for ever taking leave.
—RILKE, "The Eighth Elegy"

Return
Memorial Day Weekend 1995

Auntee, I'm coming home."

"When?"

"Memorial Day weekend."

I made the call on May Day. Less than a year had passed since I was last at home, the shortest distance ever between two visits there for me. The flight was crowded and very bumpy, almost like the pilot thought he might be galloping on a bronco instead of riding the air. I sipped on ginger ale, hoping to ease the rising nausea. Maybe Grandma Edie was right after all, I thought to myself: A person had to be crazy to fly.

I had long been fascinated with flying, but it had now lost its charm, a charm perhaps it only holds for children, anyway, before they learn to fear. Ever since I first saw Mother board an Eastern Airlines jet for San Francisco, I couldn't wait to fly. I was ten years old, and had only seen planes take off on television. *"Watch, I'll wave to you from the window."* Mother always said she waved, but I didn't see her hand that day. Maybe because the plane was parked far from the observation deck. I do remember the plumes of white smoke streaking through the firmament.

I still can't quite decide whether that early fascination with flying was for the thing itself or for what it represented. Throughout the community of Pipe Shop, flying signified prosperity. It was a sign that you had "made it," that you were doing well. It communicated one thing when you took the Greyhound bus and something else again, and better, if you flew. Whenever news of someone's imminent departure or arrival was mentioned at Ophelia's, you could count on hearing in the next breath, "Are they flying?" "Did they fly?" Flying was the next rung up from "motoring" on the social mobility ladder. In the days before flying became a novelty, the sign of status was returning home in a long shiny automobile with a horn like Satchmo's muted trumpet. The *Birmingham World* announced these comings and goings on its "Society" page: Mr. and Mrs. Isaiah Madison were motoring to visit relatives in Detroit, Michigan, or the Michigan relatives had motored to visit them.

After a while, though, the fact that flying was the transportation mode of choice of the up-and-coming was signaled by the *World,* which ran front-page photographs, in almost every issue, of someone standing on the steps of an airplane, waving at those below. I would clip them for my scrapbook and picture myself in the spot where the travelers stood.

Others could regard flying as they would, but Grandma Edie held it right up there with the moon walk. She was skeptical of the latter, and didn't hide it, spewing out, "Ain't nobody been up on God's moon." When Reggie pointed and said, "Look, Grandma, see for yourself. It's right here on television," she answered with great contempt and seeming disdain for his gullibility, "You can't believe everything they put on these televisions. These televisions can do anything." While she didn't doubt that planes took off and skimmed through the air for hours at a time, she seemed to think they contaminated the sacred firmament, and when God got ready, he would just get rid of them. In any argument about flying that she thought she was losing, Grandma would say with finality, "If God hadda wanted you to fly, he would have gave you wings," then she'd suck her tooth and walk away.

"How was the flight?" Auntee asked.

"Rugged. I need to report the pilot, who has obviously been watching too many reruns of *Bonanza.* Made me sick to my stomach."

"Didn't you take your Dramamine?"

"Uh-unh, I forgot. Look at you, Brittany; you're almost to my chest." She was a whole head taller, and sprouting breasts, which caused her great embarrassment. She kept her arms folded across her chest the way old women used to do in church. Mama called it the "I-shall-not-be-moved" posture.

We padded down a seemingly endless stretch of corridor, the thickness of the tufted carpet muffling our footsteps. Well before we reached it, I spotted the blue-green lush and vibrant colors of a mural that was standard billboard scale. As we drew nearer, I could decipher the caption: COME TO ALABAMA.

"What's this?" I paused in my tracks to see that it was an ad from the Alabama Bureau of Tourism and Travel. I took a brochure from the plastic box affixed to the wall.

We chattered the rest of the way, then walked up and down the aisles of the parking garage, searching for the car.

"We could've walked to Bessemer by now. Don't you remember where you parked?" Auntee complained.

"I thought it was on the blue level," Gina answered calmly.

"Well, evidently it's not here."

Brittany then remembered that it was on the yellow level. They had only driven through the blue to get to the yellow. In the car I cast my eyes over the brochure, still in my hand, tsk-tsk-tsking at its sentimental pitch about

> *cherished memories and time spent at the home house listening to Grandma recount stories from her childhood. . . . A time for all to come together in a special place where some of your fondest memories were made. This is Alabama.*

I'll say this is Alabama, I thought to myself, sticking the brochure in the outer pocket of my tote bag. Then began the cheery updates— Brittany's math trophy, her Girls' Club award, her Future Writers of America certificate. Barely had Brittany finished bringing me up to date when Auntee said, "Did I remember to call you about Miss Hambright?"

"No, what about her?"

"They found her dead up in that house all by herself. Had been up in there for going on four days. They say Junebug found her. Remember her nephew, Junebug? He was 'bout the only family she had left here in Bessemer, and since she been down sick, he's been the onliest one to look in on her. You know, she had got so big, couldn't hardly move around. He said he had a time getting up in that house, what with all the papers and all— schoolchildren's papers from years and years ago—dumpster loads of junk. I bet some of your papers could have been up in there. June said it's a wonder she didn't set herself on fire. He was taking garbage bags by the dozens down to that dump."

I interrupted her. "They—he threw away the papers?"

"Yeah, what was he gon' keep all that junk for?" and then Auntee rattled on. "I went to the funeral. Had it down in Jonesboro at Bethel Baptist. Coleman had the body. Had so much face powder on Miss Hambright she didn't favor herself at all."

Gina laughed, "Well, that ain't nothing new. That's par for the course with Coleman."

Out the Bessemer Super Highway, a block before where Miss Pigrom's ramshackle music studio used to be, Bessemer's two oldest black funeral homes stood side by side—Coleman and Sons and Stansell Brothers. For a time, because Coleman was the older establishment, the folks said that it was the place to let "handle the body" of your kin, especially if you had kin who cared about how you looked when the mourners and idle curiosity-seekers gazed down into your face resting on the pillow of the coffin.

Whenever anybody died, one of the first questions heard was "Who got the body?" If the answer was "Coleman," then the person breathed a sigh of relief, for this was the mortuary with a reputation for making the dead look just like they were sleeping. Many the day after a funeral when neighbors and family of the deceased sat on porches drinking beer, eating fried chicken, and swapping stories about the dead one's escapades, someone would say, "So-and-so sure did favor himself. Looked just like he would open up his eyes any minute and say, 'What you doing eyeballing me like that?'" You could substitute any name, any age, any gender to that generic statement, for Coleman's reputation was rock solid; that is, until the old man died and his wild son took over the business, managing it between joyrides and weekends in Atlanta with carloads of drunken friends. Folks used to say that the son—his name was Rayfield—must have bought blue negligees and face powder by the crate, since practically every woman that he embalmed was buried in a light blue negligee, her face thickly layered with loose powder that almost never matched the tone of the dead woman's skin. But concerned souls always proffered mourning relatives the necessary reassurance: "She sure did favor herself. Looked just like she was sleeping." And if a ravenous disease or a sudden violent death from a lover's knifing or a mangling car wreck would betray such words as bald-faced lies, then something like "Coleman did the best he could, considering" would have to do.

"Auntee, don't you know any good news?" and she pinched up her face.

Still woozy from the flight, I lay down for a nap and was awakened by the pleasingly delicate notes of "Für Elise." I followed the sound to the living room where Brittany was practicing her piano lesson.

"That sounds really good, sweetie," I said while clapping loudly.

"The recital is in June. Are you gonna come?"

"Maybe. You know, I used to play this piece," I said, flipping to the cover of the music book. I called for Gina, who came to the door, her finger stuck between the pages of *Disappearing Acts*. "Gina, didn't we used to use this same Wurlitzer music book?"

"I think so."

Brittany laughed and said, "Mama told me that you never used to like to practice your finger exercises."

"That's right, but she didn't either. What else did your mama tell you?

I know she left out the part about her playing hooky from music lessons so she could go skating in the Carver Projects. You see, once your mama got titties, she lost all interest in the piano. She wanted to get to Forrest and the cat-eyed boys who lived down there."

"Wait a minute," Gina interrupted the tale. "I can't have you telling these lies to my child. Brittany, the truth is, she wanted to skate but she was so stiff and clumsy that every time she tried, she came back home cut up and bruised, ready for a cast."

"That's not true."

"Yes it is. Brittany, ask her how she got that scar on her knee. See that scar? She got it skating down the hill in Carver Projects, busted her knee wide open. Bandages had to be changed for days."

"Wait, wait, wait. Let me finish. Brittany, she played hooky and dared me to tell anybody, and then when I said I was gonna tell Papa on her, she bribed me, said if I didn't tell, she would show me how to grow titties."

"Can't nobody show nobody how to grow titties," Brittany answered.

"I know, but I was stupid and believed everything your mama told me, because I wanted to be just like her. When Auntee bought her a brassiere at Momart, I wanted a brassiere, but didn't have a thing to put in it. I was so jealous of her having titties that I was desperate; I would have believed anything. She could have told me that gasoline would give me titties and I would have marched right to the service down the street from Mother's house and asked them to sell me some gas in a Dixie cup."

"I still can't believe that you believed me, but when I saw the look on your face that day at the foot of the Bessemer Super Highway bridge, I thought to myself, 'If she is stupid enough to think I have the power to give her titties, then Lord help her.'"

Until that day, I had always been afraid of crossing the bridge all by myself, but that Saturday, because I thought I would soon have titties, I strutted across that bridge, past the army salvage store, its window cluttered with fatigues, boots, and canteens. I even stepped confidently past the winos who leered and slouched on the stoop of Duke's Place. That day, it didn't even frighten me to pass the funeral homes. No, none of this bothered me. Titties were on my mind and fantasies of whistles from the boys at the start of school when I would pass the stall of lockers.

"How come you believed her?" Brittany wanted to know, and when I recovered from laughing at the memory of this episode, I told her, "You see, your mama told me that the same ingredients that made Papa's lemon pound cakes rise were the ones that would give me titties."

"And you bought that?"

"Not exactly, but I pushed all my doubts aside and started stealing baking powder and butter to rub in circles on my chest. You see, I had a crush on the preacher's son, Timmy, and I thought I could get him to like me if I had titties. I finally gave up the day I embarrassed myself in front of him. All the while I was waiting for mine to grow in, I borrowed one of your Mama's bras and stuffed it full of tissue paper. But this one Sunday we were at Mother's. It was after church. Reverend Lockhart and his family had come to Sunday dinner and stayed for the meeting of the Bessemer Voters League. The grown folks were doing their business in the living room, while the children played badminton in the field that ran alongside Mother's house—Timmy and his sister, Wanda Glen, Gina, Reggie, Bumbiddle, and I.

"When it came my turn to serve, I raised my arm to swat the plastic shuttlecock and the tissue fell from underneath my blouse and landed right on the grass. Nobody would have ever noticed if Gina hadn't started laughing and pointing: 'Somebody lost her titty; somebody lost her titty.'"

"Anybody could see that big white wad of tissue paper laying down on the grass. Anyway, you made it worse when you started crying and ran inside the house."

"What happened then?"

"I didn't come out for the rest of the afternoon. Needless to say, it took me years to get titties, and baking powder and butter didn't do it."

"How you know they didn't?" Gina asked, and I pushed her head against the back of the chair.

"Brittany, play some more."

"You want to play a duet? You know how to play 'Blue Moon'?"

"Who doesn't? Slide over."

"Now you sound like Florida B."

"No, she wouldn't say 'slide over'; she'd say 'move over,'" and we cracked up once again.

"I bet you wouldn't call her Florida B. to her face."

"Lord, no." Gina began to stomp around the room, imitating Miss Pigrom—chest pushed out, shoulders back, head bobbing.

"'Wrong, wrong.' Tick-tock-tick-tock. 'Wrong, wrong.' Tick-tock-tick-tock. 'Did you practice? Did you practice?'"

Then I joined in the mime.

"Andante, fortissimo, pianissimo."

Then Gina again, "Crazy-mo, No-mo."

"Gina, you have her voice down pat. She must be retired by now; she can't still be scaring children half to death?"

"No. She's down in Florida with her son. Alzheimer's."

The community was so proud of Miss Pigrom. One of our own had been to Juilliard. Though, at the time, most of us didn't really know what Juilliard was, Reverend Wells had announced in church that it was a famous school for musicians that didn't let just any old body in. Black people all across Bessemer sacrificed to give their children piano lessons with this six-foot, two-inch big-boned woman who made us quiver in our Mary Janes. Her fingers looked like the tentacles of an octopus, and my child's eye remembers at least two octaves between her thumb and pinky finger. Her face was always set in a grimace as she stomped the floor, just as Gina remembered, in time with the rebuking metronome, to each child's tentative and tangled rendition of "Minuet in G."

I never understood why Miss Pigrom wanted your fingers placed on specific keys. It seemed to me that as long as you played the right notes, the position of your fingers shouldn't matter a whole helluva lot. There was no negotiating with Florida B., however. "Over in the corner." And there you went to work it out on a paper keyboard, while the next trembling child hunched her shoulders, hoping to blot out Miss Florida B. Pigrom's towering body.

If you had the first appointment, you could often hear her thunderous playing when you reached the first step of the rickety, worm-eaten staircase leading to the studio. Her passionate playing—I still remember her rendition of "Polonaise in A major"—seemed to rattle the very walls of that ramshackle building with the professionally painted sign: FLORIDA B. PIGROM MUSIC STUDIO.

Revelations

Nobody fries fish like Auntee. She breads it just right—not too heavy, not too light—then spreads it on layers and layers of paper towels to soak the grease away. There is just the right amount of mayonnaise in her coleslaw, and just a pinch of sugar and sprinklings of caraway seeds. I like the ritual preparations—setting the table, pouring the iced tea, folding the napkins (not the blue ones that are permanently on the table in their napkin rings; they are just for decoration). Tension and old-time misunderstandings magically disappear at mealtime, and we are just hands—Auntee's, Gina's, mine, and now Brittany's—all working together. Laughing. Telling stories. Some new. Some we have told too many times to count.

As we cleared the table and Gina sudsed up the water, she asked, "You want to wash or dry?" and we both laughed at the recognition that nothing much had changed. We were girls again, back in Mother's kitchen, asking this question on any given Sunday afternoon.

"Auntee, whatever happened to that big fat scrapbook Mother used to have? The one with the brown leather cover."

"I think it's there on that stack in the den with the other ones."

"No, it's not. I looked for it."

"Hmm. Well, I don't know then. You know, come to think of it, it could have been among Mother's papers and things in the credenza. When they set her things outdoors, a lot of stuff came up missing. Her punch bowl, her silver trays. Lots of stuff, all that Junior didn't pawn before he died.

"I'm mighty glad that Mother didn't live to see him laid out dead. He had near 'bout wasted away to nothing. I don't think she could've stood it. Seeing her child like that and not being able to do anything for him, after all she had done for him all his life. He was her heart."

He was her heart, which is why no one could ever understand or accept why he rarely visited once he moved away, not even when she had the stroke. Although I still only knew a fraction of Uncle Jr.'s last miserable days, I was glad too that Mother was gone and could not see his shrinking frame, the rotting septum of his nose, and the stooping, defeated shoulders of her last-born child.

His funeral service at a local white Episcopal church was full of ritual, very different from what we would have had for him at Macedonia. But after Uncle Jr. moved back home from Washington—after losing his executive job, his house in the suburbs, his marriage to a speech therapist, his children—he joined the Episcopal Church. He said he liked the service better, but I always felt he wanted to spare himself the embarrassing questions from those who had seen him go from short pants to trousers and prophesied with Mother that he would be a doctor one day.

Once Uncle Jr. died, Auntee found it hard to talk about it. He was much like her own child; she was the one who had mainly raised him, after all. That afternoon as we remembered him, she revisited his final days.

"He sho' did suffer before he left this world. Legs full of runny sores, chills and fever. And he had lost so much weight, I could almost pick him up the way I used to do when he was just a baby."

That was hard for me to imagine. Uncle Jr. was six foot four and, in his healthy years, he weighed well over two hundred pounds. When we viewed the body at the wake—the casket was closed at the funeral—I could tell that he had lost weight, but he didn't look to be small enough for Auntee, five foot five, to carry. But neither I nor Gina saw any need to pry her loose from this image of herself as the one who had cared for her baby brother from the start of his life up to the very end.

When Uncle Jr. came back home after the divorce and the foreclosure, it seemed that he would get a second chance, a new life. His good friend Mark Green, who had gone through Howard's Dental School and returned home to establish a lucrative practice (there were so few black dentists), was well connected in Birmingham, as was his wife, Earlean, who later became an Alabama state senator. Together, they quickly found Uncle Jr. a job on Richard Arrington's history-making campaign for mayor.

Papa, especially, was proud of him again. His son was walking tall once more and wearing a crisp white shirt and tie to work at campaign headquarters, where apparently everybody liked him and wanted his long straight legs under their dinner table and his sophisticated patter ringing in their ears.

When Mama died that May 1979, the campaign was in full swing and Uncle Jr. was out late every night, and slept until well after noon the next day. He always seemed evasive when anyone asked him questions about the campaign. Eventually, we thought it best to leave him to his privacy, until

Papa mentioned the string of roughnecks parading in and out of his house. He and Papa took their meals at Auntee's, and whenever she had company, Uncle Jr. cadged cigarettes from them and sometimes money. The money was the tip-off. He was always short of cash, always cornering somebody for a loan. This one would slip him a ten, that one a twenty, and then we started putting two and two together.

Although we discovered that he was no longer working with the Arrington campaign, he insisted that he was. Papa, who had always suffered from an enlarged heart—and not just medically— stood by as Uncle Jr. persuaded him to mortgage the house to the hilt, and because he protected his only son from our curious questions, we could not intervene. When Papa died the very next year, Uncle Jr. handled all of his affairs, and by the time we knew anything, the shyster mortgagors owned Papa's property and all of Mother's elegant things.

"I never will forget the day Miss Wilson tracked me down at the school cafeteria. I was working the cash register, and my boss lady said, 'Estella, you have an emergency phone call.' My heart went to pounding, pounding; I thought Junior had dropped dead somewhere or been killed, but it was just Miss Wilson telling me to come home quick; that the police was at Mother's house with a man and they were putting her things outdoors. I hopped in the car, shaking so hard I could barely drive. It was raining that day. Not misting rain, but a hard rain, down on Mother's good furniture. I didn't know where Junior was. There was just this white man standing there with the papers saying everything was his. 'Yours?' I asked him. 'How could it be yours?' And then he told me and it liked to broke my heart. Wasn't nothing I could do. I didn't have that kinda money laying around. Junior denied that too, and I said, 'How you gon' deny this, Junior? I saw the paper with my own eyes.'"

"Auntee, I can't bear to hear any more of this."

Gina brought a bit of humor back into the conversation.

"Fred Jr. was just that way. He wouldn't tell the truth to save his soul. You could be standing with him looking at a bright blue sky, and I swear 'fore God, he'd say it was green. There was no accounting for the things he did, right down to joining that church. I won't ever forget that communion."

I had forgotten about that moment, the one note of levity in an otherwise wrenching day: blacks and whites together, truly together, not simply sitting in the same church and nodding nervously at each other, but taking the sacrament from the same cup.

"I knew when that white man told us to come up to that altar and drink from the same cup, that he had trouble on his hands. It was a right nice service up to that point, but I knew the folks from Macedonia would not go for that. I said to myself, I hope this won't keep my brother out of heaven, but I sho' ain't gon' put my mouth on that cup. I don't know where them other mouths been." And then we all just exploded, all together, whooping there in the kitchen, until the tears trickled down.

As the night wore on we remembered more and more about Uncle Jr.'s tragic end, and especially about his relationship with Mother. Why had they grown so far apart? I asked.

"Well, I told you about the letter, didn't I?"

"No, Auntee, you didn't."

She shuffled between the stove and the refrigerator, in which she was furiously stacking blue-lidded Tupperware containers heaped with food. I was not prepared for what followed, but it locked so many other things into place.

"Jr. wasn't the same after he opened the letter that Mother wrote to that preacher."

"What preacher?"

"Well, I don't really know, but folks said," and then she stopped herself. Auntee must have inherited this tendency from Grandma Edie. She'll be telling you something, and right smack dab in the middle of telling, she'll think better of what she started and pull the plug.

"Just let me say this. Mother wrote this letter to the man one time she was home from Mountain Brook. What possessed her to give the letter to Junior to mail I will never know, not for the life of me, not 'til kingdom come. But she did. Handed that letter right over to Junior and said run this to the post office. And then she went on that very day to Mountain Brook. Miss Berger picked her up.

"Well, I'll have you know, Junior didn't mail that letter; for some reason, he opened it and found out that Mother was planning to meet this man somewhere. I want to think it was up in Huntsville, but maybe it was Mobile. I can't be sure. Anyway, he was so upset I thought he would bust a blood vessel. Before I saw it, he took the letter to your daddy in Pipe Shop. He was threatening to tell Mr. Fred, but Wiley begged him not to. Wiley said he told him, 'Junior, telling Mr. Fred is just gonna make a bad situation worse.' Well, Junior calmed down. When they showed up on the side porch that day—I never will forget it as long as I live—both of 'em looked like they had shitted and stepped in it. And I said, 'What in the world is the matter?' And that's when Junior pulled the letter out of his pocket and I stood right there on that side porch and read it.

"'Well, I dee-clare,' I remember saying. 'Mother got some business telling everybody else about respecting the marriage bed and she ain't doing it herself.' The letter talked all about how much she enjoyed seeing him the last time. She didn't say where she had been with him, but I can't believe that she would bring him to Miss Berger's house. Right then, the lights started coming on. Like they say, if you don't catch it in the wash, you'll catch it in the rinse.

"I want you to know that until I read that letter, I was in the dark about the telephone calls. You see, Mother would be gone for a month or two, if she was out of the Birmingham area, but as soon as she set foot in this house, the telephone would start ringing. Ring, ring, ring. Ring, ring, ring, just ringing off the hook. If I answered, the person on the other end would hang up. Sometimes Mother would ask me, in a kind of offhand way, 'Who was that on the phone?' And I would tell her probably just somebody with a wrong number, since they had hung up. And don't you know, within minutes Mother would be on that hallway phone, talking so low that couldn't nobody hear what she was saying. She would be on that phone sometimes for hours, but never when Mr. Fred was at home.

"Then too, I started thinking about the clothes. Why would Mother need to take so many Sunday clothes to Mountain Brook, if she was only going there to work? I asked her about it one time, and she said that sometimes she went places with Miss Berger, but I didn't really believe her. What white woman was gon' show up anywhere with a black woman in Birmingham, not unless she was riding in the backseat of the white woman's car? And you know, she went to New York a whole heap of times. San Francisco too. She told us she was going to help different friends and relations of Miss Berger, and wasn't no reason to doubt her word, 'cause we always had an address and a phone number of where she was in case something happened. But after I saw that letter, I didn't know what to believe.

"Still and all, I didn't want to see Mr. Fred get hurt. I knew it would break his heart. I never knew a man to love a woman the way Mr. Fred loved Mother. Well, between me and Wiley, we talked Junior out of telling his daddy, but he fell out with Mother that very day. She knew it too. That's why she tried to buy him back with all them expensive presents. That's why he went to Howard instead of Miles. That's why he got the car. Mr. Fred didn't want him to have that car, and he almost left Mother behind that. But you know he was such a tender-hearted man. Couldn't go nowhere and Mother knew it. But she got hers; she suffered 'fore she left this world. Her conscience whipped her till the day she died. After all that going, going, going, she had to finally come right on back home and lay down every night in that bed next to Mr. Fred. Just goes to show you, sometimes the farther you travel, the less you move.

"Sometimes I felt sorry for her, and sometimes I didn't. The night she had the stroke? Mr. Fred called us. I was sitting right where you sitting, right on the end of that couch. Gina was in the rocking chair. Mr. Fred said 'Stella, come quick. Your mother is low-sick. I can't 'rouse her. She unconscious.' He had already called the ambulance and told us to meet him down at Bessemer Carraway. I was trying to get some more information out of him but he cut me off and screamed at me, and I had never heard Mr. Fred scream at nobody. He said, 'Stella, hurry up. Make haste.' Still and all, I didn't really believe him, and you know why? 'Cause Mother had just come home that very day from Mobile; I had talked to her. She had this bad habit of faking like she was sick as soon as she walked in the door from one of these jobs. Now, she would be fine up until she got home, but once she came down off that mountain or wherever she had been, oh, Lord, she was too sick to pour herself a glass of ice water. Would lay back in that bed sometimes for a week or more, but as soon as somebody called her about a job, she was well again, like Jesus or Lazarus or somebody had come in here and laid his hands on her. She hopped up from that bed, and whatever had been ailing her was gone. So for that very reason, when Mr. Fred called me that night, I took my good time getting down there. I stayed right up on this hill, right here in West Highlands. I had a great mind not to go at all. It was ten o'clock at night, and I was already in my nightgown.

"When I got down to the hospital, though—Gina went with me—and saw her hooked up to all them tubes, I knew she couldn't be faking this time, and I went to praying, 'Oh Lord, please don't let my mother die. Please don't let her die.' Junior took his time getting here too. Mother had the stroke on a Monday night, and they didn't give us much hope; they didn't even give her a week to live. I'll have you know, it was Friday before Junior got here and by Sunday he was gone again.

"I will always believe in my soul that Mr. Fred kept Mother alive for all that time. There ain't no way she would have lived eight whole years after that stroke if it wasn't for Mr. Fred. He would not leave her bedside, no longer than to go to the bathroom and take a bite of food. Most nights he slept sitting up in a chair, and when he would wake up, he would grab her good hand and just squeeze, just squeeze it, like he was squeezing the life back into Mother, and I guess he did, 'cause she came out of that coma in less than a week. He brought her back to life—such as it was. Sometimes I used to look at her folded up in that bed and wonder why the Lord didn't just take her on, just like he did Wiley. It's like I always told you, it was a blessing your daddy died, cause he would have been paralyzed just like Mother—not able to do anything for himself."

Here, just as my visit was coming to an end, Auntee opened up. That night, we talked again until long past 3 A.M., or at least Auntee did. Gina and I sat spellbound as she dug deeper and deeper into memory's trenches, coughing up the silt. But I knew that, despite all that she had excavated, much more still lay down below, and it would stay down there forever, out of resurrection's reach.

Revisitations

We went to church on Sunday. I had not been inside the walls of Macedonia since May 1981, for Papa's funeral. Just inside the double doors, ushers in bleached white uniforms stood like sentries, handing fans and printed programs to all who entered. This could have been any Sunday of my childhood, when I took a fan from the white-gloved usher and proceeded automatically down the aisle to a pew toward the front on the left. Only the ushers and the fans had changed.

In my girlhood days, the front side of the fan featured either a picture of the Last Supper or of the brunet Jesus in the Garden of Gethsemane, his hair parted down the middle, hands together in prayer, eyes lifted heavenward. But once Martin Luther King Jr. had galvanized the Birmingham area with his fiery promise to take the heart out of Dixie, his picture rivaled that of Jesus' in frequency and appeal. Of course, the backside of the fan was saved for advertisements from Shadow Lawn Cemetery or Walker-Handley and Sons, where Crockett used to work, which sold new and used furniture and promised easy payment plans, even for those with busted credit and no job.

I took my seat and examined the fan with a portrait of a black family on front. "We Are Family." The father stood erect, a head taller than the devout-looking mother. The two children—a boy and a girl—held hands. On the flip side was an ad, not for Walker Handley furniture, but for Brighton Funeral Home:

> We offer an economical burial, which includes:
> Professional services. Metal casket. Concrete vault. Grave. Hearse.
> Limo transportation.
> Price: $2,150.
> We also offer pre-need and payment plan.
> We honor all burial and insurance policies.

As the air was stifling, I soon joined the multitude of fanning hands, a blur of motion whipping up memories of all the times I had spent in Macedonia A.M.E. Zion Church. There, in that very basement, I had first imbibed the rudiments of religious and social doctrine. Memorized the beatitudes printed on white construction paper and taped all around the concrete walls. Attended Vacation Bible School, where I fought with all the other girls and boys to carry the U.S. flag down the aisle, shouted in unison the pledge of allegiance and the Nicene Creed.

Reverend Miree, long one of two assistant ministers at the church, beamed in recognition from the pulpit, and when we came to the "Visitors' Welcome," she called for me to stand.

"We have one of our own with us today," she said in her slow, deliberate way. "She's not a visitor. She was brought up right here inside the walls of Macedonia. I know some of you still remember the very beautiful way she spoke her pieces right here from the floor of this very pulpit. And the way she played the piano. We're so proud of her and glad to have her back home. She's made good, teaching at . . ." She paused. "Where is it you teach, honey?" I told her. "Oh, your people would be so proud of you, especially Miss Viola. Do say. University of Virginia. What is your church home there?" I finessed a vague answer, naturally unable to admit to this, my childhood congregation, that I had long since given up on church, although in memory of Grandma Edie I sometimes read the Ninetieth Psalm, hoping for the faith, the consolation, and uncomplicated certainty she found anchored in its verses.

After the benediction, Mrs. Young, who used to smooth down my cancans and sneak me nickels for ice cream cones, rushed over to give me a deliciously sweaty hug. She lost no time in asking why I hadn't married and had some children. "You must be too fussy. Don't you wait too long now. If you wait too long you gon' be so set in your ways ain't nobody gon' wanna marry you." And then she popped the question only Mrs. Young would dare to ask, "And when you gon' get your hair fixed? You used to have such nice thick hair. Ophelia would style it so beautiful. But now you bound and determined to look just like a porcupine 'bout the head." Before I could frame an answer, she said, "When you heard from your brothers? Reggie still got all them mangy plaits hanging way down his back?"

"Yes ma'am."

"Well, if that don't beat all. Jimmye brought some odd children into this world," she said, turning to Auntee. "Always would go their own way, don't care who didn't like it. Here the boy got all these great long plaits and the girl's head near 'bout shaved." When Miss Gaston joined in with, "When you moving back home?" Auntee flashed a look of vindication, then adjusted her saucy hat with a satin brim worn at a rakish angle.

We ambled out of the basement's dimness into the clarion July light, Mrs. Young still at our side. We walked her to her car and lingered as she unlocked the door to her red-laquered Plymouth that seemed to match the lipstick smeared beyond the outlines of her mouth. She turned again to me, and, patting my hips, said, "You just like your grandmother. Got going in your blood. Always on the move. Get yourself some babies and don't stay gone so long next time."

"Yes, ma'am."

I waved Mrs. Young on her way, searching my mind for words to justify my having left, if only to myself, for I knew that I could never justify it to all the other stalwart, standard-bearing folk back home who would never leave themselves, not even in their dreams.

From church we headed directly to Pine Hill Cemetery. At the intersection of Fifteenth Street and Ninth Avenue Gina signaled to make a left turn.

"Why aren't you taking Route 150?"

"I'm going to keep straight to Fourth Avenue; that's the most direct route right now."

"But I told you I want to go past Mother's house."

"Oh, girl, you wouldn't hardly recognize that house. It's nothing like it used to be. It's been turned into an eyeglass shop."

"I don't care. I want to see it anyway."

We pulled into the asphalt driveway of Family Vision Eye Care, now a barn-red building with metal shingles and no front porch. The honeysuckle hedge is gone and so is the abelia that once fronted the house. I snapped a picture. For a few moments we all just sat there in the car, saying nothing. As usual, Auntee spoke up first. "Well, they finally got their wish. Drove black folks right on out of the houses they worked and bought and paid for.

"I know Mother is rolling over in her grave, and everybody else in the Voters League. But at least they didn't see Ninth Avenue turn all the way to business before they died."

The Bessemer Voters League had been successful in their fight to keep the zoning board from taking over the vicinity of Ninth Avenue, knowing that it was all a scam to push black voters out of the Bessemer city limits. And when they won, Mother boasted of how the City Commission and the City Planning and Zoning Board had been outsmarted by the young black attorney, David Hood. "Do they think, hard as people work, they just gon' sit down on their rusty asses while these white folks take over their neighborhood? No sir-ee, Bob."

The cars were rushing by so fast down the four-lane highway that we had to sit a while, just idling in the car, and when Gina finally backed into the highway, I halfway listened for the gravel that was no longer there. In all, we'd sat there just ten minutes, maybe even less, but they were minutes crowded with the memories of many, many years.

We crossed over to the other side and, closeted with our own thoughts, lumbered toward Pine Hill. In my childhood years, the cemetery was a straight shot south down the Bessemer Super Highway, but when the freeway came through, it blocked access to the graveyard. Now, to get there, we took Fourteenth Street to Fourth Avenue, past the Bessemer Stadium, where Gina once strutted as a majorette, then down the two-lane highway where farmers sold fresh produce from roadside stands.

We spotted the house that marks the turnoff into the cemetery, a low-slung, double-tenant house just to the left of the dirt road that sharply curved round and round and round until we finally neared the section where all the family is scattered, except for Daddy Les and Daddy Frank and Crockett, whose bones lie in Tuscaloosa, Greensboro, and Demopolis, respectively, and Martha Faye's in Buffalo.

We drove the car as far as we could go, then piled out and trudged up the hill, passing just-dug graves, the newly turned sod thick with pebbles and shards of glass that caught the sun's bright light. Brittany slipped a time or two on clods of the stony red soil, and I grabbed her hand. Each of us took turns sweeping off the headstones the size of paving stones.

VIOLA GEE WILLIAMS

1907–1977

FRED ALVIN WILLIAMS SR.

1906–1981

FRED ALVIN WILLIAMS JR.

1942–1984

WILEY MCDOWELL

1923–1974

JIMMYE ZIEGLER MCDOWELL

1923–1979

Grandma Edie was at the far end, where the earth slopes slightly upward. Her stone read simply:

EDITH CRAWFORD
1885–1974

I couldn't help but remember all the afternoons at 1805 Eighteenth Street, the weight of the heavy Bible pressing on my thighs, struggling to mouth the words just as Grandma Edie ordered:

Thewaterswearthestonestheearthisthelordandthefulnessthereof theworkofthyhandsestablishthouit.

We all stood there sobbing, not just for ourselves, but for all of them, especially for Mama, Daddy, and Uncle Jr. with whom the years had been so stingy. Two red carnations now crisscrossed on each grave; the four of us joined hands and formed a tiny circle. I whispered, "Rest in peace."

Records

Put that camera in your pocketbook."

I had already taken several snapshots of the scene, including the only spot of green on this defoliated landscape cluttered with pipes: the grassy slope at the west end of the complex cemented with the bright white letters, among the first signs I had learned to read. The letters were still large, but not as large as I remembered from my childhood.

U.S. PIPE AND FOUNDRY. EST. 1890.
MORE THAN A PLACE TO WORK

I had already snapped the two brick pillars with wrought-iron lanterns marking the gateway to the plant and had just raised and angled my camera to get a shot of the blue-and-white water tower that reached for the sky when I heard the shout again.

"I said, Put that camera in your pocketbook." At first I could not tell just where the shouts were coming from, but then a squat white man with burnished face and forearms burst through the door of the shingled guard-house. "I'm only gon' tell you one more time to put that camera up. After that, I'm gon' call the police. What you doing here? Don't you know this is private property?"

"I didn't see a No Trespassing sign."

"I don't care what you didn't see. You can't just walk up in here, just like you please, and start taking pictures."

His words were slippery, imprecise—the unmistakable sound of tooth-lessness. I stared at him long and hard, seizing on his sunken jaws, his steel blue eyes, and the tattoo of an eagle bluing his upper arm. When he started to speak again, I saw that I was right: He didn't have a single tooth in his head.

"I said, What you doing here? What you want?"

"I'm here to see Ms. Robin Dean."

He turned back inside the guardhouse and, within a minute, was directing me to the personnel office.

"You see up yonder where that tractor at?"

"No, I don't see it."

"Look off over yonder," he said, pointing off to the side, "by the green trailer." This time I saw. "Well, you go up there and turn to your right and keep walking back a ways. You gon' pass two big buildings and a first aid station crost from them two buildings. Then keep a-going, keep a-going until you come to a small building with two pipes in front of it."

I thought to myself, from what I can see, there are pipes everywhere. Pipes of various diameters were stacked in piles six deep, stretched across almost the entire expanse of parched red gravelly soil. I thanked him and hoped no one would confiscate my camera at the personnel office. Stamping toward the yellow tractor, I passed two black men standing just outside the opening of a building that was as large as an airplane hangar. The one in the blaze orange hard hat nodded to me and I nodded back. I wanted to stop and ask them questions, but there was something uninviting and apprehensive etched in both their faces. When I rounded the next corner, out of sight of the guard, I snapped more pictures of the buildings all covered in corrugated steel.

NO APPLICATIONS TAKEN TODAY read the cardboard sign taped to the door of the personnel office. I knocked lightly at first, then again and very hard when no one answered. Finally, a chipper voice invited me into a cheap-issue office with low ceilings. Three four-drawer file cabinets lined a wall with fake-oak paneling. The speckled floor tiles seemed newly laid but stopped just short of the threshold of the door, exposing a strip of bare wood flooring, scuffed from constant traffic.

"Are you Ms. Dean?"

"Yes, I'm Mrs. Dean."

"I'm the person who talked to you on the phone. About my father's records?"

"Oh, yes, yes. Mr. Livingston hasn't come in yet, but he should be here any minute. Let me start taking down some information from you. Have a seat here."

As she disappeared through the door, I sat to the right of her desk where a pack of Camels lay on the base of a crooknecked lamp next to a clear glass globe with a red rose inside. A collage of snapshots lay underneath a chipped slab of glass. At the corner nearest me, I glimpsed a picture of what looked like Ms. Dean lying on her back in a hospital bed, a ruddy-faced baby with eyes squinted shut nestled in the crook of her arm. And then another of a toddler with a shock of bright red hair, standing in a walker, grinning to expose two little bottom teeth. She came back into the room and plopped down at her desk.

"Is this you and your baby in the photograph? I couldn't help but notice."

"Oh, that's all right. Yes, ma'am, that's my first. Sarah. She's three now. I have a little boy, Justin."

She took a stenographer's pad and a ballpoint pen from her desk drawer.

"Now tell me again why you need your daddy's employment records?"

"For information. I'm writing a book of stories about my family and people here in Pipe Shop. I grew up here, just a few blocks away."

"I see." As she started to scribble, I noticed that she was left-handed and crooked her wrist inward.

"I see you're left-handed. I am too."

She smiled and nodded. "Do you know when your father started working here?"

"No, I don't know exactly when. Maybe the 1950s. I was born in 1951, and I think he was working here then. But I can't be sure."

"When was your father born?"

"October 23, 1923."

"And when did he pass away?"

"December 6—no, December 5, 1974."

I could see from her expression that she was calculating in her head and so I volunteered, "He was fifty-one years old."

"Oh, he was young. Sounds like I hear Mr. Livingston. I'll be right back." She stood again, reached in the pocket of her jumper for a barrette, and pinned her hair off her neck. "I hope it's cooler than this where you came from?"

"Not much."

I heard a man's deep voice from the next room say that the records were down in the . . . and then his voice dropped off. Ms. Dean returned, her thongs flip-flopping on her heels. "I'm going to have to go to another building, down where we keep the files of deceased workers."

"Your records aren't computerized?"

"Oh, Lord, no, not that far back."

"Do you know how long it will take?"

"It shouldn't take too long," she said reassuringly.

"I wouldn't push you, except that I have a one o'clock appointment."

"Oh, Lord, I'll be done long before then. It's just nine-thirty now."

"May I go with you? It might go faster with both of us looking."

"Oh, no, ma'am, I'm sorry. Only employees are authorized to go through records. I won't be long."

When I'd called the plant two days before, I had been informed that there was no one in authority, not the manager, not the assistant manager, not anyone who could authorize Miss Dean to release Daddy's records to me. But when Mr. Livingston returned from his fishing trip on Monday morning, she would be sure to let him know that this was an urgent matter.

I sat for almost an hour in this tiny room, staring out the window at stacks of coal black hollow pipes, like so many Roman columns or newly-felled trees awaiting another revolution of the sawmill's blade. This was the place that had given me the first fragments of an identity and marked the rhythms of my earliest days. I have no memory of these times, but for years Mama had teased me about a habit I established when I was barely three years old.

I had been taught my name and memorized other vital information to provide anyone with in case I was ever lost. But, according to her, I would offer it indiscriminately to any person who stopped to pass the time of day. "You were just like a walking tape recorder," Mama used to say. "And when anybody, even perfect strangers, asked you a question, it was like they had pushed Play and turned up the volume. You would give your name and your daddy's name and just keep rattling on: 'My daddy works at the Pipe Shop. I live at 1805 Long Eighteenth Street. My phone number is Hamilton 58258.'" And, according to Mama, before I entered kindergarten, I listened for the three-thirty whistle, which signaled the end of Daddy's shift. "You would start squealing like a runt after teats, 'Daddy's coming home. Daddy's coming.'"

I heard footsteps in the outer room and when the woman entered, my heart started palpitating.

"Did you find them?" When she said, "Beg pardon?" I saw that it wasn't Robin Dean.

"Oh, I'm sorry. I thought you were Ms. Dean. You look just like her."

"Lots of people say that."

"Are you related?"

"No, ma'am, but everybody thinks we're kin to one another. Are you the lady what's waiting for the records?"

"Yes, I am."

"Robin shouldn't be much longer. Would you like a cold drink or a cup of coffee?"

I asked for coffee and, as she pivoted on her heels to fetch it, I remarked again how much she looked like Robin Dean. The resemblance was uncanny. She even wore a blue denim jumper with cavernous pockets that drooped on the side and had streaked blond hair permed with corkscrew curls.

She returned with the coffee in a plaid paper cup sunk down inside another one.

"The coffee gets really hot sitting on that plate, so I put it in another cup for you. You don't want to burn your tongue. Let me know if you need anything else; I'll just be in the next room here."

I asked if she had a newspaper lying around, but she said no. "Who would have time to read it," she said, and chuckled.

"Well, do you have anything on the history of the plant? Or maybe the section where my father worked? He worked in the de Lavaud section."

"Yes, I think there might be something in Mr. Livingston's office." She returned with an aged clothbound book on centrifugal casting.

I moved over to the couch, which looked more comfortable, and took out my notebook, sipping the hot coffee and scanning the booklet's pages. The de Lavaud was the casting section of the plant, where they produced cast-iron pressure pipes by pouring molten metal into molds and extracting the pipes after the molds had cooled. I started yawning over the dry, technical language of the booklet, full of references to defects in the pipes, when my eyes scrolled down to "segregation banding," a term that gave me pause.

"Segregation banding" described the hard lines that formed in the pipe when the molten metal is poured too fast. "Hot tears" were cracks in the pipes. Staring mindlessly out the window, I sat, pondering how "tears" would be pronounced. My instincts said "tares" as in the choking weeds of the grain field, but my memory said tears, hot tears, like the ones I cried the day that Daddy fainted in the de Lavaud.

It was a typical Alabama summer—sweltering, sultry, humid. It was my first summer at Mother's and I had tagged along with Papa, who was bringing Mama a bag of field peas from the farmers' market and a pair of trousers to be cleaned. He tossed them on the rocking chair. "Another dead head for you," he said. That's what everybody called the free cleaning that Mama and coworkers did on the sly for their families: dead heads. The sweat gushed down Papa's face and neck and chest, molding the wetness of his blue-striped shirt to his body, revealing the imprint of what looked to me like breasts. "Papa, I didn't know that men had titties." He and Mama were howling when the phone rang. I ran inside to answer.

"Mama, a white man wants to talk to you."

With her sandals in her hand, she ran outside and said to Papa, "Mr.

Fred, quick, drive me out to the Pipe Shop. Wiley's fainted." She was a few months pregnant with the baby she lost later that summer, the second in two years, and the buttons of her dress strained across her slightly bulging stomach. We all jumped in the car and rode the four blocks to the plant. Just inside the door we found Daddy lying on a stretcher, covered up to his neck in a white sheet. His face was ashen blue, but he was conscious and able to walk. With Mama on one side and Papa on the other, he dragged himself to the car. He could not bear the 150-degree furnace that day, and just fainted dead in his tracks.

When we reached home, Daddy went straight to bed and Mama turned the fan on his face. I didn't go back to Mother's house. I stayed at home for the rest of that day, passing back and forth through the room. I needed to see if he was breathing, to watch his chest rhythmically rising and falling, rising and falling, assuring me, moment by moment, that he was still alive.

Daddy awoke to find me looming over him.

"Are you hot, Daddy? Do you want me to fan you?"

"No, I'm all right."

I kneeled at the foot of the bed and squeezed his toes. He smiled.

"It must have been really hot in that place, Daddy."

"It was like an inferno."

"What's an inferno?"

"It's a really, really hot place. Like hell."

"Like where the Devil lives?"

"Yeah, like that."

As near as I can remember, "inferno" was one of the first words Daddy taught me that turned an abstraction learned in Sunday School into a concreteness I could see and feel. I was eight years old.

I placed the booklet on centrifugal casting on the edge of the desk and shuffled through the stack of pamphlets on the coffee table. I opened the inaugural issue of *U.S. Pipeline,* the newsletter printed for the 1991 centennial celebration of U.S. Pipe and Foundry. The bold black letters of the headline read:

BESSEMER PIPE PLANT CELEBRATES CENTENNIAL

The text enclosed within black borders began:

1991 marks the 100th year that U.S. Pipe and Foundry Company's Bessemer plant has been manufacturing and shipping pipe products for both domestic and foreign markets.

With an inducement of $96,000 and eighty acres of land from the Besse-mer Land and Improvement Company, Thomas Howard and John W. Harrison of the St. Louis, Mo. firm of Shickle, Howard and Harrison arranged to locate a large cast-iron pipe and foundry plant in Bessemer, Alabama. A parcel of land along Nineteenth Street was designated for the new plant site and construction began in 1890. The site chosen for the plant had been a cemetery; thus, construction of the plant was delayed while bodies were removed and relocated to a new cemetery site.

"I have very bad news." I was so absorbed in the brochure that I didn't hear her come in.

"I'm sorry?"

"I can't find your daddy's records."

"You can't? Where could they be?"

"I don't know. I searched and searched. That's why I was down there so long. I found some other McDowells, but not Wiley."

"Do you remember the names? Maybe my father's records were filed in another folder by mistake."

"No, I thought about that and checked. Here are the names." She showed me the names written in her slanting, left-handed strokes. Neither was Crockett nor Daddy Frank.

"The only thing I found on your daddy was his employee record card."

She held up a butter-colored card that unfolded into four sections. "I can make you a xeroxed copy of this but, I'm sorry, it's all I could find."

"I just don't understand how *all* my father's records could just disappear, just vanish without a trace. Can you keep looking? Is there anybody who might know what happened?"

"I don't think so. Most of the employees here now were hired within the last five to ten years. They're all new. Nobody's here from your father's time."

"May I use your telephone?"

"Is it a local call?" I nodded. "Just press nine to get an outside line."

I called for Gina and Auntee to pick me up and sank back down into the vinyl chair, watching this young woman raise and lower the copier's lid, flashes of light escaping from the edges. She gathered the pages from the paper trough, stapled them in the corner, and stepped toward me.

"I hope this helps. A few letters got chopped off a bit and the pages are a little smudged. The machine does that if it's a colored original. Color is hard to copy, but I think you can still read all the information."

UNITED STATES PIPE AND FOUNDRY CO.

BESSEMER, ALABAMA PLANT

EMPLOYEE RECORD CARD

AME	ADDRESS		PHONE
Wiley McDowell	1805 18th Way, Bess. Ala.		HA 58258

IRTH-DATE	PLACE
October 24, 1923	Bessemer, Ala.

ACE	HEIGHT	WEIGHT	NO. DEPENDENTS
Col.	5 ft. 10 in.	150	5 (Wife, 4 children)

EDUCATION

ADE SCHOOL	LOCATION	GRADUATE	
Pipe Shop Elem.	Bessemer, Ala.	Yes	

IGH SCHOOL	LOCATION	YEARS	GRADUATE
Brighton	Brighton, Ala.	3	No

ECHNICAL	LOCATION	YEARS	GRADUATE
Parker Vocational (Bus.)	B'ham	2	Yes

OLLEGE	LOCATION	YEARS	GRADUATE

I had forgotten. Our address had changed three times, although we never moved. It used to be 1805 Long Eighteenth Street; then it was North Eighteenth Street, then Eighteenth Way, and not long after I went to Brighton High, our phone number was changed.

There were five and a half pages in all. All except for the cover page were broken into half-inch horizontal lines and vertical columns. Daddy commenced his tenure at U.S. Pipe on July 24, 1946, in the yard. His original classification was "Laborer," earning 74½ cents an hour. On August 22, 1946, he moved to pit no. 3 at 79½. On October 12, 1946, he quit.

This would have been just after World War II. I wasn't yet born. He went back to work there as a temporary in the yard on July 12, 1950.

Then he worked the 7 A.M. to 3:30 P.M. shift at a rate of $1.79½ an hour. Why couldn't they just give him $1.80? What was with the one-half cent? I leafed through to the end to see what he made at the time of his death. It was $4.168. I was filled with rage and a sudden desire to crash something, to punch somebody out. I motioned in the air with my arm and cried out, startling the young woman who sat poring over invoices. I gripped her wrist.

"Do you know that from 1946 to 1974, my father went from making barely seventy-five cents an hour to making barely four dollars when he died in 1974?" I counted the years in my head and shouted, "That's criminal. That's criminal."

Her voice quaking, she said, "They didn't make much back then."

Gina waited in the car while Auntee came inside to find me. "We should have told you to meet us down on the road. We been hemmed up in this place for the past ten minutes."

Ms. Dean spoke up. "Didn't the guard give you directions?"

"He did, but they must not have been too good since we got so turned around." We were down the walkway when she noticed I was crying. "What's wrong with you?"

"Auntee, do you know that in all the years Daddy worked out here, he never made even five dollars an hour?"

"That ain't no surprise. Did you get the records?"

"Uh-unh. They weren't there."

"Weren't there? Where did they go?"

"I don't know, and they claim they don't know either."

"What?"

We climbed into the compact car, Auntee in back, I in front. For the next few minutes, I sat without speaking, thinking of Daddy and all of his responsibilities—a wife and four children, all those pressures on that paltry salary.

"They didn't have anything on Daddy Frank and Crockett either, Auntee. Didn't they work at the plant too?"

"Yeah, but you know Crockett hadn't worked at Pipe Shop since long before he and Grandma Edie divorced. They fired him over some kind of union mess, and after then, Reverend Turner helped him find a job delivering furniture at Walker-Handley."

I turned back around in the seat and stared out the windshield. When we neared the corner where Mr. Pat's store used to be, I started to cry again. Auntee kept right on talking, stabbing at the silence every few blocks: "You know they didn't just lose your daddy's records. I bet you anything it was something in there they didn't want you to see. Didn't no records just get up and walk away. This had to be accidentally on purpose. Just kill black folks. Get a lawyer. He'll straighten things out. He'll make them find the records and give 'em up. You need to contact somebody at the newspaper and report these people. They'll put it in the paper. You know it ain't nothing but the asbestos. They think you after the asbestos money, and they don't want to give up no more."

When I finally found my voice again, I said, "Auntee, they don't handle asbestos claims. U.S. Pipe is not responsible. It's the companies which manufactured products that were used at the plant. Plus, I don't have any proof that asbestos poisoned Daddy."

"Why don't you contact the NAACP?"

"For what? Like I said, I can't prove that they destroyed Daddy's records."

"You know they did, and you bet' not go knuckling under them."

"But it would just be my word against theirs."

"Don't matter. You got to fight it. You know they got to be in cahoots with them asbestos folks."

I was silent again.

"Well, what you gon' do?"

"I don't know yet."

All those years, I'd passed the big white luminous letters, MORE THAN A PLACE TO WORK.

"What does that mean, Daddy, 'More than a Place to Work?'"

I had finally traveled back to Pipe Shop, but was no closer to solving the riddle for myself. No longer did these bright white letters resemble the alphabets above the blackboard or the logo of Bessemer Stadium. What were they then? I resolved right then and there that I would pursue the asbestos question, try to determine what, if any, role it had played in my father's early death. I would pursue it, not for money, nor simply to honor Daddy's memory, but to continue fighting for the cause of justice.

Epilogue

I spent my final day in Bessemer in search of information from men in Pipe Shop who had worked with Daddy at the plant. I visited up and down the streets of the neighborhood, where balding, gray-haired men sat on porches in their soft-soled slippers, white T-shirts stretched across their bulging bellies. "I'm Proud to Be Drug Free" read one. Two men had black spots on their lungs and were already receiving compensation from the manufacturers of products containing asbestos (though neither would say how much). Three other cases pended and I heard mention of countless other claims awaiting settlement. Oddly, the men I talked to seemed more eager to rail against the postponed sewage system than asbestos poisoning. For years on end, they breathed the fetid air of Pipe Shop that escaped from leaky septic tanks.

The City Council of Bessemer offered them no explanations for the delay in implementing the ordinance issued five months before, right around the twentieth anniversary of Daddy's death. I had received a copy of the ordinance from the realtor who collected the rents on 1805. It had come by registered mail, and I hurriedly opened the manila envelope to read the three pages of legal paper:

IMPROVEMENT ORDINANCE NO. 2642. AN ORDINANCE TO PRO-
VIDE CERTAIN IMPROVEMENTS IN THE CITY OF BESSEMER KNOWN
AS "PIPE SHOP."

It went on to state that the "area bounded by Nineteenth Street on the north, Twelfth Street on the south, Interstate 59/20 on the east, and Twenty-second Avenue on the west . . . shall have sanitary sewers constructed thereon, all in accordance with the present requirements for sanitary sewers established by the City."

The ordinance ran to seven sections then concluded: "ADOPTED AND APPROVED this 15th day of December 1994."

But here it was May 1995, and there were still no signs of preparation for sewage lines.

How ironic. Daddy and all these other men who labored at U.S. Pipe had manufactured cast-iron pressure pipes and pipe fittings for the water and sewage industries. The pipes forged in our very neighborhood were shipped to outside sites, while the stench of septic tanks hovered over Pipe Shop. That day I learned that Daddy was called a "checker," assigned to check the pipes as they emerged from the mold, searching for defects, for signs of "segregation banding" and "hot tears." One man recalled how Daddy spoke his mind. "Your daddy had a good head on his shoulders. He was never scared to speak his mind, and that scared them Hoosiers out there at the plant. You know they don't like the kind of blacks that'll stand up to 'em, and look 'em right, straight in their eyes without blinking nary one time. Them's the ones they want to break, one way or another. I think your daddy was one of the ones working with that suit against the union and that sho' didn't win him no friends."

I had read the "Brief on Remand," but Daddy's name did not appear, just "*Joseph Terrell, Jr., et al., Plaintiffs versus United States Pipe and Foundry Company, et al., Defendants.*" The U.S. District Court of Alabama had ruled that there was a "history of racial discrimination by the company in making job assignments," and had found that the seniority system at U.S. Pipe in Bessemer had its genesis in purposeful racial discrimination."

As we left these houses, one by one, and rode through the streets of Pipe Shop, I was reminded that U.S. Pipe and Foundry had been built over what was once a cemetery. Now the community named for the foundry had become itself something of a cemetery. The neighborhood had an abandoned, desolate air, much like the photographs I saw of the abandoned towns in the museum exhibition.

Dying right along with Pipe Shop were the hopes and dreams of all those there whose vision of a prosperous future had long been bound to U.S. Pipe and Foundry and the mines and mills and furnaces in the surrounding area—Tennessee Coal and Iron, Pyne Mine, Pullman Standard, the rolling mill. The plaintiffs' brief had well documented that the ending of the dream was embedded there right in the beginning. Segregated lines of hiring, segregated lines of promotion, segregated lines of pay (the average black male's wage was roughly half that of whites, as late as 1969) ensured that blacks would not get very far ahead and that aggressive white supremacy would not be toppled from its throne.

Just at the moment that the civil rights movement surged hard against segregation's ramparts and courageous workers stepped forward to protest economic advancement long reserved for whites, industrial jobs declined amid shifting market forces. Pipe Shop's fate as a community was all but sealed, and what was happening there was being mirrored everywhere else black workers had staked their fortunes to iron and steel.

These days the papers and airwaves herald news of industry's demise and chronicle the breakdown of graveyard towns standing in the shadow of former factories. Occasionally, industries have scrambled to reinvent themselves, to rise from their ashes, fully formed as industrial museums. The headlines read:

> BETHLEHEM SEARCHES FOR A NEW HEART
>
> WANTED: BIG IDEAS FOR A STEEL MILL SITE
>
> UNEMPLOYMENT: THE THEME PARK
>
> JOHNSTOWN, PA, IS TURNING STEEL MILLS AND
>
> COAL MINES INTO TOURIST SITES

> Foundry Formation: Birmingham's Sloss furnaces made pig iron during its industrial heyday in the '50s. With the city depending more on service-economy jobs, it is now closed.

While U.S. Pipe and Foundry has not closed its doors, it is drastically transformed. The men of my father's generation are now retired, but their sons still cast iron out at the foundry, some in the de Lavaud. All told, though, they constitute half of the workforce that used to file in hard hats through those gates, meeting and passing as their shifts changed. Now, there's only one shift—seven to three—the shift that Daddy worked off and on for several years, leaving the time to help me form sentences and spin stories from long lists of words. This is a familiar tale, the changing same. Now, the company can produce more pipes in one eight-hour shift than they used to make in three, just by speeding up machinery and cutting back on hands.

With fewer jobs available, most of the younger generation has fled Pipe Shop, although there are some who make their living dealing drugs or who live off their grandmothers' Social Security checks. I listened to the older retirees, who now live fearfully behind wrought-iron gates at doors and windows, fondly remembering safer days when people sat on porches and sometimes slept on them at night.

Meanwhile, frequently on Sunday mornings, as I leaf through the *New York Times Magazine,* I happen on quarter-page ads in large block type for Bessemer Trust Company, named for the captain of industry who named the city of my birth. According to the ad, Henry Bessemer established this trust company to ensure that "he and his heirs were properly advised on tax and trust matters, so that his fortune would not be diminished as it passed to continuing generations."

We climbed into the car and rode through the streets of Pipe Shop. Crouched in the backseat of Auntee's Rambler, I cried silent tears. Out of sadness, fear, rage, guilt, relief. Relief at having left it, just as Mother had bade me do. Guilt for learning only now what Pipe Shop was all about. Sadness for what I'd left behind and yet still carried strong within me.

We rolled past the spot where Pipe Shop Elementary had stood. The school is gone. Only the concrete slab is left, hugging the red soil that surrounds it.

"Stop the car, Gina, I want to get out."

Auntee and Gina stayed behind as I walked up and planted my feet securely in the middle of the concrete slab and stared into the far corner of the field where children once twirled streamers around the Maypole. I conjured up the image of my first-grade room—the chalkboard, the letters of the alphabet stretching from end to end. Mrs. Foster standing in a dress striped like saltwater taffy, the pointer in her hand. The butcher paper we used for crayon drawings. The pilgrims in tall, flat-topped buckled hats.

I climbed back inside the car. Gina and Auntee glanced at each other, but neither spoke a word. Twisting the key in the ignition, Gina headed the car toward West Highlands. Near the end of Sixteenth Street, before we reached Daddy Frank's old house, we approached a group of girls and boys playing Little Sally Walker, one of the many ring games I had played in yards up and down the block or right in the middle of Eighteenth Street.

> *Little Sally Walker*
> *Sitting in a saucer*
> *Rise, Sally, rise,*
> *Wipe your weeping eyes.*
> *Put your hands on your hips*
> *Let your backbone slip*
> *Oh, shake it to the east,*
> *Oh, shake to the west,*
> *Oh, shake it to the one you love the best.*

Hearing the slow screech of the braking car, the children scattered to the edge of the road to let us pass, peering shyly through the window at our unfamiliar faces. As the car crawled down the street, I turned around to stare out the back window, as the children retook their places in the road. Out of the corner of my eye I glimpsed one girl's bright blue gathered dress, much like the one that Mama made me one Easter, the one I wore on my very first day at Pipe Shop Elementary. The girl moves to the center of the circle and plops down on the ground, then rises and shakes convulsively toward the one she wants to tag. The peals of the children's laughter float on the early-evening air thick with the cloying scent of honeysuckle and chinaberry trees. I wipe my hand across my nose and watch the splash of cobalt blue until it's out of sight.

May 1996
Charlottesville, Virginia

Author's Note

Memoirs are the stuff of fiction and memory's re-creations. To ensure their anonymity, some characters in this narrative are composites of others, and in several cases, names and places have been changed.

Acknowledgments

I owe tremendous debts of gratitude to several people. First, I would like to thank Auntee, whose simple imperative, "You've got to come home," instigated the process. She, along with my remaining family members—Gina, Reggie, and Bumbiddle—added memories that I had lost and corrected those I had distorted.

I thank my editor, Hamilton Cain, for understanding and respecting my vision for this project and for his guidance, support, and unwavering enthusiasm; my agent, Geri Thoma, whose patience and good humor kept me working through some challenging moments; Jennifer Chen, whose energy and attention to last-minute details has been heroic; and my brilliant and indispensable research assistant, Michael Furlough.

I have benefited greatly from conversations with Jeff Norrell, his scholarship on the Birmingham steel industry, and from essential legal documents which he made available to me during the research process. Retired workers, who wish to remain anonymous, eagerly recounted to me their experiences at U.S. Pipe and Foundry.

Janet Beizer, Ann duCille, Barbara Nolan, Marilyn Richardson, Charlene Sedgwick, Jeanne Toungara, Cheryl Wall, Orson Watson, Gwendolyn Rigby Williams, and Francille Wilson read or listened to (and sometimes both) various drafts of the manuscript, offering razor-sharp insights and editorial advice. Nancy Miller's expert eye and shaping hand are everywhere apparent in these pages. Mary Rose, of the Carter G. Woodson Institute readied the bulging manuscript for the press, not once complaining about its length.

For her bottomless generosity and encouragement at every stage of this process, I owe my dear friend, Farzaneh Milani, an especial debt. And finally, as always, thanks to M. H. S., who enables everything.